Enterprise Client Management

Using System Center 2012 R2 and Windows Server 2012 R2

Andreas Stenhall
Tim Nilimaa-Svärd

PUBLISHED BY
Deployment Artist
http://deploymentartist.com

Warning and Disclaimer

Every effort has been made to make this book as complete and as accurate as possible, but no warranty or fitness is implied. The information provided is on an "as is" basis. The authors and the publisher shall have neither liability nor responsibility to any person or entity with respect to any loss or damages arising from the information contained in this book.

Feedback Information

We'd like to hear from you! If you have any comments about how we could improve the quality of this book, please don't hesitate to contact us by visiting http://deploymentfundamentals.com, send an email to feedback@deploymentfundamentals.com or visit our Facebook site http://facebook.com/deploymentfundamentals.

About the Authors

Andreas Stenhall

Andreas Stenhall is a Senior Technical Architect at Coligo, specializing in the Windows client in terms of deployment, management, and optimization for enterprises and governments. When not providing hands-on consulting services, Andreas lectures, leads workshops, and teaches courses on Windows client and server. He has spoken at various Microsoft conferences, including prominent TechEd events both in the US and in Europe.

Andreas is deeply involved in the community and has been awarded the Microsoft Most Valuable Professional title of "Windows Expert – IT Pro" every year since 2009. He also has run the Swedish-speaking community www.alltomwindows.se for 10 years, as well as an English-language blog for IT professionals, named "The Experience Blog" (www.theexperienceblog.com). He is the author of the book *Windows 8 in the Enterprise*.

You can connect with Andreas on Twitter @AndreasStenhall and on LinkedIn at http://linkedin.com/in/andreasstenhall.

Tim Nilimaa-Svärd

Tim Nilimaa-Svärd is the Product Manager for Enterprise Client Management at Lumagate, working with Configuration Manager and Intune. While working with consulting services, Tim mainly helps customer design and implement management solutions for server, client, and BYOD based on Configuration Manager and Intune. He also conducts workshops and presents on topics in the Enterprise Mobility area.

In the community, Tim is known both for his work with the Session Downloader tool (http://infoworks.tv), which allows you to download session videos and slide decks from events such as TechEd and the now retired Microsoft Management Summit (MMS), and the Hydration Kit for Windows Azure. He also has been a speaker at multiple Microsoft events, such as at MMS.

You can connect with Tim on Twitter @TimNilimaa and on LinkedIn at http://linkedin.com/in/timnilimaa.

Contents

Contents

Introduction

Enterprise Client Management is the essential source for any IT professional wanting to fully take advantage of the benefits of managing Windows clients in an enterprise environment. At the same time, what you learn in this book will enable you to give your end users a really good user experience and the best means to perform their work effectively.

Times are changing, and effectively managing your Windows clients is becoming more and more essential. as Also, new types of devices have come into use, and security and efficiency are becoming even more important.

The scope of this book is to guide you via hands on examples and with real-world experience how to manage your enterprise Windows clients, using both new and existing software. There are certain parts of this book that require you to use the latest Windows versions, i.e. Windows 8.1 and Windows Server 2012 R2, but we all know that Windows 7 is deployed across millions and millions of devices out there. Therefore we cover both Windows 7 and Windows 8.1 in this book.

Managing the entire life cycle of the Windows client is essential. That includes deploying operating systems, applications, Windows updates, and antimalware protection, as well as providing inventory reporting and also maintaining configuration at an enterprise level. The tool we use to accomplish this is System Center 2012 R2 Configuration Manager, which in practice means you can manage every aspect of your Windows clients using one tool.

To add further value to your users and to give you additional features, we use other System Center products, such as Service Manager, Data Protection Manager, and the Microsoft Desktop Optimization Pack to demonstrate a top-of-the line, automated, and secure client environment that also provide a really good user experience for your end users.

The audience for this book is both aspirants who want to start using System Center Configuration Manager and those already running it. The experienced reader receive tips and tricks on how to further extend the use of existing investments.

Say Hello (Possibly Again) to ViaMonstra Inc.

In this book, you work with the fictive company ViaMonstra Inc., which is a company located in New York and has around 3000 employees.

BTW, the name ViaMonstra comes from *Viam Monstra*, Latin, meaning "Show me the way."

Structure of the Book

The first chapter deals with basics of Active Directory and what lays the foundation of any Windows environment. The second chapter describes how to install and configure System Center 2012 R2 Configuration Manager.

Chapter 3 deals with operating system deployment (OSD), and in Chapter 4, you learn how to deploy applications and what the possibilities are for deploying applications to other, non-Windows types of devices. Chapter 5 guides you on how to keep your Windows clients up to date with the latest Windows updates.

Chapter 6 deals with user profiles and data in the enterprise, and in Chapter 7, the entire concept of "bring your own device" and its opportunities are explored.

Security is dealt with in Chapter 8, and in Chapter 9 you learn about remote access and mobility. In Chapter 10, you learn how Service Manager can help you do things more efficiently. Speaking of efficiency, PowerShell is the only topic in Chapter 11. As you probably know, PowerShell is great for automating things.

How to Use This Book

We have packed this book with step-by-step guides, which means you can implement your solution as you read along.

In numbered steps, all names and paths are in bold typeface. We also have used a standard naming convention throughout the book when explaining what to do in each step. The steps normally are something like this:

- On the **Advanced Properties** page, select the **Confirm** check box, and then click **Next**.

Code and sample scripts are formatted like the following, on a grey background.

```
OSDMigrateMode=Advanced
```

The step-by-step guides in this book assume that you have configured the environment according to the information in the "ViaMonstra Inc." section later in this chapter, as well as in Appendix A.

Sample Files

All sample files used in this book can be downloaded from http://deploymentfundamentals.com.

Additional Resources

In addition to all the tips and tricks provided in this book, you can find extra resources on our blogs (www.theexperienceblog.com and www.infoworks.tv), like articles and even more tips and tricks drawn from issues we've encountered in the real world while deploying, implementing, and simply dealing with enterprise client management.

Topics Not Covered

This book does not cover any consumer-related topics regarding Windows client, nor does it contain any information on installing or managing printers in the enterprise.

ViaMonstra Inc.

Again, ViaMonstra Inc. is the fictive company you use throughout this book. Here, we describe the company in more detail, as well as the management solution built for that company.

In addition to the information in this chapter, you can find detailed instructions on how to install and configure the servers and clients in Appendix A. If you want to follow all the step-by-step guides in this book, you need to have your environment set up as described in Appendix A. In the appendix, you use the sample files included with this book; all these files can be downloaded from http://deploymentfundamentals.com.

> **Note:** The password for the accounts created by the hydration kit is P@ssw0rd (including the Administrator account).

ViaMonstra Inc. was invented for the very purpose of having a "real" company for which to implement a management solution. In the real world, these management solutions come from multiple consulting engagements we have done. For purposes of this book, we have consolidated them into a single generic scenario.

Virtual Machines

In the step-by-step guides, what we call Build-While-Reading, you use the following virtual machines;

- **DC01.** A **Windows Server 2012 Standard R2** machine, fully patched with the latest security updates, and configured as Active Directory Domain Controller, DNS Server, Certificate, and DHCP Server in the **corp.viamonstra.com** domain.
    - Server name: **DC01**
    - IP Address: **192.168.1.200**
    - Roles: **DNS**, **DHCP** and **Domain Controller**
- **CM01.** A **Windows Server 2012 Standard R2** machine, joined to the **corp.viamonstra.com** domain as a member server.
    - Server name: **CM01**
    - IP Address: **192.168.1.214**
    - Role: **System Center 2012 R2 Configuration Manager**
- **FS01.** A **Windows Server 2012 Standard R2** machine, joined to the **corp.viamonstra.com** domain as a member server.
    - Server name: **FS01**
    - IP Address: **192.168.1.213**
    - Role: **File Services**

- **DPM01.** A **Windows Server 2012 Standard R2** machine, joined to the **corp.viamonstra.com** domain as a member server.
    - Server name: **DPM01**
    - IP Address: **192.168.1.219**
    - Role: **System Center 2012 R2 Data Protection Manager**
- **SM01.** A **Windows Server 2012 Standard R2** machine, joined to the **corp.viamonstra.com** domain as a member server.
    - Server name: **SM01**
    - IP Address: **192.168.1.220**
    - Role: **System Center 2012 R2 Service Manager**
- **PC0001.** A **Windows 7 SP1 x64 client**, joined to the **corp.viamonstra.com** domain.
    - Client name: **PC0001**
    - IP Address: **DHCP**
    - Role: **Client**
- **PC0002.** A **Windows 8.1 x64 client**, joined to the **corp.viamonstra.com** domain.
    - Client name: **PC0002**
    - IP Address: **DHCP**
    - Role: **Client**

Software Requirements

To be able to follow some of the step-by-step guides in this book, you need access to Microsoft Desktop Optimization Pack 2014 (MDOP). MDOP is currently available as an evaluation found on TechNet or MSDN web sites if you have a current subscription to one of those services.

The MDOP products used in the book are Advanced Group Policy Management (AGPM), User Experience Virtualization (UE-V), and Microsoft BitLocker Administration and Monitoring (MBAM).

Chapter 1

Active Directory Infrastructure

Active Directory is a fundamental piece of every Windows environment. From a Windows client perspective, it provides, among many things, authentication services and configuration in the form of group policies. From a management perspective, it is the one place where management is done for users, security groups, and group policies. This chapter deals with the basics of Active Directory and how to manage group policies in the enterprise using the Advanced Group Policy Management tool .

Forest and Domain Functional Levels

Depending on what Windows server operating system version you are running on your domain controllers in your current environment, you will see feature improvements if you are running the latest and greatest forest and domain functional levels.

> **Note**: As of Windows Server 2012 R2, the Windows Server 2003 domain and forest functional levels are deprecated, and you should move to a forest and domain functional level of at least Windows Server 2008.

Forest Functional Level Features

Over the years there have been few new features when it comes to the forest functional level. The one major new feature that was introduced with the Windows Server 2008 R2 forest functional level was the Active Directory Recycle Bin. The Recycle Bin is a way to restore deleted objects while still having your Active Directory online and operating.

There are no new features in Windows Server 2012 forest functional level. Also, there are no new features in Windows Server 2012 R2 when selecting the Windows Server 2012 R2 forest functional level.

Domain Functional Level Features

The domain functional level is limited to each domain in a forest, and there have been several feature additions since Windows Server 2008. One of them is fine-grained password policies that lets you have multiple password policies in your organization. Also another new feature is Distributed File System (DFS) replication for the SYSVOL share containing all Group Policy objects, for instance, and better replicate them between the domain controllers.

There have also been significant enhancements in the Kerberos authentication area, specifically better encryption that comes with raising the domain functional level to Windows Server 2008 level. As of Windows Server 2008 R2, a feature called "authentication mechanism assurance" was introduced that allows you to control access to file resources depending on whether the user has authenticated using a username and password or the user has authenticated by using a smart card.

The Windows Server 2012 domain functional level adds further improvements to Kerberos. One such improvement is that the token is compressed, which avoids problems with authentication when a user is a part of many groups, for instance. Also, to be able to fully utilized Dynamic Access Control which was introduced with Windows Server 2012, there is a need to raise the domain functional level to Windows Server 2012.

In Windows Server 2012 R2, there is only one new feature introduced in the Windows Server 2012 R2 domain functional level, and that is new forest-based authentication policies that can be used to control which machines a user can log on to.

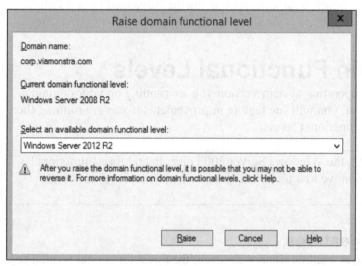

Raising the domain functional level will typically give you more bells and whistles to work with in your Active Directory.

Note: To raise the functional level of either the domain or the forest you need to have domain controllers running the corresponding OS version of the forest or domain functional level you are raising it to. For instance, to be able to run the Windows Server 2012 R2 forest functional level, you need at least one domain controller running Windows Server 2012 R2 in the forest. We strongly recommend having a homogenous setup of domain controllers running the same version of Windows. Raising the forest and domain functional levels is done in the Active Directory Domains and Trusts console.

Active Directory Schema

The schema in Active Directory is what defines properties or attributes that can be stored for each object, for instance the computer name for a computer object or the logon name for a user object.

With most new versions of Windows, there are new attributes added to the Active Directory schema that introduce new features. For example, in Windows Server 2012, new attributes were added for the user objects to support defining one or more primary devices for a user. To be able to use the primary device feature, there is really no need to install domain controllers using Windows Server 2012; you can simply extend the schema to use a primary device for folder redirection and/or roaming user profiles.

To be able to use new features such as multi-factor authentication when using Work Folders (detailed in depth in Chapter 6) requires you to upgrade your schema to Windows Server 2012 R2 level.

Extending the schema to the latest version is done by taking the adprep tools from the support\adprep folder which can be found on the Windows Server 2012 R2 ISO and executing it in your existing environment.

Extend the Schema to Windows Server 2012 R2

Extending the schema in your existing domain, without the need to replace your domain controllers with Windows Server 2012 R2, enables you to instantly use some of the new features introduced with Windows 8.1 and Windows Server 2012 R2.

> **Note**: ViaMonstra is only running on Windows Server 2012 R2, so the following steps are valid only if you want to upgrade your current domain's schema to Windows Server 2012 R2 level. If you install a Windows Server 2012 R2 domain controller in your environment where you have pre-Windows Server 2012 R2 domain controllers, adprep will be run automatically. You can use adprep, however, to prepare the schema extensions beforehand.

1. From a Windows Server 2012 R2 ISO, copy the adprep folder from the support folder to a domain-joined server in your existing domain.

2. Start a cmd.exe with a user account that holds the privileges of Schema Admins.

3. Type the following command:

   ```
   adprep /forestprep
   ```

4. Type the following command:

   ```
   adprep /domainprep
   ```

Analyze the Active Directory Schema

There is a great little tool you can use to see what attributes the Active Directory schema consists of. The tool is called ADSchemaAnalyzer. It is installed in C:\Windows\ADAM when the role Active Directory Lightweight Directory Services is installed and can then be used to examine the schema in detail and also compare schemas.

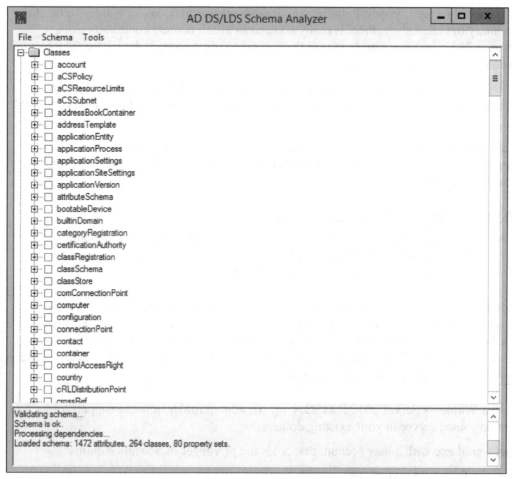

Use ADSchemaAnalyzer to view all Active Directory schema attributes.

Organizational Units

Very simply put, you can say that apart from user accounts and computer accounts, the "folder structure" in Active Directory consists of organizational units or OUs.

In most organizations, it can be tricky to change the entire OU structure because there are likely to be dependencies for applications that force you to keep the structure as it is. Keep in mind when creating new OUs that they can be used for delegating rights, which is discussed later in this chapter in the "Rights Delegation" section.

Group Policies

Today, group policies provide the most common way to centrally alter the configuration of your Windows clients, and they play a key role in keeping your clients secure and configured the way you want them to be.

Note: With Windows 8.1 and Windows Server 2012 R2, Microsoft introduced something called Desired State Configuration (DSC). We believe this technology will grow in use in future Windows versions. There are no pre-configured scenarios or cases for the Windows client in the current Windows 8.1 release, but keep an eye out for this in future releases. Desired State Configuration is an extension of PowerShell, which is covered in detail in Chapter 11.

Historically, the number of group policy settings that you can manage has increased significantly with each new Windows version released after Windows XP. In Windows XP, there were about 800 settings that you could configure; in Windows Vista, that was doubled to 1600, and with Windows 7, it was increased to around 2400 settings. As for Windows 8 and Windows 8.1, that number did not grow much, but now you can configure some 3000 settings using group policies.

New Group Policy Features in Windows 8.1

In Windows 8.1 and Windows Server 2012 R2, Microsoft has enhanced group policy in terms of three areas: improved IPv6 support for printers and in item-level targeting; improved logging to the Event Log / Group Policy log; and last but not least, a totally new feature that caches group policies for improving startup times, which is a very common problem in enterprises. The caching only applies if you are running group policies in synchronous mode, which always is the case if you have enabled the policy setting "Always wait for the network at computer startup and logon."

Activate Group Policy Caching

This, and following guides, assumes you have set up DC01 per the instructions in Appendix A.

1. On **DC01**, log on as **VIAMONSTRA\Administrator**, using a password of **P@ssw0rd**. Then start the **Group Policy Management** console.

2. Expand **Forest: corp.viamonstra.com**.

3. Expand **Domains**.

4. Expand **corp.viamonstra.com**.

5. Right-click **corp.viamonstra.com**, choose **Create a GPO in this domain, and Link it here**, and complete the following:

   Name the group policy **GPO Caching** and then click **OK**.

6. Right-click the **GPO Caching** group policy and choose **Edit**, which starts the **Group Policy Management Editor** console.

7. Under **Computer Configuration**, expand **Policies / Administrative Templates / System / Group Policy**.

8. Double-click the setting **Configure Group Policy Caching**.

9. Set the policy to **Enabled**, leave the default settings for the time values, and then click **OK**.

10. Close the **Group Policy Management Editor** console.

Central Store

Having a central store for group policies will make the lives of everyone who manages group policies in your organization easier. If you create a central store, you put all your Group Policy template files (ADMX and ADML files) in one location and make sure that everyone is using the same files when editing group policies.

Take, for instance managing, Office Group Policy settings where the policy definitions (ADMX files) are not available by default. You need to download them and add them to the Group Policy Management console when you want to edit an Office setting. If you do that on your machine and then a colleague of yours wants to edit that GPO from another machine, your colleague will see your Office settings as "Extra registry settings" as they lack the Office policy definitions in their local store.

Instead, copying those policy definition files to the central store ensures that everyone managing group policies uses the same policy definitions.

> **Note**: By default, the Group Policy Management console is designed to look for a central store of policy definitions in the SYSVOL share (for example, \\corp.viamonstra.com\SYSVOL\ corp.viamonstra.com\Policies\PolicyDefinitions). If a central store of group policies is not found, the console uses the content of the local PolicyDefinitions folder.

Create (or Update) the Central Store

1. On **DC01**, log on as **VIAMONSTRA\Administrator**. Again, using a password of **P@ssw0rd**.

2. Using **File Explorer**, navigate to **C:\Windows** and copy the entire **PolicyDefinitions** folder to **C:\Windows\SYSVOL\domain\Policies**.

> **Real World Note**: The preceding steps are also valid if you already have a central store in place for previous operating system versions. In such cases, you need to replace the contents in PolicyDefinitions in the SYSVOL share with all ADMX and ADML files from a Windows 8.1 machine. Also note that the Windows client does have some Group Policy templates that only exist on the client, so in the real world, you would copy PolicyDefinitions from a Windows 8.1 client as well to the SYSVOL share.

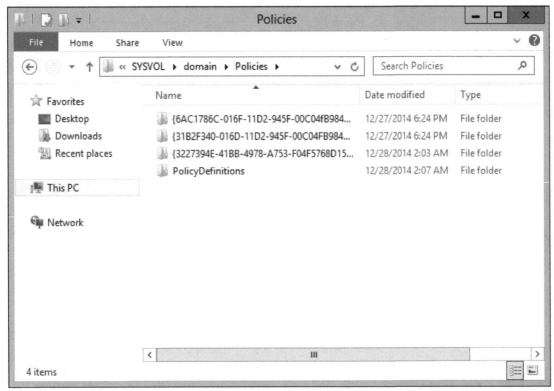

A central store is actually just the PolicyDefinitions folder being stored in the Policies node in the SYSVOL share.

Verify the Central Store Operation

1. On **DC01**, log on as **VIAMONSTRA\Administrator**.

2. Using the **Group Policy Management** console, edit the **Default Domain Policy** group policy.

3. In the **Computer Configuration / Policies** node, select **Administrative Templates**.

4. Note what the title says. When central store templates are being used, it says **Administrative Templates: Policy definitions (ADMX files) retrieved from central store**. Close the **Group Policy Management Editor**.

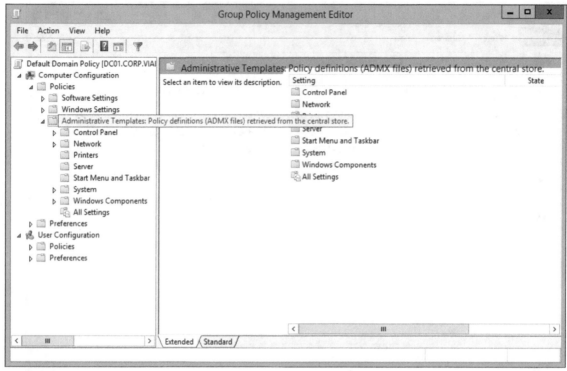

In the Group Policy Management Editor, you can see under Administrative Templates whether the policy definitions were loaded from the local store or the central store.

Managing Group Policies in the Enterprise

As we have clearly stated, group policies are essential for configuring Windows clients and maintaining the configuration. One of the biggest challenges with group policies is that there is no traceability of what has been changed in a particular group policy object, who did it, or when.

To address this issue, everyone managing group policies should use Microsoft's Advanced Group Policy Management (AGPM) tool which comes as a feature in the Microsoft Desktop Optimization Pack (MDOP).

> **Note**: AGPM is a part of MDOP that requires a separate addition to your software assurance license agreement. It is strongly recommended that MDOP is added to your current license, and not only for AGPM. The MDOP package contain other tools that are essential for managing clients in the enterprise. Another tool that is part of MDOP and covered later in this book is Microsoft BitLocker Administration and Monitoring which lets you manage BitLocker drive encryption in an enterprise way. Other tools in the MDOP include Diagnostics and Recovery Toolset (DaRT) for recovery of machines and User Experience Virtualization (UE-V) for roaming application settings. UE-V is covered in Chapter 6 in this book.

AGPM lets you take full control over the group policies and gives you the means to have a version history of all changes. You can easily go back in time if a certain policy setting did not have the effect you wanted or if someone made a mistake editing a group policy.

Installing and Working with AGPM

AGPM consists of a server component and a client component, and it has support for various roles so that you can not only delegate who can do what, but also have a review process to make sure that only changes that meet your corporate standards are deployed to production.

Prepare for AGPM Installation

In AGPM, you can have several roles; therefore, to determine what users should be allowed to do, you create four security groups. The roles which are available are:

- **Administrator (Full Control)**. Users belonging to this group can do everything in AGPM, such as editing a GPO and deploying it to production.

- **Editor**. A user belonging to this group can edit group policy objects and request that a new group policy is created, deleted, or restored.

- **Approver**. A user who holds the approver role can deploy the changes made by the editor to production.

- **Reviewer**. This role is just for those reviewing the settings in each group policy object.

Real World Note: Many organizations do not use this role-based setup but instead use only the version control and traceability. However, it is a best practice to set up AGPM so you are prepared for if or when the need to go one step further arises.

So to accommodate for these roles, create a security group for each role:

1. On **DC01**, log on as **VIAMONSTRA\Administrator**.

2. Open **Active Directory Users and Computers**.

3. Expand **corp.viamonstra.com**.

4. Expand the **ViaMonstra** OU, then select the **Security Groups** OU.

5. In the **Security Groups** OU, create a **Global** security group named **AGPM_Administrators**.

6. Repeat creating a global security group with the following names:

   o **AGPM_Editors**

   o **AGPM_Approvers**

   o **AGPM_Reviewers**

7. To the **AGPM_Administrators** group, add the group **Domain Admins**.

Install the AGPM Server Components

This procedure installs the AGPM 4.0 SP2 Server components and preferably is done on one of the domain controllers. This guide assumes you have set up DC01 per the instructions in Appendix A. If not, you need to make sure Microsoft .NET Framework 3.5 is installed because that's a requirement for AGPM 4.0 SP2.

Note: This requires that you have the MDOP 2014 ISO file, which contains AGPM 4.0 SP2, and that you mount it to be accessible from within the virtual machine, i.e. mount it using Hyper-V or VMware mounting capabilities. In this guide, the MDOP 2014 ISO file is mounted as D:.

1. On **DC01**, log on as **VIAMONSTRA\Administrator**.

2. Open **File Explorer**.

3. Double-click **D:** to bring up the splash screen for **Microsoft Desktop Optimization Pack for Software Assurance 2014**.

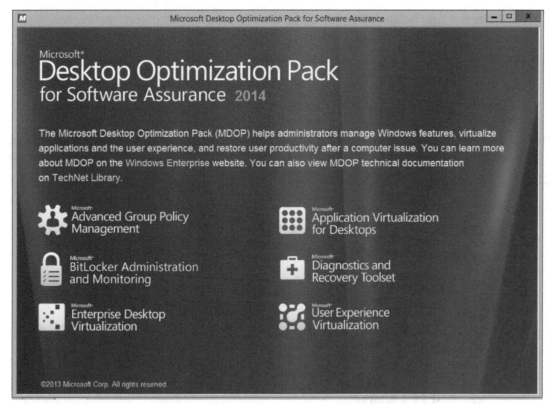

MDOP contains six tools that add additional value to your Windows environment. This book covers three of them.

4. Click **Advanced Group Policy Management**.

5. Click the **64-bit** link next to **AGPM 4.0 SP2 Server**. If the **User Account Control** dialog box appears, choose **Yes** to proceed with the installation.

6. On the **Welcome to the Setup Wizard for Microsoft Advanced Group Policy Management – Server** page, click **Next**.

7. On the **Microsoft Software License Terms** page, select the **I accept the license terms** check box and click **Next**.

8. On the **Application Path** page, accept the default settings and click **Next**.

9. On the **Archive Path** page, accept the default settings and click **Next**.

10. On the **AGPM Service Account** page, select **Local System** and click **Next**.

11. On the **Archive Owner** page, click **Browse** button and complete the following:

    Type **AGPM_Administrators**, click **Check Names**, and click **OK** followed by **Next**.

12. On the **Port Configuration** page, accept the default settings and click **Next**.

13. On the **Languages** page, accept the default settings and click **Next**.

14. On the **Ready to Install Microsoft Advanced Group Policy Management – Server** page, click **Install**.

15. On the **The installation of Microsoft Advanced Group Policy Management – Server is complete** page, click **Finish**.

Install the Client Part of AGPM

In ViaMonstra, all management of group policies will be done on DC01 so that is where you install the AGPM Client.

> **Real World Note**: In your enterprise environment, you must install the AGPM client on any machine that you use to manage group policies. It is recommended that you use one or only a few management stations for all group policy management.

1. On **DC01**, log on as **VIAMONSTRA\Administrator**.

2. Open **File Explorer**.

3. Double-click **D**: to bring up the splash screen for MDOP.

4. Click **Advanced Group Policy Management**.

5. Click the **64-bit** link next to **AGPM 4.0 SP2 Client**. If the **User Account Control** dialog box appears, choose **Yes** to proceed with the installation.

6. On the **Welcome to the Setup Wizard for Microsoft Advanced Group Policy Management – Client** page, click **Next**.

7. On the **Microsoft Software License Terms** page, select the **I accept the license terms** check box and click **Next**.

8. On the **Application Path** page, accept the default settings and click **Next**.

9. On the **AGPM Server** page, in the **DNS name or IP address** text box, enter **DC01**, and then click **Next**.

10. On the **Languages** page, accept the default settings and click **Next**.

11. On the **Ready to install Microsoft Advanced Group Policy Management – Client** page, click **Install**.

12. On the **The installation of Microsoft Advanced Group Policy Management – Client is complete** page, click **Finish**.

Define Roles for AGPM Access

Now you need to set up AGPM for the different roles. In the Group Policy Management console, the change control node is where all group policies are managed using AGPM. Any changes done to group policies outside of AGPM and the Change Control node will be overwritten when you deploy a group policy from within AGPM. Therefore it is advisable that you make sure to remove all rights for users to do normal editing of group policies.

1. On **DC01**, start the **Group Policy Management** console.

2. Expand **Forest: corp.viamonstra.com / Domains / corp.viamonstra.com**, and click **Change Control**.

> **Note:** If you get an access denied error when clicking on the Change Control node, make sure you added the Domain Admins group as a member to the AGPM_Administrators group. If needed log out, and log in again.

3. Click the **Domain Delegation** tab.

4. In **These groups and users have these roles for the selected GPO in the archive**, click the **Add** button and complete the following steps:

   a. Enter **AGPM_Editors**, and then click **Check Names** followed by **OK**.

   b. In the drop-down list, choose the **Role** named **Editor** and then click **OK**.

   c. Repeat and add **AGPM_Approvers** and **AGPM_Reviewers**, choosing the corresponding **Role**.

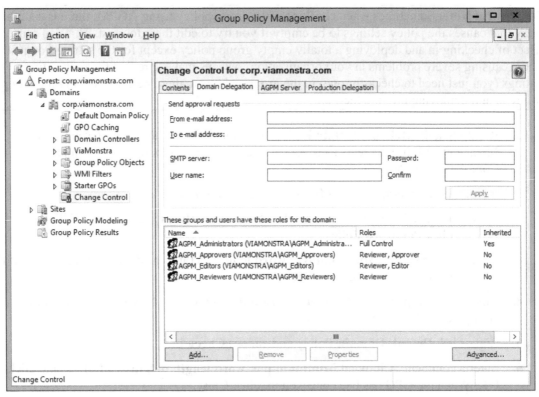

By adding all the roles to AGPM, all GPOs you take control of with AGPM will be handled according to the specified permissions for each role.

Take Control of the Group Policies

1. On **DC01**, using the **Group Policy Management** console, in the **Change Control** node.

2. In the **Contents** tab, click the **Uncontrolled** tab.

3. Right-click **Default Domain Policy**, choose **Control**, and then click **OK**. When control has been taken, click **Close**.

4. Click the **Controlled** tab to see that the **Default Domain Policy** is now being controlled by AGPM.

Edit and Deploy a Group Policy

1. Using the **Group Policy Management** console, in the **Change Control** node.

2. Right-click the **Default Domain Policy**, choose **Check Out**, and then click **OK**. When the policy has been checked out, click **Close**. The group policy is now checked out by you and is ready for editing.

Real World Note: Sometimes when checking out a group policy using AGPM, there is a slight delay that causes the policy settings to be empty if you try to edit them too fast. This can cause the effect of checking in and deploying a totally empty group policy except for the setting you just made, causing severe problems in your organization. Always make sure that the preexisting settings (you just need to check for one) in the group policy are there before checking the group policy in and deploying it to production.

3. Right-click the **Default Domain Policy** and choose **Edit**. The regular Group Policy Management Editor appears as if you were editing a group policy the "regular" way. Complete these steps:

    a. Under **Computer Configuration**, expand **Policies**.

    b. Expand **Windows Settings**, then **Security Settings** and **Account Policies**, and click **Password Policy**.

    c. Double-click **Minimum password length**, set it to be **8 characters** instead of the default 7, and then click **OK**.

4. Close the **Group Policy Management Editor** and return to **Change Control** in the Group Policy Management console.

5. Right-click **Default Domain Policy** and choose **Check in**.

6. Enter a comment "**Changed Minimum password length to 8 instead of 7.**" and click **OK**. When the GPO has been checked in, click **Close**.

Note: Up until this point, you have made a change to a GPO but still have not deployed it to production and all the client machines. If you choose to have delegated control over the group policies, now is where an approver would come in to play and have the chance either to approve or reject the change. As you are using a plain AGPM role structure, i.e. you are de facto AGPM_Administrators, you can go ahead and deploy this GPO to the production environment.

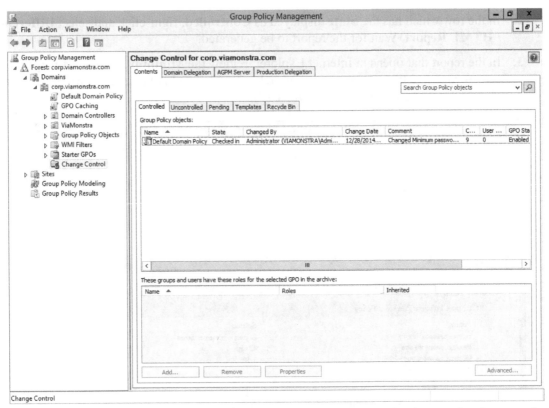

Checking in the changes you've made is essential, but apart from checking in the changes, the policy must also be "deployed," which is the AGPM term for saying "make the GPO changes available" to the targeted machines or users.

7. Right-click **Default Domain Policy** and choose **Deploy**; then click **Yes** in the **Deploy GPO** dialog box. When the GPO has been deployed, click **Close**. At this point, the GPO is put into the SYSVOL share and is immediately available to be applied for your clients.

Real World Note: If you change the linking or WMI filter on a Group Policy object, you can do this only in the GPMC view. When you deploy the GPO using AGPM, that change will be lost. Therefore, if you do change the WMI filter or link the GPO to another OU, make sure you go to AGPM and choose Import from production to make sure that these changes are saved. Otherwise, AGPM will not be aware of them.

Check Differences in Group Policies

One of the most useful features in AGPM is that you can check what has changed in a particular group policy over time. This is really good for traceability when troubleshooting possible errors that occur in your environment.

1. Using the **Group Policy Management** console, in the **Change Control** node, right-click the **Default Domain Policy** and select **History**.

2. In the row which has the **State** displayed as **Controlled**, right-click and select **Differences / HTML Report**. Wait for the report to be generated.

3. In the report that opens in Internet Explorer, review the **Minimum password length setting** and note that the change is highlighted in blue and indicates the current value (8 characters) as well as the previous value (7).

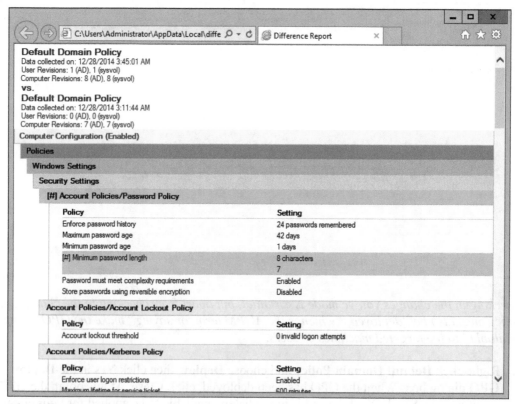

The difference feature is really good for tracking changes in GPOs historically, and the changes are highlighted and easy to spot.

4. Close **Internet Explorer**, and then close the **History for Default Domain Policy** window.

Revert a Group Policy Change

As we are only human, mistakes do occur. The power of AGPM is that you can quickly revert to an older group policy and deploy that to production easily.

1. Using the **Group Policy Management** console, in the **Change Control** node, right-click the **Default Domain Policy**, choose **History**, and then click the **Unique Versions** tab.

2. Right-click the **Default Domain Policy** that has the **State** labeled as **Controlled**.

3. Click **Deploy**, followed by **Yes**. When the group policy has deployed, click **Close**.

You have now reverted to the previous group policy settings, where the minimum password length was set to the default of 7.

Group Policy Infrastructure Health Check

As group policies are vital to the configuration of your clients, it is imperative that you have a fully working infrastructure on the backend. Windows Server 2012 introduced a GPO health check tool, which checks your infrastructure from a GPO point of view to analyze whether there are problems related to replication or inconsistences in the SYSVOL share that stores all group policy objects.

Check the Health of Your Infrastructure

1.   On **DC01**, start the **Group Policy Management** console.

2.   Expand **Forest: corp.viamonstra.com**.

3.   Expand **Domains**.

4.   Click **corp.viamonstra.com**.

5.   Click the **Detect Now** button located in the lower right corner to initialize the health check.

Any errors in replication or inconsistencies are displayed so that you can take further actions on resolving the issues detected. Use this check regularly to verify a fully operational infrastructure for delivering group policies to your Windows clients.

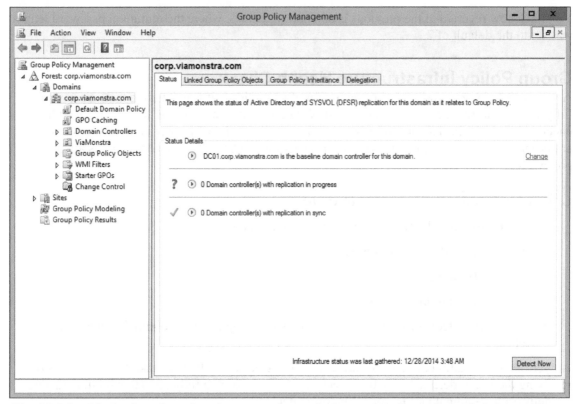

The GPO health check tool verifies the status of your domain controllers, the replication, and a few other aspects that need to be in place for a fully functional group policy environment on the machines in your Active Directory.

Volume Activation

We don't think anyone considers licensing and activation to be fun. There is nothing much to say about it because you need your machines to be both licensed and activated. Most enterprise environments running Windows 7 (or Windows Server 2008 R2) have a Key Management Service (KMS) server setup that activates machines automatically.

Windows 8, along with Office 2013, introduced a new way of activating client machines: that is, Active Directory-based activations. You also can do KMS-based activations as before, or use Multiple Activation Key (MAK) activation for scenarios in which you do not have at least 25 machines to activate (the KMS-based activation minimum).

Also note that Windows Server 2012 brings a graphical user interface to volume activation for the first time, meaning it is a separate role called "Volume Activation." Configuring the volume activation role basically means that you can use the GUI to install either a KMS server or Active Directory-based activations.

Active Directory-Based Activation vs. KMS Activation

Active Directory-Based Activation (ADBA) basically means easier and more secure activation than ever. Having the activation done via the regular communication with domain controllers requires the machine to be a part of the domain, meaning you have total control over which machines can be activated in your environment.

Really small businesses benefit from the fact that you can skip MAK activation and rely solely on ADBA for Windows 8.1, as there are no limits on the number of clients you need to have.

Requirements for Using ADBA

To be able to use ADBA, you must extend the Active Directory schema to a minimum of Windows Server 2012 schema. This does not mean you need to introduce Windows Server 2012 (or 2012 R2) domain controllers in your environment, but you need to take the adprep utility from the Windows Server 2012 or Windows Server 2012 R2 installation media/ISO (located in the support/adprep directory) and run that command from any domain member in the domain. This extends the schema of the Active Directory to house the new activation objects.

Coexistence of ADBA with Your Current KMS Infrastructure

In an enterprise environment, you most likely already have a KMS infrastructure activating not only your Windows 7 machines but also Office 2010. That is the case for ViaMonstra. The point is that if you do have KMS in place, you can and must continue to use KMS to be able to activate Windows 7 and Office 2010 for as long as you have these products in your environment. ADBA is applicable only for Windows 8 and 8.1, Windows Server 2012 and 2012 R2, and Office 2013.

> **Note**: Previously there has been no elegant (read GUI) way of activating a KMS server. Starting with Windows Server 2012, there is a new role made specifically for activation. It is called the Volume Activation role.

Rights Delegation

In a large organization, you simply cannot grant, for example, domain administrator rights to everyone who needs to edit a security group. Instead, what you should use is Active Directory rights delegation to delegate rights to only a particular OU or particular objects.

A commonly used example of delegating rights to a particular OU is one in which you appoint a specific account to be able to join computers to the domain and to only a certain OU during deployment time. In those cases, you want to minimize what the user account can do and let that user have as few privileges as possible. Rights delegation in Active Directory is very powerful in creating granular control and access to certain parts of an Active Directory.

Delegate Rights for a User to a Particular OU

In this example, you delegate rights for the Domain Users group to modify the Description attribute of any security group located in the ViaMonstra OU.

1. On **DC01**, start the **Active Directory Users and Computers** console.

2. Expand the node **corp.viamonstra.com**.

3. Right-click the **ViaMonstra** OU and choose **Delegate Control**.

4. On the **Welcome to the Delegation of Control Wizard** page, click **Next**.

5. On the **Users or Groups** page, click the **Add** button and complete the following:

    Enter **Domain Users**, click **Check Names**, followed by **OK**, and then click **Next**.

6. On the **Tasks to Delegate** page, select the **Create a custom task to delegate** option, and then click **Next**.

7. On the **Active Directory Object Type** page, select **Delegate control of: Only the following objects in the folder** and complete the following:

    Scroll down to **Group objects**, select the check box, and then click **Next**.

8. On the **Permissions** page, select the **Property-specific** check box and complete the following:

    Scroll down to **Write Description**, select the check box, and then click **Next**.

9. On the **Completing the Delegation of Control Wizard** page, click **Finish**.

Now the Domain Users group, i.e. every user in your organization, can add a description to a group. This is a demonstration of how powerful delegating rights for only certain properties and attributes in Active Directory can be.

Using the Delegation of Control Wizard can delegate rights on small parts of objects in your Active Directory.

Real World Note: Some other examples from the field include the needs for the helpdesk to enable and disable computer accounts and for having user control-specific security groups. In both these scenarios, rights delegation on an OU in Active Directory come in very handy.

Chapter 2

Configuration Manager Infrastructure

For more than 10 years, Microsoft has developed its management platform—from Microsoft Systems Management Server 1.0, released back in 1994, to today's people-centric IT. A lot has changed with the shift from system-focused, or rather device-focused, management to have the end user in focus in the latest releases. In the Configuration Manager 2012 R2 release, there is now even a Site System Role called Intune Connector which shows that management has stretched out of the datacenter into the cloud and onto the Internet. There are some features, however, that have to reside within the corporate network, and the Pre-Boot Execution Environment (PXE) service is one of them.

Configuration Manager is an extremely comprehensive product for managing not only clients or servers from Microsoft but also OS X, Linux, HP UX, and Solaris systems. Using the cloud-based Intune service, it also is possible to use MDM (Mobile Device Management) functionality for management of iOS, Windows RT, Android, and even non-domain joined Windows 8.1 devices.

Sites

As of Configuration Manager 2012, the required hierarchy in a Configuration Manager environment has changed drastically. From previous needs for multiple primary sites, now the only need for multiple primary sites more or less comes down to whether your environment will include more than 100,000 devices. If your environment will use fewer devices than that, you'll most likely do just fine with one primary site.

Primary vs. Secondary

A Configuration Manager installation must have at least one primary site. This site can then be connected to up to 24 other primary sites when connected to a hierarchy using a Central Administration Site. Each primary site also can have up to 250 secondary sites connected to it. Communication between a primary site server and a secondary site server is based on replication using SQL, which is why a secondary site is perfectly placed at a location where a large number of clients are located so that all their communication to the primary site server can be collected by the secondary site server acting as a proxy and then sent off to the primary site server using SQL instead of HTTP communication.

Site System Roles

Each site in Configuration Manager consists of at least one site system that holds one or more site system roles. One can think of these different roles as different services within a normal Active Directory domain where different servers hold different roles, as well. Not only are there servers holding the special Active Directory FSMO (Flexible Single Master Operations) roles, such as the RID Master or Primary Domain Controller Emulator role, but there also are more common roles like DNS and DHCP.

The absolutely most common role is the Distribution Point role, which is a role whose purpose is to hold content and deliver it to clients that need it. Even though it is the most common role, it is not a required role for a Configuration Manager site or environment. The Management Point role, however, is a mandatory role. You simply cannot manage Configuration Manager clients without it. The Management Point role acts as a form of domain controller in that it gives clients policies that they should evaluate and act upon. A policy can be to install a specific application or operating system.

Content Management

There are two major things to consider when designing a new Configuration Manager infrastructure. The first one is to size it according to the number of clients and to arrange with secondary sites where needed. The second thing is to make sure that clients out in the network can get content and that the content gets close to the clients so that it only has to travel as few times as possible over network links.

Back in the 2007 version of Configuration Manager, secondary sites were used for two things: One was to proxy network traffic from clients sending status updates and requesting policy information. The second thing was to enable a distribution point to throttle how much network traffic it could use to get content from the primary site server during specific hours. In Configuration Manager 2012 and later, that is possible for a distribution point, as well. This makes the need for secondary sites less frequent.

However, it is not only to preserve network usage that you need to think ahead when it comes to content. You also need to make sure that you know where content ends up on your Configuration Manager servers.

Creating Folder Structure and NO_SMS_ON_DRIVE.SMS

Once the bits and bytes for a distribution point, or the Site Server role, are installed on a server, it will calculate which volume is most appropriate to host the content library.

One way to make sure that a volume is left unused by Configuration Manager is to place an empty file called NO_SMS_ON_DRIVE.SMS in the root of the volume. During setup of a distribution point, there are also options to select the primary and secondary volume for the content library.

When the content library is staged, it is done by accessing content from a source directory. Each application's deployment type, package, operating system image, driver package, and so on has its own source path. These sources can be anywhere on the network; however, it is good practice to store them in one organized location.

Organize the Source Folders

This, and following guides, assumes you have set up CM01 per the instructions in Appendix A.

1. On **CM01**, log on as **VIAMONSTRA\Administrator**, using a password of **P@ssw0rd**. Then using **File Explorer**, navigate to the **D:** drive.

2. Create a folder in the root of the drive called **SCCM_Source$** and open the folder.

3. In **D:\ SCCM_Source$**, create four new folders called **Applications**, **OSD**, **Packages**, and **Software Updates**. Then open the **OSD** folder.

4. Within the **OSD** folder, create six new folders called **Custom Settings**, **Driver Packages**, **Driver Sources, MDT Toolkit Files, Boot Images**, and **OS Images**.

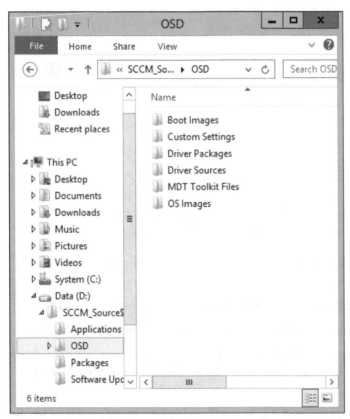

Keeping a good structure of source files makes an upgrade much easier. It's also far easier to take backups of one folder than many.

5. Navigate back to the root of the drive, right-click the **SCCM_Source$** folder and select **Properties**.

6. In the **SCCM_Source$ Properties** dialog box, select the **Sharing** tab and click **Advanced Sharing**.

7. In the **Advanced Sharing** dialog box, select **Share this folder** and click **Permissions**.

8. In the **Permissions for SCCM_Source$** dialog box, select **Full Control** to **Everyone** and click **OK** twice to come back to the properties dialog box.

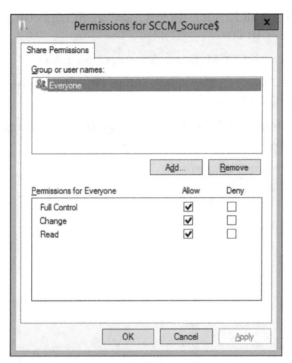

By setting Everyone Full Control on the share, you only need to take care of NTFS permissions since Everyone no longer includes the Unauthenticated Users group.

9. Back at the **SCCM_Source$ Properties** dialog box, select the **Security** tab and click **Advanced**.

10. In the **Advanced Security Settings for SCCM_Source$** dialog box, click **Add**.

11. Click **Select a principal** in the **Permissions Entry for SCCM_Source$** dialog box.

12. In the **Select user, Computer, Service Account, or Group** dialog box, change **Object Types** to include **Computers**, enter **CM01** in the **Enter the object name to select** field, and click **OK**.

13. Back at the **Permission Entry for SCCM_Source$** dialog box, make sure that **Applies to** is set to **This Folder, subfolders and files**, select **Full control**, and click **OK**.

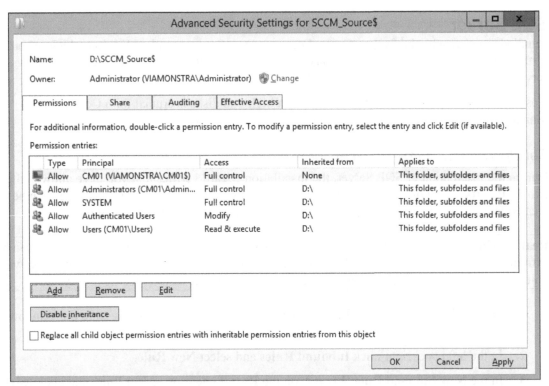

When the site server accesses the source folder, it does so using the share, and thus it does not use its SYSTEM credentials but rather its Active Directory Account credentials.

14. Click **OK** to close the **Advanced Security Settings for SCCM_Source$** dialog box and then close the **SCCM_Source$ Properties** dialog box, as well.

Installing the Primary Site

Running the primary site server in a virtual machine is supported by Microsoft as long as you follow the guidelines for hardware requirements that apply to a physical machine. Running the primary site server on hardware that isn't capable of delivering the performance needed will make your job a lot harder and take more time. Due to the nature of how Configuration Manager is built on SQL Server technologies, it is important to have hard drives that can deliver a lot of IOPS (Input / Output Per Second). It is in fact the number one priority when sizing hardware for a primary site server. If you cannot host your database disks on SSD drives, at least make sure that they will be hosted on dedicated traditional mechanical disk drives. If you are using a SAN, make sure to get dedicated LUNs and disk ports.

Real World Note: Running the site server in a VM gives many benefits, such as less hardware dependency, because the VM can be running on different hosts. You also could make a snapshot of your VM before you make any large updates, such as installing a service pack.

SQL Server

Bundled together with the System Center license is SQL Server Standard Edition which, when installed on the same server as the primary site server, supports up to 50,000 clients (Windows servers, Windows clients, and/or Linux/UNIX systems).

Hosting the database and temp database files on high-end disks is crucial for a Configuration Manager site server, whereas the program files can be hosted on slow volumes.

Set Up Windows Firewall Exceptions

During the installation of SQL Server, the installation wizard verifies that you have allowed the two TCP ports that SQL Server uses for connectivity from other servers. Although they can be created later, you will create them before so you don't get the warning during setup.

> **Real World Note**: Creating firewall rules using group policies for both servers and clients can be extremely efficient and works very well in larger environments. It is important to control on what objects those group policies apply using security groups instead of OUs for flexibility.

1. On **CM01**, start **Windows Firewall with Advanced Security** by pressing the Windows logo key to enter the **Start screen**, typing **wf**, and pressing **Enter**.

2. In the left pane, right-click **Inbound Rules** and select **New Rule**.

3. In the **New Inbound Rule Wizard**, on the **Rule Type** page, select **Port**, and click **Next**.

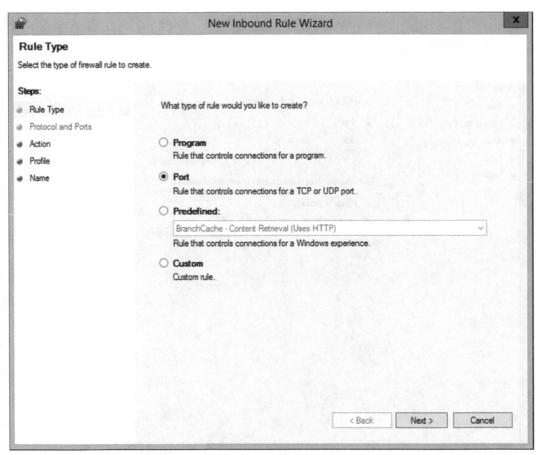

The built-in firewall in Windows has been greatly improved over the years, and we recommend using it for all clients and servers.

Real World Note: Rules can be created based on TCP or UDP ports, but also to allow specific applications, binaries, to accept incoming connections or allow outgoing connections when specific criteria are met, such as the traffic is encrypted or that the client is on the "domain" network.

4. On the **Protocol and Ports** page, make sure **TCP** is selected, enter **1433, 4022** as **Specific local ports**, and click **Next**.

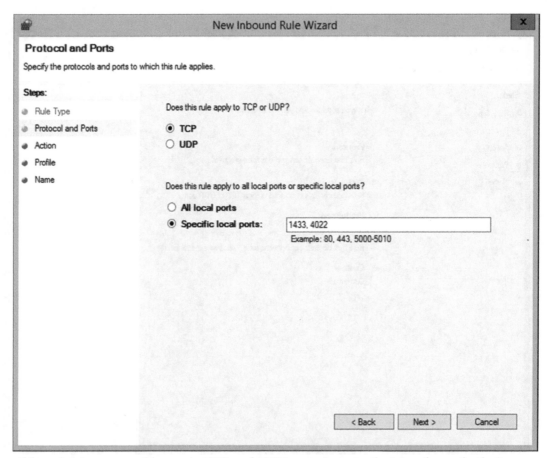

Although it is not possible to mix TCP and UDP ports in one rule, it works perfectly fine to mix an array of ports and ranges. Individual ports in an array are defined by colons and ranges are defined using a hyphen.

5. On the **Action** page, make sure **Allow the connection** is selected and click **Next**.

6. On the **Profile** page, clear the **Private** and **Public** check boxes, but leave **Domain** selected and click **Next**.

7. On the **Name** page, in the **Name:** text box, type **SQL Server Ports**. Optionally, type text explaining that this rule is for the SQL Server for the Configuration Manager primary site server. Then click **Finish**.

8. Close the **Windows Firewall with Advanced Security** window.

Install SQL Server 2012 Standard with SP1

Although this installation design works perfectly in a lab scenario, in a production environment, you would want to add additional RAID volumes for the content library, database files, temp database files, and all SQL log files. Configuration Manager is really SQL-intensive, which means that the disks that have the SQL files on them should be able to deliver a lot of IOPS.

1. On **CM01**, start **SQL Server 2012 SP1 Setup** (setup.exe) from the SQL Server 2012 Standard with SP1 (x64) installation media.

2. In the **SQL Server Installation Center**, navigate to **Installation** and click **New SQL Server stand-alone installation or add features to an existing installation**.

3. On the **Setup Support Rules** page, after the **Setup Support Rules** have been processed, click **OK**.

4. Wait until the main **SQL Server 2012 Setup** wizard starts, then on the **Product Key** page, click **Next**

5. On the **License Terms** page, select the **I accept the license terms** check box, and if applicable for you, select the check box to send usage data to Microsoft. Then click **Next**.

6. On the **Product Updates** page, if your environment does not have Internet connectivity, you see an exception that SQL Server Setup could not search for updates, which is ok for this setup. Click **Next**.

7. After the setup files installation has been completed, on the **Install Setup Files** page, click **Install**.

8. Again **Setup Support Rules** are processed, and you will see a warning for **Windows Firewall**. Ignore that warning for now (you already configured the firewall), and click **Next**.

9. On the **Setup Role** page, make sure **SQL Server Feature Installation** is selected, and click **Next**.

10. On the **Feature Selection** page, select **Database Engine Services**, **Reporting Services – Native**, and **Management Tools – Complete**, and then click **Next**.

11. When the operation is done, on the **Installation Rules** page, click **Next**.

12. On the **Instance Configuration** page, change the **Instance root directory** to **D:\MSSQL**, but leave the **Instance ID** as it is and click **Next**.

13. On the **Disk Space Requirements** page, click **Next** after examining the calculation.

14. On the **Server Configuration** page, on the **Service Accounts** tab, change the **Account Name** for the **SQL Server Database Engine** to **NT AUTHORITY\SYSTEM** (In the drop-down list, select Browse, type in System and click OK).

15. In the **Collation** tab, make sure the **Database Engine** is set to use the **SQL_Latin1_General_CP1_CI_AS** collation, and then click **Next**.

16. On the **Database Engine Configuration** page, add the **VIAMONSTRA\Administrator** account as **SQL Server administrators** by clicking **Add Current User**. Also add the **CM01\Administrators** group, by clicking **Add** (will be renamed to BUILTIN\Administrators after being added). Note the paths for all file types in the **Data Directories** tab, and then click **Next**.

17. On the **Reporting Services Configuration** page, make sure **Install and configure** is selected and click **Next**.

18. On the **Error Reporting** page, if applicable for you, select the check box to send error reports to Microsoft and click **Next**.

19. After the operation is completed, on the **Installation Configuration Rules** page, click **Next**.

20. On the **Ready to Install** page, note that the complete unattended file for this SQL Server installation has been saved in the **Configuration file path**, and then click **Install** to start the SQL Server 2012 SP1 installation.

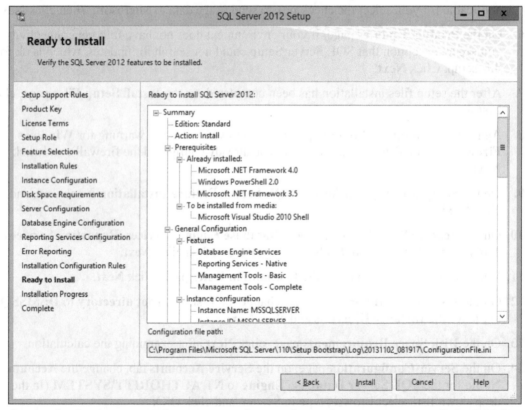

Saving the ConfigurationFile.ini is a good way to know that you can reinstall the SQL Server exactly the way it was set up in the first place.

21. On the **Complete** page, when the installation is complete, review the **Status** for each **Feature** and then click **Close** to complete the installation.

22. Close the **SQL Server Installation Center**.

Limit SQL Server Memory

1. On **CM01**, start the **SQL Server Management Studio** located among the apps on the **Start screen**.

2. When prompted to **Connect to Server**, make sure that the **Server name** is **CM01** and then click **Connect**.

3. In the **Object Explorer** window, right-click the **CM01** instance to the left and click **Properties**.

Note: If the Object Explorer isn't visible, press F8.

4. Select the **Memory** node.

5. Set the **Minimum server memory** to approximately 50% of your server's total RAM, i.e. **8192** if you gave your VM 16 GB.

6. Set the **Maximum server memory** to approximately 80% of your server's total RAM, i.e. **13312** if you gave your VM 16 GB.

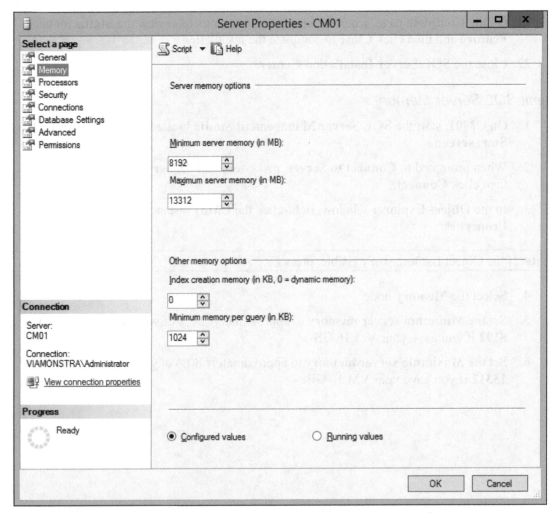

Limiting the SQL memory might seem like a small thing to do, but it can have great performance impact compared to leaving it at the default.

7. Click **OK** to save the new values and close the **Server Properties** dialog box.

8. Close **Microsoft SQL Server Management Studio**.

You also can set the server memory options using the following SQL script:

```
EXEC sys.sp_configure N'show advanced options', N'1'  RECONFIGURE
WITH OVERRIDE

GO

EXEC sys.sp_configure N'min server memory (MB)', N'8192'

GO

EXEC sys.sp_configure N'max server memory (MB)', N'13312'

GO

RECONFIGURE WITH OVERRIDE

GO

EXEC sys.sp_configure N'show advanced options', N'0'  RECONFIGURE
WITH OVERRIDE

GO
```

Prerequisites

In addition to a primary site in Configuration Manager requiring at least SQL Server Standard
Edition, a set of other software and server features must be installed prior to the installation of the
site server. Depending on the site server roles that you are running on a server, different Windows
Server roles and features are required. Microsoft keeps an updated list of all requirements at
http://technet.microsoft.com/en-us/library/gg682077.aspx#BKMK_SupConfigSiteSystemReq.

Real World Note: Just as you can use the hydration kit for this book, there are many other
installation resources in the community. One that can help you install all the prerequisites is the
Prerequisites Installation Tool developed by Nickolaj Andersen and available at
http://www.scconfigmgr.com/2013/12/18/configmgr-2012-r2-prerequisites-installation-tool.

Windows Server Roles and Features

ViaMonstra runs all necessary site server roles on the primary site server, and therefore the following Windows Server roles and features are required:

- .NET Framework 3.5

   HTTP Activation

   Non-HTTP Activation

- .NET Framework 4.5

   ASP.NET 4.5

- BITS Server Extensions

- Remote Differential Compression

- IIS

   o Common HTTP Features

      ▪ Default Document

      ▪ Static Content

   o IIS 6 Management Compatibility

      ▪ IIS 6 Metabase Compatibility

      ▪ IIS 6 WMI Compatibility

   o Application Development

      ▪ ASP.NET 3.5

      ▪ ASP.NET 4.5

      ▪ .NET Extensibility 3.5

      ▪ .NET Extensibility 4.5

      ▪ ISAPI Extensions

   o Security

   Windows Authentication

When adding Windows Server roles and features, there are sometimes requirements to other features, as well. When required, those other features also must be installed. There is a complete list of requirements that Microsoft updates at http://technet.microsoft.com/en-us/library/gg682077.aspx#BKMK_Win2k12SiteSystemPrereqs.

Install Necessary Windows Server Roles and Features

1. On **CM01**, start the **Server Manager** if not already started.

2. From the menu in the upper right corner, click **Manage** and **Add Roles and Features**.

3. On the **Before you begin** page, click **Next**.

4. On the **Select installation type** page, make sure **Role-based or feature-based installation** is selected and click **Next**.

5. On the **Select destination server** page, make sure **Select a server from the server pool** is selected and **CM01.corp.viamonstra.com** is selected in the **Server Pool**, and then click **Next**.

6. On the **Server Roles** page, select **Web Server (IIS)**. When prompted to add required features for each role, make sure **Include management tools (if applicable)** is selected and click **Add Features**. Then click **Next**.

7. For the following steps, when prompted, always make sure that **Include management tools (if applicable)** is selected and click **Add Features**.

8. On the **Features** page, expand **.NET Framework 3.5 Features**, make sure **.NET Framework 3.5 (includes .NET 2.0 and 3.0)** is selected, and select **HTTP Activation**.

9. Expand **Background Intelligent Transfer Service (BITS)** and select **IIS Server Extension**.

10. Select **Remote Differential Compression**, and click **Next**.

11. On the **Web Server Role (IIS)** page, click **Next**.

12. On the **Select role services** page, under **Security**, select **Windows Authentication**.

13. Still on the **Select role services** page, under **Management Tools**, expand **IIS 6 Management Compatibility**, select **IIS 6 WMI Compatibility**, and then click **Next**.

14. On the **Confirmation** page, click **Install** to start the installation.

15. When the text changes to **Configuration successfully completed**, click **Close** to close the **Add Roles and Features Wizard**.

Software

To install Configuration Manager, there is some other software that needs to be installed beforehand. Deployment Tools, Windows Preinstallation Environment (Windows PE), and User State Migration Tool (USMT) are all needed by Configuration Manager and bundled into Windows Assessment and Deployment Kit (ADK). The ADK was previously known as Windows Automated Installation Kit (WAIK) before its name changed with Windows 8.

Install Windows Assessment and Deployment Kit for Windows 8.1
In this guide we assume you downloaded Windows ADK 8.1 from Microsoft.

1. On **CM01**, start **adksetup** from the Windows ADK 8.1 installation source.

2. On the **Specify Location** page, accept the default settings, and click **Next**.

3. On the **Join the Customer Experience Improvement Program (CEIP)** page, if applicable for you, select **Yes** to join the CEIP. Then click **Next**.

4. On the **License Agreement** page, click **Accept**.

5. On the **Select the features you want to install** page, clear all features except **Deployment Tools, Windows Preinstallation Environment (Windows PE),** and **User State Migration Tool (USMT)** and then click **Install**.

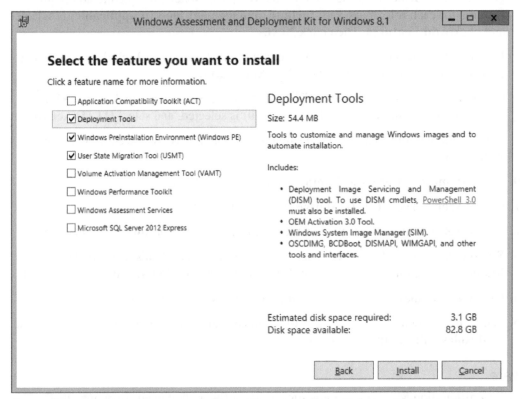

In smaller environments, some people prefer to install the Volume Activation Management Tool on the same server as Configuration Manager. In that case, make sure to use the full version of SQL Server that you already installed. Having SQL Server Express also kills performance of your site server.

6. When the **Welcome to the Windows Assessment and Deployment Kit for Windows 8.1** page appears, click **Close** to complete the installation.

Configuration Manager 2012 R2

The Configuration Manager 2012 R2 installation isn't very complex. You just need to know what to do before you start the setup because it does not do everything for you even though the wizard is great. Although we've taken you through the steps needed to run the necessary site roles on your server, there are some things outside the server that need to be done before the installation starts. Although none of the following steps are truly necessary in order to complete the installation of the site server, they are all recommended and you will get warnings if you skip them.

Extending the Active Directory Schema

By extending your Active Directory domain's schema, you enable Configuration Manager to write site information into the Active Directory Container *System Management* which the Configuration Manager client can use to find the correct site and management point to talk to.

Even though extending the Active Directory schema is an easy task to perform, it is important to know that it is an action that cannot be reversed.

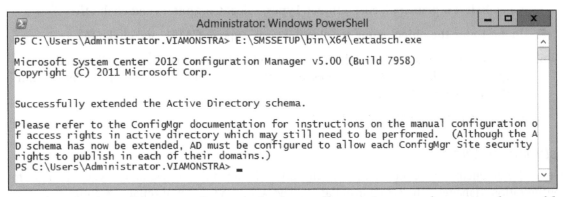

Extending the Active Directory schema can be done only once; however, the command can safely be executed more than once. If the schema has been extended for SCCM 2007, it does not need to be done again.

System Management Container

In order for the site servers to be able to store data in Active Directory so that the Configuration Manager clients can look up the correct management point, a container must be created within Active Directory where each site server has access to create and delete objects. A common practice is to create a security group in the Active Directory domain of which all site servers, not all Configuration Manager servers, are members.

Create a System Management Container

1.   On **DC01**, start **ADSI Edit**.

2.   On the **Action** menu, select **Connect to** and then press **OK** in the **Connection Settings** dialog box.

3. Double-click **Default naming context**.

4. Double-click **DC=corp,DC=viamonstra,DC=com**.

5. Right-click **CN=System** and select **New / Object**.

6. In the **Create Object** wizard, select **container** and click **Next**.

7. In the **Value:** text box, type in **System Management** and click **Next**.

8. Click **Finish** to close the wizard.

Set Permissions on the System Management Container

1. In **ADSI Edit**, double-click **CN=System**, right-click **CN=System Management**, and select **Properties**.

2. Select the **Security** tab and click **Advanced**.

3. In the **Advanced Security Settings for System Management** dialog box, click **Add**.

4. Click **Select a principal**, click **Object Types**, select **Computers** and click **OK**.

5. In the **Enter the object name to select** text box, type in **CM01**, and click **OK**.

6. In the **Permissions** list, select **Full control** and make sure that **Type** is **Allow** and **Applies to** is **This object and all descendant objects**. Then click **OK** in the **Permission Entry for System Management** window.

7. Click **OK** twice and close **ADSI Edit**.

Installing the Site Server

When all prerequisites are completed, you can start with one of the easiest things when it comes to Configuration Manager – the actual installation. The wizard helps you through the entire installation, and although you could do an unattended installation of Configuration Manager, the GUI version isn't so painful that you can't stand it once or twice.

Real World Note: After Configuration Manager is installed, changing the server name or the domain membership of the server is no longer supported.

Although you do not need to do so, it has become quite common to create the database before you install Configuration Manager. For this environment, there isn't a need for it, but for larger installations (above 5,000 clients), we do recommend that you at least take a look at how the databases are going to grow. The reason is to get the best performance you can. Kent Agerlund has created an Excel spreadsheet to help with sizing a database for Configuration Manager: http://blog.coretech.dk/kea/system-center-2012-configuration-manager-sql-recommendations/.

Furthermore, it is important to run the installation with Domain Administrator credentials, or you need to verify that the account running the SQL Reporting Services is a member of the built-in Active Directory group Windows Authorization Access Group and have Allow on the Read tokenGroupsGlobalAndUniversal permission, or role-based access to reports will not work.

> **Note**: To complete this step-by-step guide, you must have an Internet connection in the virtual machine. If you need help getting the Internet to work in the virtual machine, please see Johan Arwidmark's guide on how to set up virtual routers in the lab environment at http://tinyurl.com/cln7fd2.

1.   On **CM01**, using **File Explorer**, create the **D:\Setup\CM2012DL** folder.

2.   Start **setup.exe** from the **SMSSETUP\BIN\X64** folder on the **System Center 2012 R2 Configuration Manager** installation ISO.

3.   On the **Before You Begin** page, click **Next**.

4.   On the **Getting Started** page, leave **Install a Configuration Manager primary site** selected and the **Use typical installation options for a stand-alone primary site** check box cleared, and click **Next**.

5.   On the **Product Key** page, enter your **Product Key** or select to install the evaluation edition and click **Next**.

6.   On the **Microsoft Software License Terms** page, select **I accept these license terms** and click **Next**.

7.   On the **Prerequisite Licenses** page, select all three check boxes to accept all license terms and click **Next**.

8.   On the **Prerequisite Downloads** page, select the **Download required files** option, type in the **D:\Setup\CM2012DL** path, and click **Next**.

9.   After all prerequisites have been verified, on the **Server Language Selection** page, select all the additional languages that you want to install. These languages will be available in reports and for the ConfigMgr console. When done, click **Next**.

10. On the **Client Language Selection** page, select all the languages that you want to install. These languages will be used in the agent as well as in the Software Center. Then click **Next**.

11. On the **Site and Installation** page, enter **P01** as the **Site Code** and **ViaMonstra Headquarters Primary Site** as the **Site Name**, and then click **Next**.

> **Real World Note:** Defining a naming convention for site code as well as site names can be a challenge in some organizations. If you are planning for an implementation project, make sure to book some time in the project calendar for this process because it often takes a while to reach consensus. Also note that there is no supported way of changing the site code after the site server has been installed other than reinstalling the whole site.

12. On the **Primary Site Installation** page, select **Install the primary site as a stand-alone site** and click **Next**. Then answer **Yes** on the popup question asking whether you are really sure that you would like to continue.

13. On the **Database Information** page, nothing needs to be changed as the FQDN for the server is populated in the **SQL Server Name** and a suggested name for the database has been populated, as well. Click **Next** to continue.

14. On the second **Database Information** page, that is new as of the R2 Configuration Manager release, it is possible to change the path for the SQL data file and log file. In this scenario, the paths that are already entered work. Click **Next**.

15. On the **SMS Provider Settings** page, click **Next** without alternating the FQDN.

16. On the **Client Computer Communication Settings** page, select **Configure the communication method on each site system role** and click **Next**. Leave the check box cleared and then click **Next**.

17. On the **Site System Roles** page, make sure that both **Install a management point** and **Install a distribution point** are selected and then click **Next**.

18. On the **Customer Experience Improvement Program** page, choose whether to join the Customer Experience Improvement Program (CEIP) and then click **Next**.

19. On the **Settings Summary** page, validate all settings before clicking **Next** to start the Prerequisite Check.

20. After the check is complete, on the **Prerequisite Check** page, click **Begin Install**.

21. The installation normally takes between 10 and 20 minutes, when it is done all actions should be marked green as successful. When the installation is complete, click **Close**.

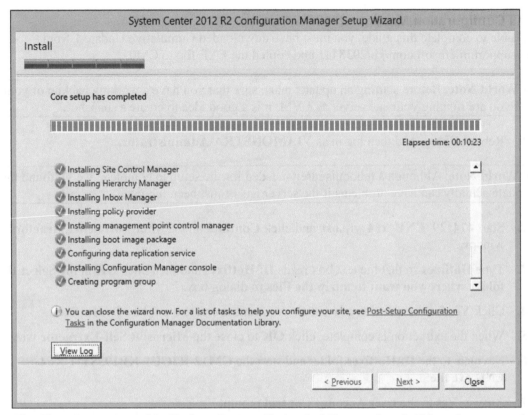

The Close button is enabled before the installation is fully completed. Although you can close the wizard, it is a good idea to keep it open until the installation is completed and you can see that all actions were completed successfully. Otherwise, you need to check the installation log files to make sure that everything worked out fine.

Installing Updates to the Primary Site Server

All software is written by humans, and no human is free from error. So every now and then a fix, or a cumulative update, is released for Configuration Manager. Some of the fixes address bugs with the client software, some with the server software, and some contains new features.

With Configuration Manager 2012, Microsoft announced that it was moving away from releasing individual hotfixes. Instead it would bundle many hotfixes together in cumulative updates and was looking at quarterly releases. However, hotfixes still are released.

When Configuration Manager 2012 R2 was released, it contained a severe problem related to how the client downloads the WIM file during PXE. In order to get a working PXE deployment, a hotfix or better yet Cumulative Update 1 must be installed. The update addresses problems with the distribution point and the site server, as well as the client software. This results in a scenario in which the client must get updates during the task sequence or the fixes will not be used.

Install Configuration Manager 2012 R2 CU1

To be able to complete this guide, you must have downloaded Cumulative Update 1 from http://support.microsoft.com/kb/2938441 and copied the EXE file to CM01.

> **Real World Note**: Before starting an update, make sure that you have a working backup of your site. If you are running your site server as a VM, it is a good idea to create a snapshot.

1. Reboot **CM01**, and then log in as **VIAMONSTRA\Administrator**.

> **Real World Note**: Although a reboot is rarely needed for the setup to complete, we've found that the update actually can have problems if the server hasn't just been rebooted.

2. Start **474129_ENU_x64_zip.exe** and click **Continue** in the **Microsoft Self-Extractor** window.

3. Type **Hotfixes** so that the text box reads **D:\Hotfixes** and then click **OK** in the **Select the folder where you want to unzip the files to** dialog box.

4. Click **Yes** for the question of whether you want to create the folder **D:\Hotfixes**.

5. When the extraction is complete, click **OK** to close the **Microsoft Self-Extractor** wizard.

6. Navigate to the **D:\Hotfixes** folder and start the **CM12-R2CU1-KB2938441-X64-ENU.exe** file.

7. Answer **Yes** to the **User Account Control** prompt.

8. On the **Welcome to Setup for Cumulative Update 1 for System Center 2012 R2** page, click **Next**.

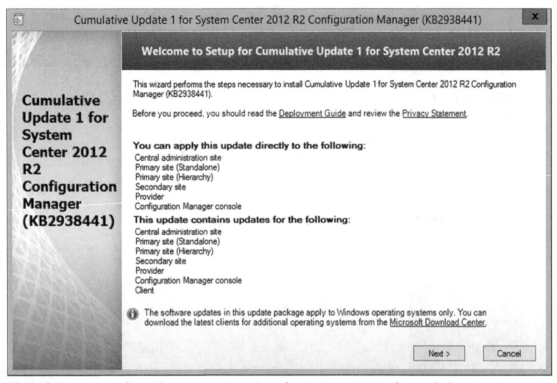

The information on the welcome page is quite informative, ranging from a link to a deployment guide to listing what the update contains and where you can install it.

9. On the **Microsoft Software License Terms** page, select **I accept these license terms**, and then click **Next** after reviewing the license terms.

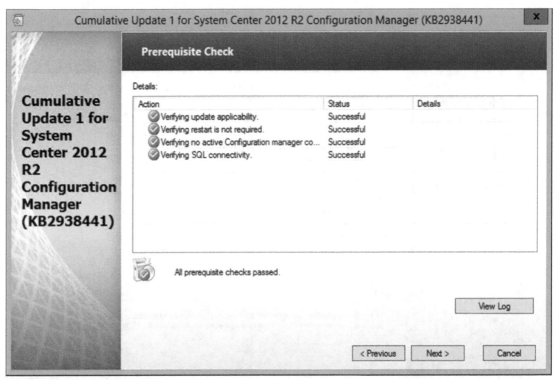

Although a pending restart can be dismissed, it is a good idea to reboot the server and get all green lights.

10. On the **Prerequisite Check** page, after the prerequisite check is complete, click **Next**.

11. On the **Console Update Option** page, leave the **Install the update for the Configuration Manager console** check box selected and click **Next**.

12. On the **Database Update** page, make sure that **Yes, update the site database** is selected and click **Next**.

13. On the **Deployment Assistance Options** page, all three check boxes should be left selected. Simply click **Next**.

Note: During the next three wizard pages the wizard creates packages that can be used for updating the Configuration Manager infrastructure and clients.

14. On the **Update Package for Configuration Manager Servers** page, click **Next**, leaving everything at its default.

15. On the **Update Package for Configuration Manager Consoles** page, click **Next**, leaving everything at its default.

16. On the **Update Package for Configuration Manager Clients** page, click **Next**, leaving everything at its default.

17. On the **Setup Summary** page, after reviewing the information, click **Install** to start the installation.

Note: During the installation of the update, the site server is unavailable for clients, servers, and operators.

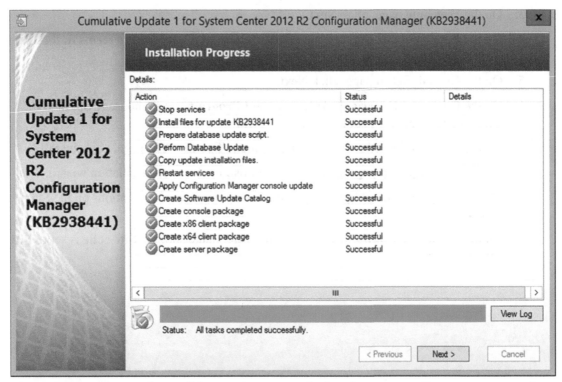

The update progress updates all bits and pieces on the local site server. Remote servers and clients must be updated manually later on by using the packages created by this update program in Configuration Manager.

18. When the update is complete, on the **Installation Progress** page, click **Next**.

19. On the **Installation Complete** page, click **Finish** to close the update wizard.

Microsoft Deployment Toolkit 2013

Even though the Microsoft Deployment Toolkit (MDT) can be used as a stand-alone product to deploy operating systems and applications during the OS installation, it can be integrated with Configuration Manager to deliver more functionality and flexibility to the OS installation process. Not only are all scripts from MDT available during OSD, but the task sequence templates and the MDT database also can be used.

Install and Integrate MDT with Configuration Manager

In this guide we assume you have downloaded MDT 2013 to CM01.

1. On **CM01**, make sure that no ConfigMgr consoles are running.

2. Start **MicrosoftDeploymentToolkit2013_x64.exe** from the downloaded media.

3. On the **Welcome** page, click **Next**.

4. On the **End-User License Agreement** page, check the **I accept the terms in the License Agreement** check box and click **Next**.

5. On the **Custom Setup** page, click **Next**.

6. On the **Customer Experience Improvement Program** page, choose to opt in to the CEIP if applicable for you, and then click **Next**.

7. On the **Ready to install Microsoft Deployment Toolkit 2013** page, click **Install**.

8. When the **Completed** page appears, click **Finish** to close the installation wizard.

9. Start **Configure ConfigMgr Integration**, found among the applications on the **Start screen**.

10. On the **Configure ConfigMgr Integration** page, make sure the **Site code** is set to **P01**, and click **Next**.

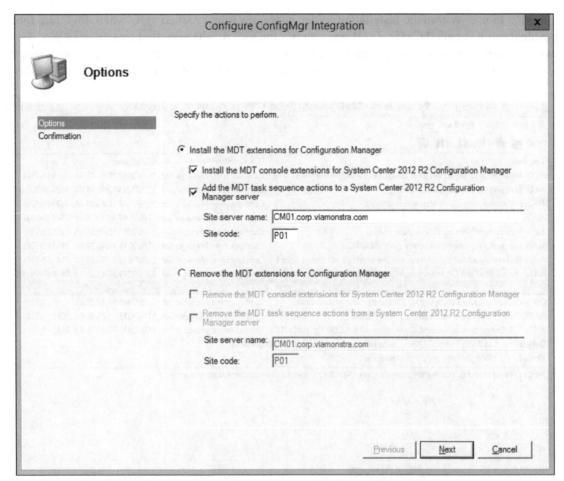

Installing the integration with MDT and Configuration Manager must be done everywhere the console is used. However, having the lower check box selected in required only the first time because the task sequence actions will already be there after the first time.

11. The process is quick, and when the **Configuration** page appears, click **Finish** to close the installation wizard.

Post Installation Configuration

Even though the actual installation is done, there are a couple of steps that still need to be done before the Configuration Manager site can be used by clients.

Configuration Manager is a log file-intensive solution to say the least. Just with the product installation, there will be several of log files located in the logs folder in the installation directory. But the actual installation log files are located at the root of the system drive, e.g. C:\. Reading log files is extremely essential for the Configuration Manager administrator, and thus it is important to know where to find them all, which one is used for what, and in the end, how to read them. Although one could simply use Notepad to read them, there is a far more advanced and yet simple program to use. Within the installation folder, there is a folder named tools where this little tool resides, and it is called CMTrace. When you run the tool for the very first time, it asks you whether you want to use this program as the default viewer for log files. We strongly recommend that you answer yes to this question, as it will make your life a lot easier when reading log files.

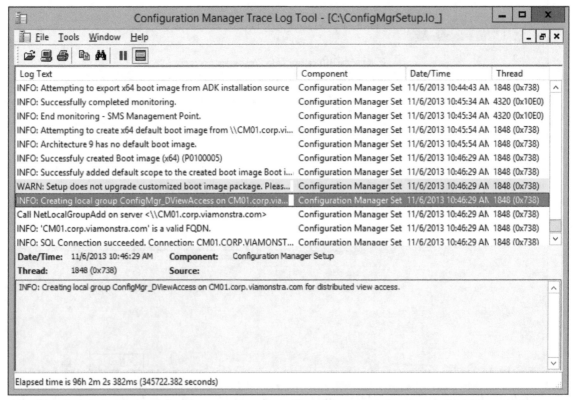

CMTrace viewing the installation log for Configuration Manager. Default behavior for CMTrace is to mark lines containing specific words yellow or red depending on whether the line contains a warning or an error.

Note: Microsoft keeps a fairly updated list with log files and their usage at http://technet.microsoft.com/en-us/library/hh427342.aspx.

Configure IE Enhanced Security

While you work with different features of Configuration Manager, there are times when you need to access the Internet. In the lab environment, we need to do that from the site server. In order for everything to work smoothly, you need to disable the Internet Explorer Enhanced Security setting found in Server Manager.

Turn Off IE Enhanced Security Using Server Manager

1.   On **CM01**, start **Server Manager**.

2.   Select **Local Server** on the left side.

Using the Server Manager settings can be changed for the local server as well as for multiple remote servers.

3.   On the **Local Server** page, click **On** next to **IE Enhanced Security Configuration** on the right side.

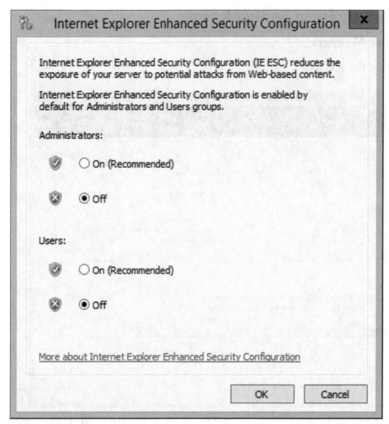

Setting the Internet Explorer Enhanced Security Configuration to Off for Administrators isn't recommended in a production environment; however, it makes life a lot easier throughout this book.

4. In the **Internet Explorer Enhanced Security Configuration** window, set the IE ESC setting to **Off** for both **Administrators** and **Users**, and then click **OK**.

Boundaries

As a best practice, you should define each network location in your environment that has clients that you are going to manage as a boundary. Boundaries are portions of your environment defined using Active Directory sites, subnets, IPv6 prefix, or IP address ranges.

Real World Note: Because the Configuration Manager client and Configuration Manager server calculate the subnet identifier differently, there is the possibility of a mismatch; therefore, it is best to avoid boundaries based on subnet identity. An example scenario is one in which a supernet is defined using 192.168.0.0/16, for example, and a client is located on the 192.168.1.0/24 subnet. The client then reports 192.168.1.0 as the subnet identifier to the server, which tries to match that against 192.168.0.0 and does not find a match, even though it actually is within what was once entered.

1. On **CM01**, start the **ConfigMgr console** if it not already started and navigate to the **Administration** workspace.

2. Expand **Overview** and **Hierarchy Configuration**, and then click **Boundaries**.

3. Click **Create Boundary** on the ribbon.

4. In the **Create Boundary** dialog box, enter **ViaMonstra HQ** as **Description**; change **Type** to **IP address range**; set **Start IP address** to **192.168.1.1** and **Ending IP address** to **192.168.1.254**; and then click **OK** to complete the addition of the first boundary.

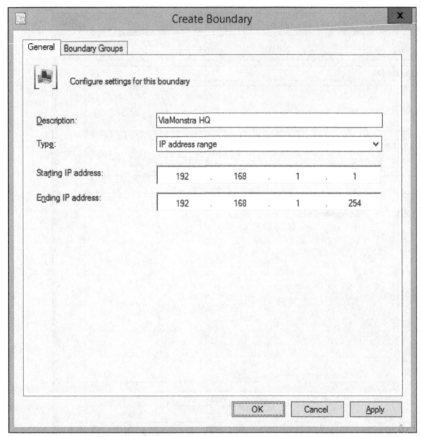

Adding boundaries can be a tedious task in a large environment; however, it can be automated using the PowerShell commands New-CMBoundary and Add-CMBoundaryToGroup.

Create a Boundary Group

A boundary without a boundary group, BG for short, can really be used too much; so even if you only have one boundary, you still need a boundary group to set site assignments and define which distribution points should be used. This is an important configuration when working with an implementation of Configuration Manager that has multiple geographical locations, especially if the bandwidth between the locations isn't the best.

1. Select **Boundary Groups** on the left-hand menu under **Hierarchy Configuration**.

2. Click **Create Boundary Group** on the ribbon.

3. Enter **ViaMonstra HQ** in the **Name** field in the **Create Boundary Group** dialog box.

4. Click **Add**, and in the **Add Boundaries** dialog box, select the newly created boundary and then click **OK**.

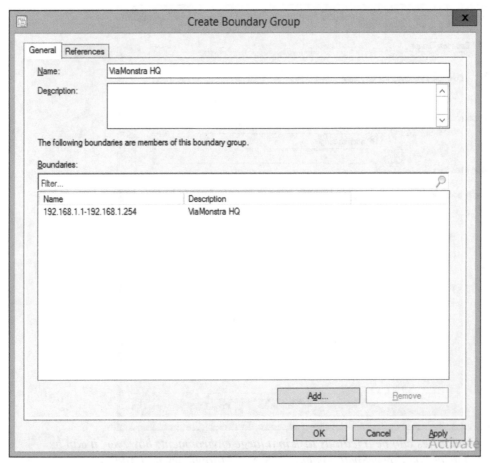

Multiple boundaries can be added to each boundary group.

5. Back in the **Create Boundary Group** dialog box, select the **References** tab and select **Use this boundary group for site assignment**.

6. Click **Add** below **Site system servers** in the **References** tab, and in the **Add Site Systems** dialog box, select **\\CM01.corp.viamonstra.com** and click **OK**.

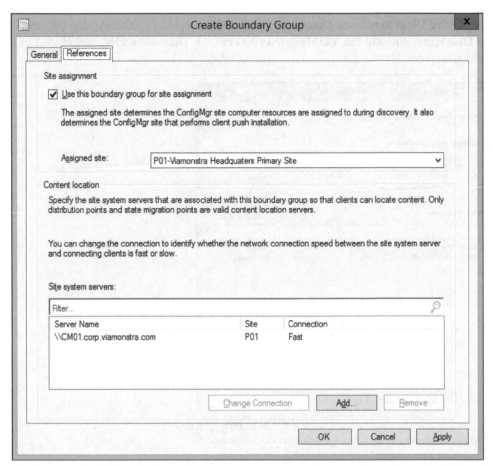

Only when the "Use this boundary group for site assignment" is selected will the site server write the boundary information to Active Directory. Adding multiply site system servers can allow for a form of redundancy even if the other site system server isn't at the same location. In that case, select the server and click Change Connection to mark the site server to be on a slow link, changing how the clients interact with the server.

7. Once again back in the **Create Boundary Group** dialog box, click **OK** to complete the creation of a boundary group and close the window.

Configure Discovery Methods

In Chapter 6 you are going to deploy client settings to users, and for that you need to enable user discovery in ConfigMgr 2012 R2.

1. On **CM01**, start the **ConfigMgr Console**.

2. In the **Administration** workspace, expand **Hierarchy Configuration / Discovery Methods**.

3. Right-click **Active Directory User Discovery** and select **Properties**.

4. In the **Active Directory User Discovery Properties** window, enable Active Directory User Discovery, and add the **ViaMonstra / Users** OU. Then click **OK**, and click **Yes** to run the discovery.

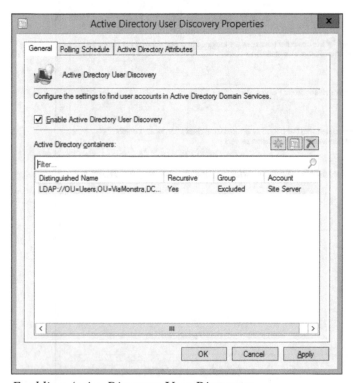

Enabling Active Directory User Discovery.

5. Using **CMTrace**, review the **C:\Program Files\Microsoft Configuration Manager\Logs\adusrdis.log** file.

6. In the **Assets and Compliance** workspace, select **Users**. Press **F5** or click the **Refresh** button to refresh the view. You should now see one member (VIAMONSTRA\Don).

Note: It may take a while for the collection to refresh, but you can view progress via the colleval.log file. If you want to speed up the process, you can manually update membership on the collections by right-clicking on a collection and selecting Update Membership.

Add Site System Roles

In this guide you add the Reporting service point site system role, and also create a service account in Active Directory to use for the role.

1. On **DC01**, start **Active Directory Users and Computers** and navigate to the **ViaMonstra / Service Accounts** OU.

2. On **Action** menu, select **New / User**.

3. Enter **CM_RSPA** in both **Full name** and **User logon name**, and then click **Next**.

4. Enter **P@ssw0rd** as password for the new account and confirm it. Clear the **User must change password at next logon** check box, select both **User cannot change password** and **Password never expires**, and then click **Next**.

5. Click **Finish** to close the **New Object – User** wizard.

6. Right-click the newly created user account and select **Properties**.

7. Enter **ConfigMgr 2012 Reporting Service Point Account** as the **Description**, and then click **OK**.

8. On **CM01**, start the **ConfigMgr console** if it is not already started and navigate to the **Administration** workspace.

9. Expand **Overview** and **Site Configuration**, and then click **Servers and Site System Roles**.

10. Right-click the **CM01.corp.viamonstra.com** server and select **Add Site System Roles**.

11. On the **General** page, click **Next**.

12. If your server requires a proxy in order to connect to Internet, select the check box that indicates that a proxy should be used and enter the address and port the proxy server uses. Also, if needed, enter credentials for accessing the proxy server. Then on the **Proxy** page, click **Next**.

13. On the **System Role Selection** page, select **Reporting services point** and then click **Next**.

14. On the **Reporting service point** page, click **Verify**, and then click **Set** and **New Account**.

15. On the **Windows User Account** page, enter **VIAMONSTRA\CM_RSPA** as the **User name** and enter the account password; then click **OK** to close the window.

16. Back on the **Reporting service point** page, click **Next**.

17. On the **Summary** page, review the summary and then click **Next** to allow the wizard to configure the Site System role.

18. When the **Completion** page appears, click **Close** to exit the wizard.

Create Collection Structure

Collections within Configuration Manager are a way to group users or devices. As of Configuration Manager 2012, there is no longer a possibility to mix users and devices in the same collection due to how collections are built. A collection can have members based on a query, so-called *dynamic membership*, or based on a specific Resource ID within Configuration Manager, so-called *direct membership*. In addition, a collection can *include* or *exclude* all members of a different collection.

Software Distribution 5 items

Search		
Icon	Name	Limiting Collection
	SD Adobe Photoshop CS5 (NY-US)	LC All New York, NY, US Systems
	SD Adobe Photoshop CS5 (STHLM-SE)	LC All Stockholm, SE Systems
	SD Igor Pavlov 7-Zip (LP-UK)	LC All Liverpool, UK Systems
	SD Igor Pavlov 7-Zip (STHLM-SE)	LC All Stockholm, SE Systems
	SD Twitter Tweetdeck (NY-US)	LC All New York, NY, US Systems

With the use of limiting collections with detailed membership rules, one can be sure that a system can be part of only one Adobe Photoshop collection, for example, because it can be only a Stockholm or a New York system, not both at the same time. This assumes the limiting collection's membership rules are created correctly, of course.

Each collection can be used as a target for application deployment, deploying client settings, power management, or maintenance windows settings. With role-based administration, collections are used to limit what users or devices a Configuration Manager administrator has access to. Last, collections can be used to simply group resources based on logical information such as OU membership, OS version, hardware model, or membership of Active Directory groups.

1. On **CM01**, start the **ConfigMgr console** if it is not already started and navigate to the **Assets and Compliance** workspace.

2. Expand **Overview** and then click **Device Collections**.

3. Right-click **Device Collections** and select **Folder / Create Folder**.

4. In the popup window, enter **Software Distribution** and click **OK**.

5. Repeat steps 3 and 4 for **Software Updates**, **OS Deployment**, **Endpoint Protection**, **Search Collections**, **Limiting Collections**, and **Maintenance Windows**.

6. Expand **Device Collections** and select **OS Deployments**.

7. Right-click **OS Deployments** and select **Create Device Collection**.

8. On the **Create Device Collection Wizard** page, enter **OSD Windows 7 SP1 Enterprise Edition x64** in the **Name** field.

9. Click **Browse** next to **Limiting collection**, and select **All Systems** in the **Select Collection** window and click **OK**.

10. Back on **Create Device Collection Wizard** page, click **Summary**. Click **OK** on the popup message informing you that the collection has no membership rules.

> **Note**: These collections will be based on Direct Rule membership, therefor there is no need to enter the Membership Rules page.

11. Click **Next** on the **Summary** page.

12. When the **Completion** page appears, click **Close**.

13. Repeat steps 7–12 for **OSD Windows 8.1 Enterprise Edition x64**.

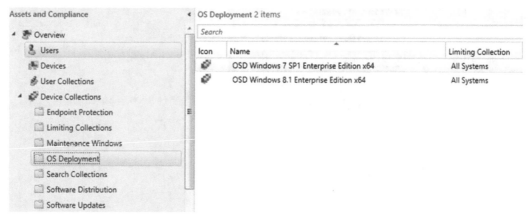

Keeping a clean folder structure among collections makes the life easier because folders cannot be hidden using the role-based administration feature in Configuration Manager. A prefix for all collections makes it easier to find them when browsing in other views, such as reporting services.

14. Select the main **Device Collections** node, and click **Create Device Collection** on the ribbon.

15. On the **Create Device Collection Wizard** page, in the **Name** field, type in **All Windows 8.1 Systems**.

16. Click **Browse** next to **Limiting collection**, and select **All Systems** in the **Select Collection** window and click **OK**.

17. Back on the **Create Device Collection Wizard** page, click **Next**.

18. On the **Membership Rules** page, click **Add Rule** and select **Query Rule**.

19. Enter **All Windows 8.1 Systems** in the **Name** field on the **Query Rules Properties** dialog box, and then click **Edit Query Statement**.

20. On the **Criteria** tab, click the **Orange star** in the **Query Statement Properties** dialog box.

21. In the **Criterion Properties** dialog box, click **Select**.

22. Select **System Resource** as the **Attribute class** and **Operating System Name and Version** as **Attribute** in the **Select Attribute** dialog box, and then click **OK**.

23. Back in the **Criterion Properties** dialog box, alter **Operator** to **is like**, enter **%Workstation 6.3** in the **Value** field, and click **OK**.

24. Click **OK** in the **Query Statement Properties** dialog box and also in the **Query Rule Properties** dialog box.

*A query rule is based on WQL and looks a lot like SQL. In contrast with normal strings, a %
is used as "anything," whereas * is the most common symbol in other languages.*

25. When back on the **Create Device Collection Wizard** window, click **Next** on the
    Membership Rules page.

26. Click **Next** on the **Summary** page, and then **Close** on the **Completion** page.

Backup of the Primary Site Server

Configuring ConfigMgr backup is outside the scope of this book; however, unlike with
ConfigMgr 2007, you should not use the built-in backup maintenance task, but instead use the
built-in SQL Backup. Not only is it much faster, it also doesn't stop any ConfigMgr services while
running.

For details on this, Enterprise Client Management MVP Steve Thompson has an excellent guide
on his blog: https://stevethompsonmvp.wordpress.com/2013/06/07/sql-server-backup-
recommendations-for-configuration-manager.

Chapter 3

Operating System Deployment

In Configuration Manager, operating system deployment (OSD for short) is divided into three different scenarios that you can execute: *new computer*, *refresh*, and *replace*. Each scenario builds upon components such as an operating system image, some drivers, and a boot image. Everything is assembled into a complete enterprise client using precise steps called tasks in an order defined in a task sequence.

Real World Note: Task sequences can be used to perform nearly any steps, in the default operating system or another operating system such as WinPE. A normal thing to use task sequences for other than OSD is for deploying sequences of applications, though the need for it has mostly been replaced with the new application model.

The new computer scenario is not only for new computers as the name suggests. Each time a deployment should not consider what is already on the computer, the new computer scenario is the way to go. It always repartitions the disk and formats those new partitions. Depending on the hardware specifications on the computer, the task sequence partitions the disk differently in order to support BIOS and UEFI systems and also virtual machines that will not need an additional partition for BitLocker support.

As the name suggests, computers running the refresh scenario reinstall an operating system on the computer. The key in that sentence is that the scenario reinstalls *an* operating system rather than *the* operating system since this is the scenario used when upgrading a computer from Windows 7 to Windows 8.1, for instance.

Real World Note: Because all operating system installations are performed unattended, there isn't a need to go with the lazy middle way and perform an actual upgrade of operating systems, but instead reinstall the computer with the new version of Windows. To be able to rule out upgrade issues during troubleshooting is always a time-saver for helpdesk.

Prepare for OS Deployment

In addition to the ConfigMgr 2012 R2 setup you did in the preceding chapter, for OSD you also need to configure a network access account, and assign permissions in Active Directory for domain join operations.

Configure the Network Access Account

The network access account is used to access content during deployment.

1. On **CM01**, using the **ConfigMgr console**, in the **Administration** workspace, expand **Site Configuration** and select **Sites**.

2. Right-click **P01 - ViaMonstra Headquarters Primary Site**, select **Configure Site Components** and the select **Software Distribution**.

3. In the **Network Access Account** tab, configure the **VIAMONSTRA\CM_NAA** user account (select New Account) as the network access account. Use the new **Verify** option to verify that the account can connect to **\\DC01\s** network share. Then click **OK** twice.

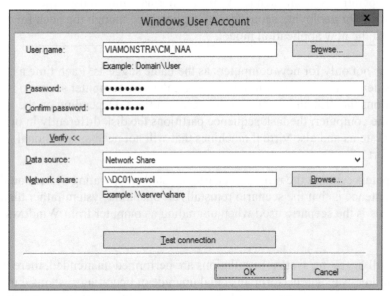

Verifying the network access account.

Configure Active Directory Permissions

To have the machines join the domain, you need to allow the join account (CM_JD) permissions to manage computer accounts in the ViaMonstra / Workstations OU. In this guide, we assume you have downloaded and extracted the book sample files to C:\Setup on DC01.

1. On **DC01**, in an elevated (run as Administrator) **PowerShell** command prompt, configure **Execution Policy** in PowerShell by running the following command:

```
Set-ExecutionPolicy -ExecutionPolicy RemoteSigned -Force
```

> **Real World Note:** In Windows Server 2012 R2 the default execution policy is already set to RemoteSigned, but the hydration kit process hardens that policy, so it needs to be configured.

2. Grant permissions for the **CM_JD** account to the **ViaMonstra / Workstations** OU by running the following command:

```
C:\Setup\Scripts\Set-OUPermissions.ps1 -Account CM_JD
-TargetOU "OU=Workstations,OU=ViaMonstra"
```

The Set-OUPermissions.ps1 script grants the minimum permissions needed to create and update computer objects in the OU that is specified. The permissions granted by the script are:

- **This object and all descendant objects.** Create Computer objects, and Delete Computer objects.

- **Descendant Computer objects.** Read All Properties, Write All Properties, Read Permissions, Modify Permissions, Change Password, Reset Password, Validated write to DNS host name, and Validated write to service principal name.

Operating System Images

As of System Center 2012 SP1 Configuration Manager, there is only support to deploy operating system images. These images are stored in Windows Imaging Format (WIM) files and include all the files for a complete operating system. In fact, as of Windows Vista, this is the format that any Windows installation is shipped in, and an install.wim file can be found on the ISO that is released by Microsoft, as well.

With Configuration Manager, you can capture a PC that not only has an operating system installed but also is configured for your organization and has the most common line of business applications installed already. A captured PC can then be deployed to other PCs using bootable media, such as a DVD, thumb drive, or network boot.

Add an Operating System Image

In this guide, we assume you have copied the install.wim file from a Windows 8.1 Enterprise x64 ISO to D:\SCCM_Source$\OSD\OS Images\Windows 8.1\x64 (you need to create the folders).

> **Real World Note:** You also can add a custom WIM image that you have created. See the following section for more information on custom reference images.

1. On **CM01**, start the **ConfigMgr console**.

2. Select the **Software Library** workspace.

3. Expand **Operating Systems**, and click **Operating System Images**.

4. Click **Add Operating System Image** on the ribbon.

5. On the **Add Operating System Image** page, enter the full UNC path to the WIM file in the **Path** field (in this example, **\\CM01\SCCM_Source$\OSD\OS Images\Windows 8.1\x64\install.wim**), and then click **Next**.

6. On the **General** page, accept the default name, and click **Next**.

7. On the **Summary** page, click **Next**.

8. When the **Completion** page appears, review the **Details** and click **Close**.

Custom Reference Image

It is possible both with Configuration Manager and Microsoft Deployment Toolkit to create reference images that include software or settings that are unique for your organization or departments within your organization.

A good practice is to try keeping the number of images to a minimum, typically one or two, or they will start requiring too much work just to keep them up to date. Typical beneficial things that can be included in a reference image are C++ Runtimes, .NET Framework, and perhaps Office. Among the things that should *not* be included in an image is software that not all PCs or users receiving the image use. Most monitoring and antivirus software and drivers are no-no's when it comes to creating a reference image. Also, it is a best practice to always capture the reference image from a virtual machine.

Boot Images

During the setup process, many tasks are performed. Two of them are repartitioning and formatting the disk that the operating system is to be installed on. For many of these steps, a requirement is that no processes are running from the hard drive. Therefore, special boot media is used called the Windows Preinstallation Environment, WinPE for short, during different phases of the installation.

One of the most common scenarios for using WinPE is during the initial boot in a new computer, also known as *bare metal*, deployment scenario, or in other words, when you have no prior operating system on the machine.

Out of the box, Configuration Manager comes with two boot images based on the version of Windows Assessment and Deployment Kit, one 32-bit and one 64-bit. Configuration Manager 2012 R2 uses Windows Assessment and Deployment Kit 8.1, which is built upon WinPE version 5.0 that in turn is built using Windows version 6.3, more commonly known by its product name Windows 8.1.

Create a MDT Boot Image

To complete the following steps, you must first have completed the Microsoft Deployment Toolkit installation and integration with Configuration Manager covered in Chapter 2.

1. On **CM01**, start the **ConfigMgr console**.

2. Select the **Software Library** workspace.

3. Expand **Operating Systems**, and click **Boot Images**.

4. Click **Create Boot Image using MDT** on the ribbon.

5. On the **Package Source** page, enter **\\CM01\SCCM_Source$\OSD\Boot Images\MDT 2013 Boot Image x64** in the **Package source folder** field and click **Next**.

6. On the **General Settings** page, enter **MDT 2013 Boot Image x64** in the **Name** field and **5.0** in the **Version** field, and then click **Next**.

7. On the **Options** page, select **x64** as **Platform** and click **Next**.

8. On the **Components** page, accept the default settings, and click **Next**.

9. On the **Customization** page, accept the default settings, click **Next**.

> **Note:** In a production environment, uncheck the Enable command support (testing only) checkbox in order to block users from starting a command prompt by pressing F8 during WinPE. It can be a quite good feature to have enabled during testing and troubleshooting but can also be a security risk in production.

10. On the **Summary** page, click **Next**, and answer **Yes** on the **User Account Control** popup.

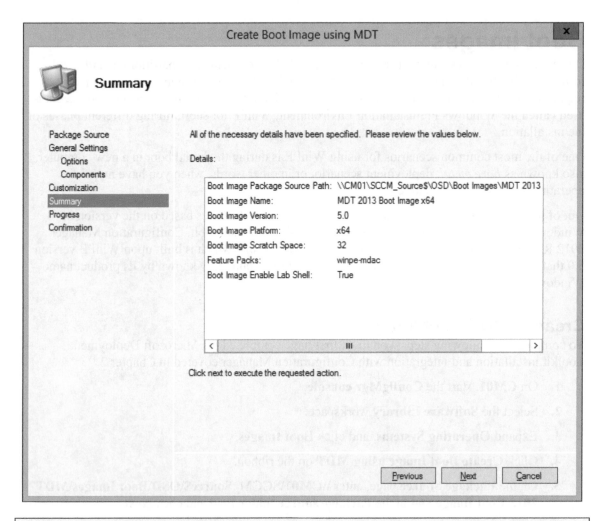

Note: Generating a boot image can take some time depending on your server's performance. This is a good time for a quick coffee break.

    11. On the **Confirmation** page, click **Finish** to close the wizard.

PXE

Although PXE, or network, boot isn't required for OSD, it is possibly one of the highest valued components within Configuration Manager for many technicians because it allows end users and technicians to install computers over the network. When not using PXE boot for OSD, one can boot the PC using a CD, DVD, or thumb drive. Or the initial installation can be started within an already existing operating system. In the latter case, the Configuration Manager client downloads the boot image, stages it on the hard drive, and then changes the boot order so that it can boot into WinPE.

PXE requires a quite good network connection, and the PXE service must answer the client's broadcast request; therefore, it is a good practice to allow only nearby distribution points to answer client requests. On a larger network, where one server answers to clients on multiple subnets, you typically use so-called IP Helpers to forward the broadcast requests from clients to specific IP addresses that just happen to be that subnet's closest distribution point. To get all this in place, it can be a good idea to meet with the network team and bring a treat or two.

> **Real World Note**: If you skipped the part of upgrading to at least Cumulative Update 1, the PXE feature will not work properly in Configuration Manager 2012 R2 due to a bug. This bug caused a lot of hair pulling during the first few implementations of Configuration Manager 2012 R2.

Enable the PXE Feature on a Distribution Point

1. On **CM01**, start the **ConfigMgr console** if it is not already started and navigate to the **Administration** workspace.

2. In the **Distribution Points** node, right-click **CM01.corp.viamonstra.com** and select **Properties**.

3. In the **PXE** tab, select **Enable PXE support for clients**, and click **Yes** in the **Review Required Ports for PXE** window that informs you of the required network ports for the PXE feature.

4. Still in the **PXE** tab, select **Allow this distribution point to respond to incoming PXE requests**, which is no longer grayed out.

5. Clear the **Require a password when computers use PXE** check box, and then click **OK** in the **CM01.CORP.VIAMONSTRA.COM Properties** dialog box.

It is possible to follow the installation of the PXE feature in the SMSPXE.log log file located in the C:\Program Files\Microsoft Configuration Manager\Logs folder.

Deploy a Boot Image to PXE-Enabled Distribution Points

1. On **CM01**, start the **ConfigMgr console** if it is not already started.

2. Select the **Software Library** workspace.

3. Expand **Operating Systems**, and click **Boot Images**.

4. Right-click **MDT 2013 Boot Image x64** and select **Properties**.

5. In the **Data Source** tab, select **Deploy this boot image from the PXE-enabled distribution point**, and then click **OK** to close the dialog box.

Driver Management

Although we run only virtual machines in the examples in this book, drivers are essential in a real-world scenario. In Configuration Manager, there are two environments in which we need to provide drivers. The first and most obvious is for operating system deployment so that the newly installed PC will have all the drivers needed to run the operating system and use all features. The other environment that needs drivers is closely related to the first one. In order to download the operating system image in WinPE, the boot image needs network drivers to connect to the distribution point where the operating system image resides.

Driver management is a significant task, and we could write a book solely on the topic. Here, we will cover the basics and give you our opinion on how to manage drivers within Configuration Manager, though there are different approaches.

Drivers, typically acquired from the PC vendor's website, often need to be unpacked so that we have the INF, CAB, and SYS files. These files are then placed in the SCCM_Source$\OSD\Driver Sources folder in a folder structure based on Vendor / Model / OS / Architecture / Device. The complete path for the Windows 8.1 (x64) wireless network driver from Broadcom for the DELL Precision M4700, for example, would be SCCM_Source$\OSD\Driver Sources\Dell\M4700\Windows 8.1\x64\WLAN.

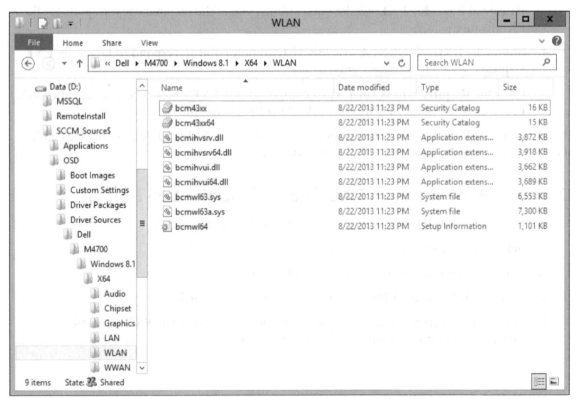

Unpacked drivers in a repository ready to be added to Configuration Manager.

Drivers are then imported into the driver repository and bundled up into driver packages that are stored in the Driver Packages folder next to the Driver Sources folder. All drivers also are stored in the content library for distribution to distribution points, with the result that all drivers are stored several times.

Import Drivers

To complete the following step, you must first have copied the Dell M4700 x64 drivers to the D:\SCCM_Source$\OSD\Driver Sources\Dell\M4700\Windows 8.1\x64 folder on CM01 (you need to create the folders). A good source for drivers that work well with Configuration Manager are the Dell Driver CAB files. For testing purposes, another good source for drivers to use to follow the step-by-step guide are the Hyper-V drivers from the Integration Services Setup ISO that can be mounted to the VM using the Action menu on the Hyper-V Virtual Machine Connection window.

1. On **CM01**, select the **Software Library** workspace in the **ConfigMgr console**.

2. Expand **Operating Systems**, and click **Drivers**.

3. Click **Import Driver** on the ribbon.

4. On the **Locate Driver** page, in the **Source folder** field, enter **\\CM01\SCCM_Source$\OSD\Driver Sources\Dell\M4700\Windows 8.1\x64** and click **Next**.

5. On the **Driver Details** page, click **Categories**.

6. In the **Manage Administrative Categories** dialog box, click **Create**.

7. In the **Create Administrative Category** dialog box, enter **DELL M4700** and click **OK**.

8. Back in the **Manage Administrative Categories** dialog box, click **Create** once more.

9. In the **Create Administrative Category** dialog box, enter **Windows 8.1 x64** and click **OK**.

10. Back in the **Manage Administrative Categories** dialog box, click **OK**.

11. Back on the **Driver Details** page, click **Next**.

12. On the **Add Driver to Packages** page, click **New Package**.

13. In the **Create Driver Package** dialog box, enter **Dell M4700 for Windows 8.1 x64** in the **Name** field, enter **\\CM01\SCCM_Source$\OSD\Driver Packages\Dell M4700 for Windows 8.1 x64** in the **Path** field, and then click **OK**.

14. Back on **Add Driver to Packages** page, note that the newly created package is listed and selected in the previously gray only area, and then click **Next**.

15. Do not select any packages on the **Add Driver to Boot Images** page, and instead click **Next**.

16. Review the information on the **Summary** page, and then click **Next**.

17. When everything is done, the **Completion** page appears. Click **Close** to complete the wizard.

Repeat the steps for all the drivers you want to import. The drivers are now ready to be distributed to distribution points and used during task sequences.

Although it is possible to use the automatic feature to install only compatible drivers during task sequences, there are some limitations to this default method. It is therefore often a good practice to explicitly specify which drivers to install on specific hardware during a task sequence. This can be done using the Apply Driver Package action with conditions to match the make and model of the PC, as described later in this chapter, in the "Edit the Task Sequence" section.

Task Sequences

A task sequence is like a cooking recipe: it contains what to do and when. The main difference is that when the task sequence is done, you won't have a cake but a freshly baked computer installation.

Create a Task Sequence

To complete the following steps, you must first have completed the Microsoft Deployment Toolkit installation and integration with Configuration Manager covered in Chapter 2.

1. On **CM01**, start the **ConfigMgr console** if it is not already started.

2. Select the **Software Library** workspace.

3. Expand **Operating Systems**, and click **Task Sequences**.

4. Click **Create MDT Task Sequence** on the ribbon.

5. On the **Choose Template** page, make sure the template is set to **Client Task Sequence** and click **Next**.

6. On the **General** page, enter **Windows 8.1 Enterprise Edition (x64)** as the **Task sequence name** and click **Next**.

7. On the **Details** page, select **Join a domain** within the **Join Workgroup or Domain** group, and then enter **corp.viamonstra.com** in the **Domain** field.

8. Click **Set** next to the **Account** field; enter **VIAMONSTRA\CM_JD** in the **User name** field and the accounts password twice; then click **OK** to close the **Windows User Account** dialog box.

9. Back on the **Create MDT Task Sequence** page, enter **ViaMonstra Inc.** as the **Organization name** and then click **Next**.

10. On the **Capture Settings** page, make sure **This task sequence will never be used to capture an image** is selected and click **Next**.

Real World Note: It is a good practice to capture reference images outside of Configuration Manager in a stand-alone MDT environment. That way the reference image can be used in a solution in which a Configuration Manager agent isn't used. That, however, requires a separate WSUS implementation so that the reference image always has the latest patches.

11. On the **Boot Image** page, click **Browse** next to the **Specify an existing boot image package** option, and in the **Select a Package** dialog box, select the **MDT 2013 Boot Image x64 5.0 en-US** image and click **OK.**

12. Back on the **Boot Image** page, click **Next**.

13. On the **MDT Package** page, select **Create a new Microsoft Deployment Toolkit Files package**, and then enter **\\CM01\SCCM_Source$\OSD\MDT Toolkit Files\MDT 2013** in the **Package source folder to be created (UNC Path)** field. Click **Next**.

14. Enter the following data on the **MDT Details** page and click **Next**:

    o **Deployment Toolkit Files** in the **Name** field.

    o **2013** in the **Version** field.

    o **Microsoft** in the **Manufacturer** field.

15. On the **OS Image** page, click **Browse** next to the **Specify an existing OS image** option.

Note: Although the wizard indicates there is a possibility to create a new OS image at this step, what actually is possible is creating an OS Image package. Creating an image itself must be done during a capture, either manually or using a task sequence.

16. In the **Select a Package** dialog box, select the **Windows 8.1 Enterprise en-US** image and click **OK**.

17. Back on the **OS Image** page, click **Next**.

18. Leave the **Deployment Method** as **Zero Touch Installation** and click **Next**.

19. On the **Client Package** page, make sure that **Specify an existing ConfigMgr client package** is selected and click **Browse**.

20. In the **Select a Package** dialog box, select **Microsoft Corporation Configuration Manager Client Package** and click **OK.**

Real World Note: From time to time, Microsoft releases hotfixes that apply to the Configuration Manager client. In the community, a script has been written, thanks to Michael Murgolo and Chris Nackers, that automatically installs the latest hotfix. You learn to setup this solution next.

21. Back on the **Client Package** page, click **Next**.

22. On the **USMT Package** page, make sure the **Specify an existing USMT package** option is selected and click **Browse**.

23. In the **Select a Package** dialog box, select **Microsoft Corporation User State Migration Tool for Windows 8** and click **OK**.

24. Back on the **USMT Package** page, click **Next**.

25. On the **Settings Package** page, select **Create a new settings package**, enter **\\CM01\SCCM_Source$\OSD\Custom Settings\Windows Client Settings Package** in the **Package source folder to be created** field, and then click **Next**.

26. On the **Settings Details** page, enter the following data and then click **Next**:

   OSD Custom Settings Windows Client in the **Name** field

27. On the **Sysprep Package** page, click **Next**.

28. On the **Summary** page, review the summary and then click **Next**.

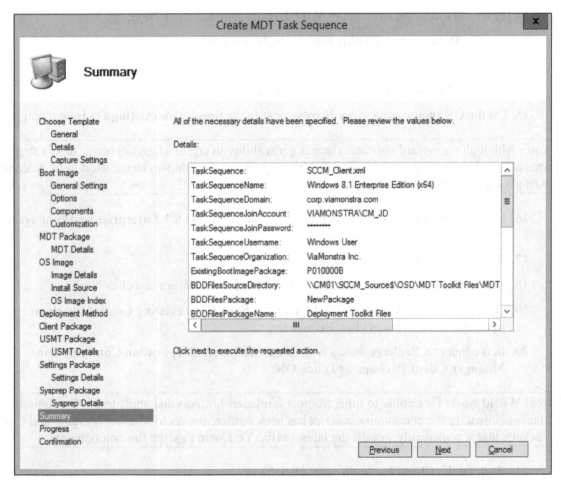

There are a lot of steps needed to be done for the first Task Sequence, it is a good idea to review all settings on the summary page before proceeding.

29. Close the wizard by clicking **Finish** on the **Confirmation** page.

Update the ConfigMgr Client Package

As you learned when creating the task sequence there is a community solution for automatically install the latest client version. For this to work you need to modify the ConfigMgr Client Package. In this guide we assume you have copied the book sample files to D:\Setup on CM01.

You can also download the script from http://blogs.technet.com/b/deploymentguys/archive / 2013/06/04/automatically-populate-the-patch-property-for-the-configmgr-client-installation-script-update.aspx. The script is copyright © 2014 by Microsoft Corporation, and for usage rights, please review the Microsoft legal statement in the script.

1. On **CM01**, using **File Explorer**, navigate to the **C:\Program Files\ Microsoft Configuration Manager\Client** folder.

2. Inside the **Client** folder, copy the **D:\Setup\Scripts\SCCMClientHotfixPath.wsf** file.

3. Still inside the **Client** folder, copy the **D:\SCCM_Source$\OSD\MDT Toolkit Files\MDT 2013\Scripts\ZTIUtility.vbs** file there too.

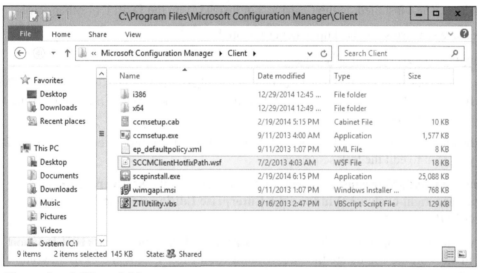

The updated Client folder.

4. In the root of the **Client** folder, there are two folders named **i386** and **x64**. Within each of those two folders, create a new folder named **Hotfix**.

5. Within each **Hotfix** folder, create a folder named after the KB-id for the hotfix or CU that you would like to automatically install. Cumulative Update 1 is **KB2938441**.

> **Note:** You only need the latest Cumulative Update in the folder since they replace each other.

6. Using **File Explorer**, navigate to the **C:\Program Files\Microsoft Configuration Manager\hotfix\KB2938441\Client** folder.

7. Copy the **i386\configmgr2012ac-r2-kb2938441-i386.msp** hotfix to the **C:\Program Files\Microsoft Configuration Manager\Client\i386\Hotfix\KB2938441** folder.

8. Copy the **x64\configmgr2012ac-r2-kb2938441-x64.msp** hotfix to the **C:\Program Files\Microsoft Configuration Manager\Client\x64\Hotfix\KB2938441** folder.

9. In the **ConfigMgr Console**, in the **Software Library** workspace, in the **Application Management / Packages** node, right-click the **Configuration Manager Client Package**, select **Update Distribution Points**, and then click **OK**.

Edit the Task Sequence

While the MDT task sequence adds a lot of new features to the OSD feature in Configuration Manager, there are some known issues that must be taken care of:

- UEFI deployments don't work
- By default, the password for the local administrator account is blank
- Windows is not installed on the C: drive, but instead is on the D, E, F or other drive
- In replace scenarios, the backup is never restored
- Changing the OU dynamically doesn't work

In addition to the issues with the MDT task sequence, we inherit the known issue with the RTM code in Configuration Manager and OSD using PXE does not work (or takes much more time to complete) as discussed earlier.

To address the known issues with MDT, as well as the issue with Configuration Manager 2012 R2 RTM code, you need to edit the task sequence:

1. Using the **ConfigMgr console**, select **Task Sequences** in the **Software Library** workspace, right-click the **Windows 8.1 Enterprise Edition (x64)** task sequence and select **Edit**.

2. In the **Initialization** group, select the first **Format and Partition Disk (UEFI)** action, and in the **Volume** list, delete the three volumes at the top so only the **OSDisk** volume persists.

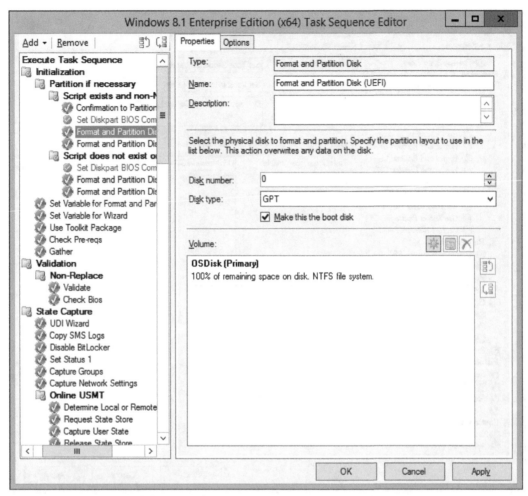

The partitions removed from the first Format and Partition Disk (UEFI).

3. In the **Initialization** group, select the second **Format and Partition Disk (UEFI)** action, and in the **Volume** list, delete the first three volumes.

Real World Note: Without these two changes in the Initialization group, the task sequence will fail when deploying to UEFI machines.

4. In the **Install** group, select **Set Variable for Drive Letter** and configure the following:

    OSDPreserveDriveLetter: **True**

Real World Note: If you do not change this value, your Windows installation will end up in E:\Windows. This behavior was introduced in Configuration Manager 2012 SP1 and is still around in Configuration Manager 2012 R2.

79

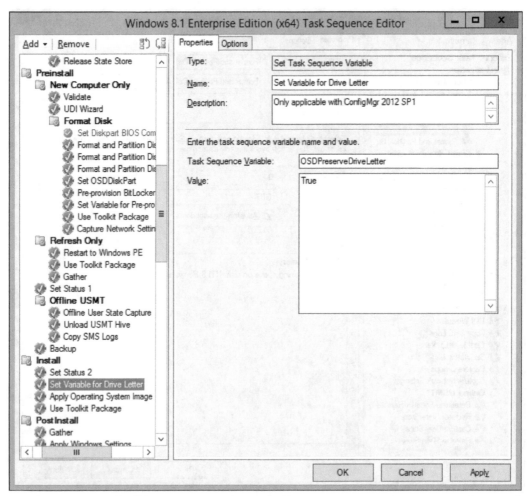

Configuring the OSDPreserveDriveLetter variable.

5. In the **Post Install** group, select **Apply Windows Settings** and configure the following:

- Select **Randomly generate the local administrator password and disable the account on all supported platforms**. Optionally, for the lab environment, you can enable the account and assign a password of **P@ssw0rd**.

- Time zone: Select the same time zone that the **CM01** server is using.

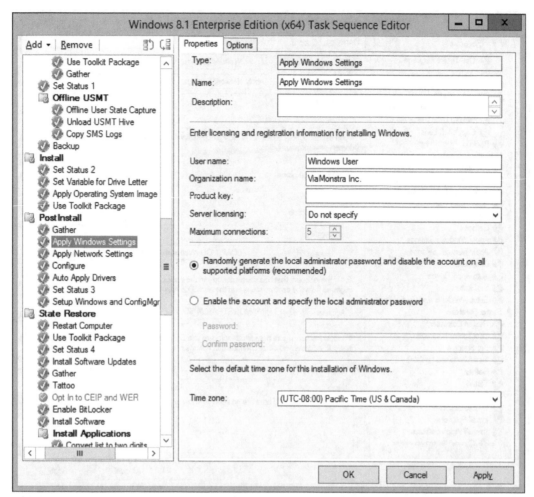

When not using BitLocker, keeping the local administrator account disabled doesn't add any security because tools like LockSmith (included in Microsoft Desktop Optimization Pack, MDOP) can enable the account and reset the password. It is a good practice, however, to prevent online attacks.

Real World Note: The default task sequence assigns a blank administrator password, which is really bad. You need to set a password for the UDI components to work. This was introduced in MDT 2012 Update 1 when the standard client task sequence was merged with the UDI task sequence. Microsoft did not change this for MDT 2013.

6.   In the **Post Install** group, select **Apply Network Settings**, and configure the **Domain OU** value to use the **ViaMonstra / Workstations** OU (browse for values).

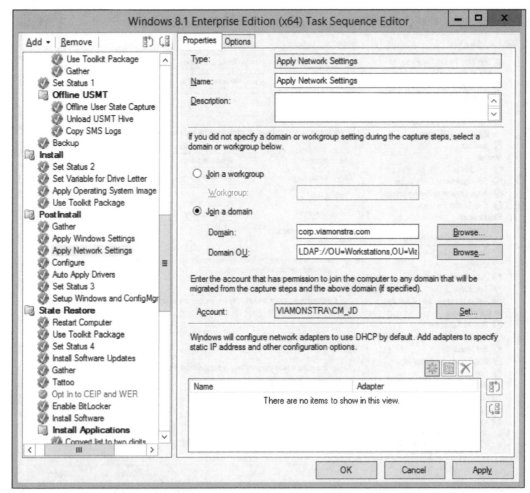

Using advanced features in the CustomSettings.ini file, you can change the Domain OU based on whether the computer is a stationary or laptop device. When possible, it's a good design GPO- and migration-wise.

Real World Note: You need to set the Domain OU value to something and not leave it blank; otherwise, the rules cannot overwrite it.

7. In the **Post Install** group, select **Set Status 3**; then from the **Add** menu, select **General / Set Task Sequence Variable** and use the following properties:

    o   Set the **Name** to **Set TS Variable SMSClientInstallProperties**.

    o   Set **Task Sequence Variable** to **SMSClientInstallProperties**.

    o   Set **Value** to **FSP=CM01** (assuming CM01 is your site server's name).

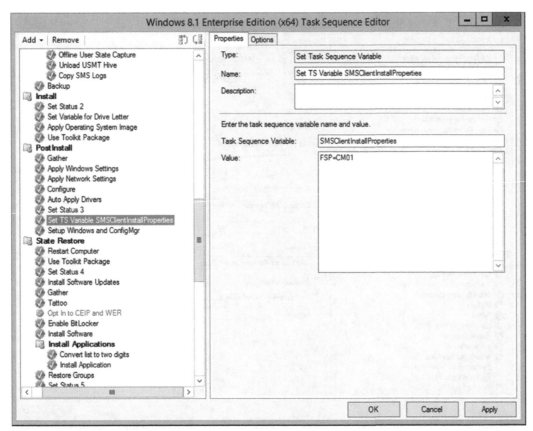

Without the SMSClientInstallProperties variable, the script to automatically populate the PATCH property will fail.

Real World Note: Even if you haven't installed the Fallback Status Point role, the SMSClientInstallProperties variable must be populated for the patch-script to work properly. The client installation will not fail because the client is unable to contact the FSP. This is more of a dummy value just to make sure that the variable exists.

8. With the newly added step **Set TS Variable SMSClientInstallProperties** selected on the left-hand side, add a **Run Command Line** task from the **Add** menu and complete the following:

    a. Enter **Set ConfigMgr Client PATCH Paths** in the **Name** field, and in the **Command line** field enter **cscript SCCMClientHotFixPath.wsf**.

    b. Select the **Package** check box and click **Browse**.

    c. Select the **Configuration Manager client Package** in the dialog box and click **OK**.

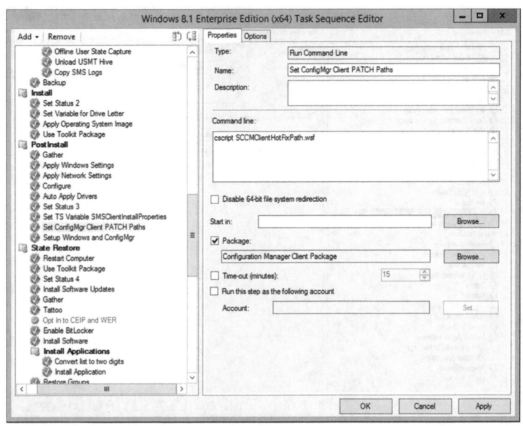

Using a package together with the Run Command Line task gives you the ability to push out files that you can use during OSD instead of having to make sure that the files are accessible over the network.

Note: Another way to do this is to always update the task sequence and point out the PATCH parameter to the Setup Windows and ConfigMgr step. That however requires that you know the Package ID of the package that includes the hotfix and that you keep track if you are deploying x86 or x64 since the hotfixes are architecture dependent.

9. In the **PostInstall** group, disable the **Auto Apply Drivers** action. (Disabling is done by selecting the action and, in the Options tab on the right-hand side, selecting the **Disable this step** check box.)

10. After the disabled **PostInstall / Auto Apply Drivers** action, add a new group name **Drivers**.

11. After the **PostInstall / Drivers** group, add an **Apply Driver Package** action with the following settings:

    a.   On the **Properties** tab:

- Name: **Dell Precision M4700**

- Driver Package: **Dell M4700 for Windows 8.1 x64**

    b.   On the **Options** tab, add a **Query WMI** condition using the **Add Condition** button, with the following query:

> **SELECT * FROM Win32_ComputerSystem WHERE Model LIKE '%Precision M4700%'**

    c.   Click **Test query** in the **WMI Query Properties** dialog box to verify the syntax. It should return "contains valid syntax." Then click **OK**.

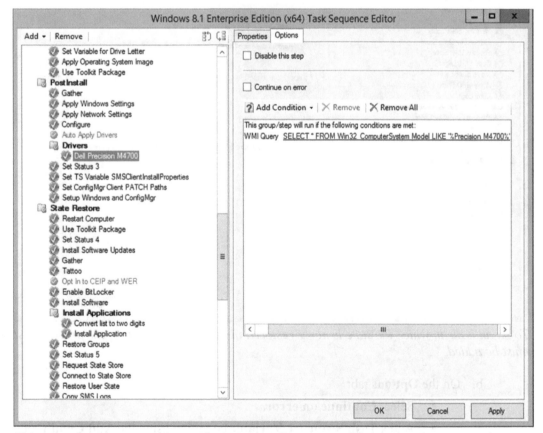

Using conditions on steps in a task sequence allows you to have one task sequence for multiple scenarios, such as multiple computer models, operating systems, locations, and so forth. Done right, they can be very powerful.

12. In the **State Restore** group, after the **Set Status 5** action, add a **Request State Store** action with the following settings:

    a.   On the **Properties** tab:

- Request state storage location to: **Restore state from another computer**
- Select **If computer account fails to connect to state store, use the Network Access account**.

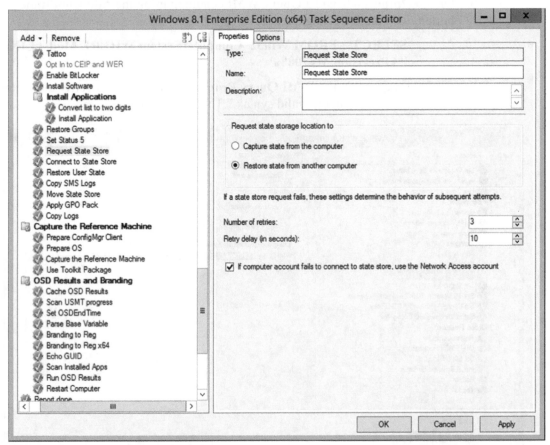

To fix an issue in which the state is never restored in the replace scenario, the preceding step must be added.

    b.   On the **Options** tab:

- Select **Continue on error**.
- Add a **Task Sequence Variable** condition using the **Add Condition** button, with the following values:
  - Variable: **USMTLOCAL**
  - Condition: **not equal**
  - Value: **True**

Many variables are populated in the Gather step. More information about them can be found in the help file for the MDT console.

13. In the **State Restore** group, after the **Restore User State** action, add a **Release State Store** action with the following settings on the **Options** tab:

- Select **Continue on error**.

- Add a **Task Sequence Variable** condition using the **Add Condition** button, with the following values:

  - Variable: **USMTLOCAL**

  - Condition: **not equal**

  - Value: **True**

14. Click **OK** to save the changes.

Deploy Task Sequence

Before any clients can install an operating system using the task sequence, it must be deployed to a collection that holds clients or to the collection named All Unknown Computers. In the latter case, a distribution point also must be configured to support Unknown Computers. Basically, All Unknown Computers is a collection containing two fake device resources that represent all devices that are as yet unknown to Configuration Manager in any way. You might know about them, but unless they have been introduced to Configuration Manager in some way, such as having had a client previously or been entered manually into the database, they are unknown.

> **Real World Note**: It can be a security issue to deploy a required task sequence to All Unknown Computers when a distribution point that supports Unknown Computers answers to requests on a network where guests or bad people can connect their devices. In the good (or at least not that bad) scenario, you install your corporate image on a customer's device when they've configured their device to boot from network as a first boot device in their boot order. In the really bad scenario, you install your corporate image on a (virtual) device that a hacker can use to gain access to your corporate network.

1. On **CM01**, start the **ConfigMgr console** if it is not already started.

2. Select the **Software Library** workspace.

3. Expand **Operating Systems**, and click **Task Sequences**.

4. Select the **Windows 8.1 Enterprise Edition (x64)** task sequence and click **Deploy** on the ribbon.

5. On the **General** page of the **Deploy Software Wizard**, click **Browse** next to **Collection**.

6. In the **Select Collection** dialog box, click **OS Deployment** on the left, select **OSD Windows 8.1 Enterprise Edition 8.1 x64** on the right, and then click **OK**.

7. Click **OK** on the warning message informing you that the collection does not contain any resources.

8. Back on the **General** page, click **Next**.

9. On the **Deployment Settings** page, change **Make available to the following** to **Only media and PXE**, and then click **Summary**.

> **Real World Note:** Using the option to make a deployment available only to media and PXE makes sure that end users don't try to reinstall their PC from within Windows using Software Center.

10. On the **Summary** page, click **Next** after reviewing all the settings.

11. On the **Completion** page, click **Close**.

Distribute Task Sequence Content

As we said earlier, a task sequence is in many ways like a recipe for a cake. As with a cake recipe, there must be a list of ingredients needed during the actual baking. We've created the recipe, and we've also said what collection of computers should bake the cake, or at least get baked as a cake. All the necessary ingredients must be deployed, however, so that they are ready.

You also can see all the requirements, which are called *References* when it comes to task sequences.

View Task Sequence References

1. On **CM01**, start the **ConfigMgr console** if it is not already started.

2. Select the **Software Library** workspace.

3. Expand **Operating Systems**, and click **Task Sequences**.

4. Select the **Windows 8.1 Enterprise Edition (x64)** task sequence and click the **References** tab below the Task Sequences list.

In this view, it is not only possible to see what software is required for this task sequence, but also how many distribution points are targeted and their compliance, that is how many of them actually have the content.

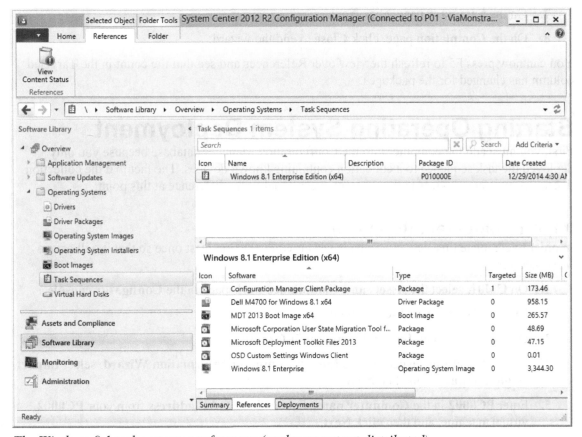

The Windows 8.1 task sequence references (packages not yet distributed).

Distribute Task Sequence References

1. With the **Windows 8.1 Enterprise Edition (x64)** task sequence still selected, change back to the **Home** tab on the ribbon and click **Distribute Content**.

2. On the **General** page of the **Distribute Content Wizard**, click **Next**.

3. On the **Content** page, review what content will be distributed and then click **Next**.

4. On the **Content Destination** page, click **Add** and then select **Distribution Point**.

5. In the **Add Distribution Points** dialog box, select the **CM01** distribution point and click **OK**.

6. Back on the **Content Destination** page, click **Summary**.

7. On the **Summary** page, click **Next**.

8. On the **Completion** page, click **Close** to end the wizard.

You can now press F5 to refresh the view over References and see that the count in the Targeted column has changed for the packages.

Starting Operating System Deployment

First, you must add the computer into the Configuration Manager database because you only deployed the task sequence to a collection containing known devices. The fact that the collection doesn't contain any devices at the moment doesn't make any difference at this point.

Import Computer Information

In order to complete this step, you must have started PC0002 at least once so that it will have a MAC address.

1. On **CM01**, select the **Assets and Compliance** workspace in the **ConfigMgr console.**

2. Expand **Overview** and select **Devices**.

3. On the ribbon, click **Import Computer Information**.

4. On the **Select source** page of the **Import Computer Information Wizard**, select **Import single computer** and click **Next**.

5. Enter **PC0002** in the **Computer name** field and the **MAC address** from your **PC0002** virtual machine, and then click **Next**.

6. On the **Data Preview** page, click **Next**.

7. On the **Choose Target Collection** page, select **Add computers to the following collection** and then click **Browse**.

8. In the **Select Collection** dialog box, click **OS Deployment**, select **OSD Windows 8.1 Enterprise Edition x64**, and then click **OK**.

9. Back in the **Import Computer Information Wizard**, click **Summary**.

10. Review the details on the **Summary** page and click **Next**.

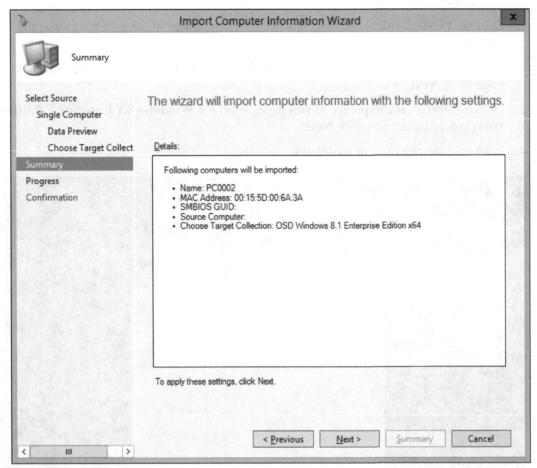

Although Configuration Manager accepts both SMBIOS GUID and MAC address during the Import Computer Information Wizard, only one of them is needed.

11. On the **Confirmation** page, click **Close** to end the wizard.

Note: It can take some time before the collection membership is updated. To speed up the process, select the All Systems collection and click Update Membership, and when the Member Count has increased, do the same on the OSD Windows 8.1 Enterprise Edition x64 collection.

Deploy PC0002

Your PC0002 client is now ready to be booted and start installing Windows 8.1. This client will be used in later guides.

1. Start the **PC0002** virtual machine, and press **F12** (or **Enter** if using UEFI) to start the PXE boot.

2. After the boot image is downloaded, on the **Welcome to the Task Sequence Wizard** page, click **Next**.

3. On the **Select a task sequence to run** page, select the **Windows 8.1 Enterprise Edition (x64)** task sequence and click **Next**.

4. Wait until the deployment completes.

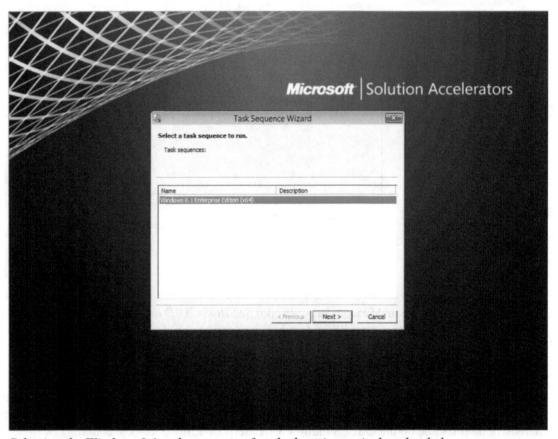

Selecting the Windows 8.1 task sequence after the boot image is downloaded.

Chapter 4

Application Deployment

Historically, IT technicians ran around the campus or office structure to install applications. Over time, that work habit evolved to gold images with all of the latest applications bundled into that image of computer software, only to be out of date the second it was done. Before System Center 2012 Configuration Manager, most organizations deployed a base image with some standard applications to the PCs and after that deployed software to PC(s) that an end user normally used. Eventually, users became more dynamic and started to have more than one device, and with that came the *application model* that allows users to get the application, regardless of what computer and platform they are using. At the same time, a shift from computer-based deployment to user-based deployment has been necessary.

With System Center 2012 R2 Configuration Manager, you also now can deploy applications to Apple PCs and mobile devices, as well. We will not cover those scenarios, however, because they follow the same technique.

Application Model

In the application model, each application is constructed mainly of two building blocks, deployment types and metadata. The benefit of having the metadata separated from the actual installation information is the support of localized information that can be used during interaction with users, such as software deployment notifications. The metadata can contain information such as support information, the name of the application, or the applications icon that is used in the Software Catalog, a web portal where users can order software for their devices.

Deployment Types

The first deployment type is created automatically during the creation of the application itself based on what you select in the wizard, except when working with script-based installation types as the first deployment type.

Create an Application

In this guide we assume you have downloaded the MSI versions of 7-Zip 9.20 and copied the x86 version (7z920.msi) to the D:\SCCM_Source$\Applications\Igor Pavlov\7-Zip\9.20\x86\ folder, and the x64 version (7z920-x64.msi) to the D:\SCCM_Source$\Applications\Igor Pavlov\ 7-Zip\9.20\x64\ folder on CM01 (you need to create the folders).

1. On **CM01**, start the **ConfigMgr console**.

2. Select the **Software Library** workspace.

3. Expand **Application Management** and click **Applications**.

4. Click **Create Application** on the ribbon, or right-click **Applications** and select **Create Application**.

5. In the **Create Application Wizard**, select **Manually specify the application information** and click **Next**.

6. On the **General Information** page, enter the following values and then click **Next**:

   o Enter **7-Zip 9.20** in the **Name** field.

Note: The Name field must be unique for each application in the application model. It is therefore a good practice to enter the version of the application.

---

   o Enter **Igor Pavlov** in the **Publisher** field.

   o Enter **9.20** in the **Software version** field.

7. On the **Application Catalog** page, click **Next**.

Note: Information added in the Application Catalog step will be visible for the end user when browsing the Application Catalog website or the company portal. For a global organization, it is possible to enter localized information for each application, and based on the user's settings on the client operating system side, the end user will see the information in his or her language, assuming that an administrator has written any.

---

8. Click **Add** on the **Deployment Types** page.

9. On the **General** page of the **Create Deployment Type Wizard**, in the **Location:** text box, enter the UNC path to the 7-ZIP .msi file, **\\CM01\SCCM_Source$\Applications\ Igor Pavlov\7-Zip\9.20\x86\7z920.msi**, and then click **Next**.

Note: Configuration Manager prompts you that the publisher for 7z920.msi cannot be verified. Click Yes anyway.

---

10. On the **Import Information** page, note that **Name**, **Detection Method** and **User Experience** have been detected from the MSI file and entered by the wizard.

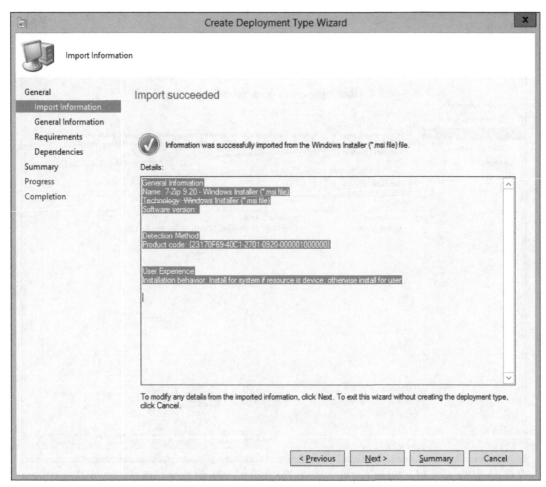

When importing an MSI file in the Create Deployment Type Wizard, the wizard most often reads out all needed information automatically from the MSI file.

11. Because you are going to add requirements for this application so that it is installed only on machines that are of 32-bit architecture, go ahead and click **Next** (otherwise, one could click Summary on this screen).

12. On the **General Information** page, click **Next**.

13. On the **Requirements** page, click **Add**.

14. In the **Create Requirement** dialog box, change **Condition** to **Operating system** and select both **All Windows 7 (32-bit)** and **All Windows 8.1 (32-bit)**, each found by expanding the corresponding OS node. Then click **OK** to close the window.

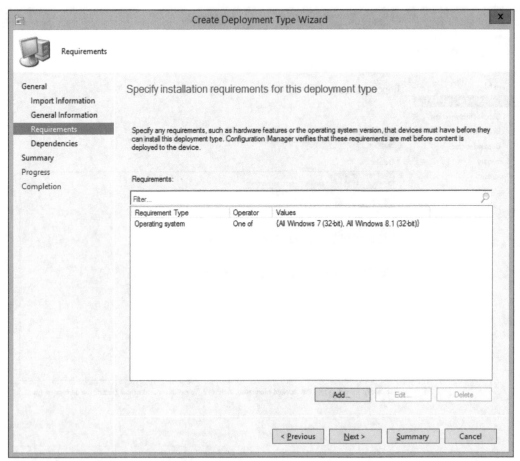

It is possible to add a lot of requirements for a deployment type, but the operating system requirement type is by far the most common one.

15. Back on the **Requirements** page, click **Summary**.

16. Click **Next** after reviewing all information on the **Summary** page.

17. When the **Completion** page appears, click **Close** to finish adding the deployment type.

18. Back on the **Deployments Types** page of the **Create Application Wizard**, click **Next**.

19. Review the information on the **Summary** page and click **Next**.

20. When the **Completion** notice appears, review the information and click **Close** to complete adding the application.

Add an Additional Deployment Type

1. With **7-Zip 9.20** still selected in the **Applications** workspace, click **Create Deployment Type** on the ribbon.

2. Make sure that **Type** is set to **Windows Installer (*.msi file)**; in the **Location:** field, enter the full UNC path to the 7-Zip 9.20 x64 MSI file, **\\CM01\SCCM_Source$\Applications\Igor Pavlov\7-Zip\9.20\x64\7z920-x64.msi**; and click **Next**.

> **Note:** Configuration Manager prompts you that the publisher for 7z920-x64.msi cannot be verified. Click Yes anyway.

3. On the **Import Information** page, again note that **Name**, **Detection Method** and **User Experience** have been detected from the MSI file and entered by the wizard.

4. Because you are going to add requirements for this application so it is installed only on machines that are of 64-bit architecture, go ahead and click **Next** (otherwise, one could click Summary on this screen).

5. On the **General Information** page, click **Next**.

6. On the **Requirements** page, click **Add**.

7. In the **Create Requirement** dialog box, change **Condition** to **Operating system** and select both **All Windows 7 (64-bit)** and **All Windows 8.1 (64-bit)**, each found by expanding the corresponding OS node. Then click **OK** to close the window.

8. Back on the **Requirements** page, click **Summary**.

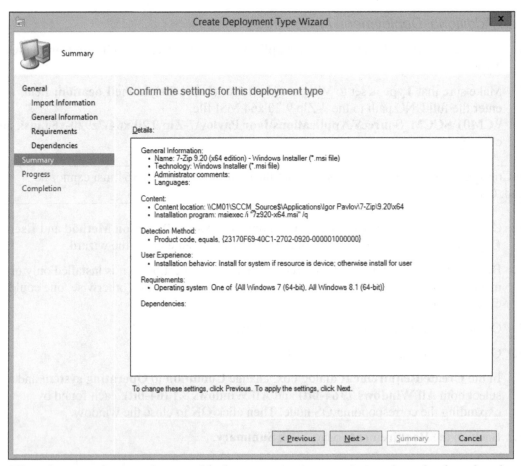

When the wizard is complete, it adds the customizations you've made to the data that the wizard was able to get by itself.

9. Click **Next** after reviewing all information on the **Summary** page.

10. When the **Completion** page appears, click **Close** to finish adding the deployment type.

Create another Application

In this guide we assume you have downloaded the MSI versions of 7-Zip 9.22 and copied the x86 version (7z922.msi) to the D:\SCCM_Source$\Applications\Igor Pavlov\7-Zip\9.22\x86\ folder, and the x64 version (7z922-x64.msi) to the D:\SCCM_Source$\Applications\Igor Pavlov\ 7-Zip\9.22\x64\ folder on CM01 (you need to create the folders).

1. Use the "Create an Application" guide to create an application of 7-Zip 9.22.

2. Use the "Add an Additional Deployment Type" guide to create an extra (x64) deployment type for 7-Zip 9.22.

Dependencies

For each deployment type in an application, there can be one or more dependencies, which are other items in the application model that are required to exist on a device before the deployment type in question can be installed. Each dependency is added in a dependency group that can include one or more items with an OR-relationship that allows the administrator to create sophisticated and/or scenarios in the dependency tree. Additionally, each dependency can be added with the feature that Configuration Manager should automatically install that dependency if it does not already exist on the targeted device. This feature makes it unnecessary to create advanced task sequences or scripts to deploy a series of applications to an end user.

Real World Note: There is an undocumented supported limit of five dependencies in a direct descending chain.

Create Application Dependency

In this guide, we assume you have copied the Sources\sxs folder from a Windows 8.1 Enterprise x64 ISO to the D:\SCCM_Source$\Applications\Microsoft\.NET Framework\3.5.1\Windows 8.1\x64 folder (you need to create the folder), and that you copied the book sample files to D:\Setup on CM01. We also assume that you have downloaded TweetDeck from http://www.tweetdeck.com/download/pc/latest to the D:\SCCM_Source$\Applications \Twitter\Tweetdeck\3.4.0\MSI\x86 folder on CM01 (you need to create that folder too).

Although these examples show you how to configure the free program TweetDeck, basically any MSI files can be used, with the caveat that the installation might not work.

1. On **CM01**, start the **ConfigMgr console** if it is not already started.

2. Select the **Software Library** workspace.

3. Expand **Application Management** and click **Applications**.

4. Click **Create Application** on the ribbon.

5. Enter the following path in the **Location** field and click **Next**:

   \\CM01\SCCM_Source$\Applications\Twitter\Tweetdeck\3.4.0\MSI\x86\ TweetDeck.msi

6. On the **Import Information** page, click **Summary**.

7. Review the information on the **Summary** page and then click **Next**.

8. Click **Close** on the **Completion** page to complete the wizard.

9. Again, click **Create Application** on the ribbon

10. On the **General** page, select **Manually specify the application information** and then click **Next**.

11. On the **General Information** page, enter **.NET Framework 3.5.1** in the **Name** field, **Microsoft** in the **Publisher** field, and **3.5.1** in **the Software version** field; then click **Next**.

Real World Note: In the application model, the Name field is a unique key, which means that each and every application most have a unique name. It is therefore a good idea to include a version number in the Name field even when the Software Version field is populated.

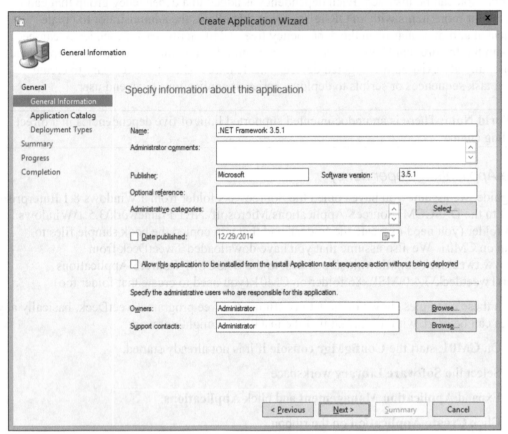

Although only Name is a required field in the Create Application Wizard, populating some more fields is recommended.

12. On the **Application Catalog** page, click **Next**.

13. On the **Deployment Types** page, click **Add**.

14. On the **General** page, set **Type** to **Script Installer** and then click **Next**.

15. On the **General Information** page, enter **Microsoft .NET Framework 3.5.1 for Windows 8.1 x64** in the **Name** field and then click **Next**.

16. On the **Content** page, enter the following information and then click **Next**:

    o   Content location: **\\CM01\SCCM_Source$\Applications\Microsoft\.NET Framework\3.5.1\Windows 8.1\x64\sxs**

    o   Installation program: **DISM /Online /Enable-Feature /FeatureName:NetFx3 /All /LimitAccess /Source:.**

- o   Uninstall program: **DISM /Online /Disable-Feature /FeatureName:NetFx3**

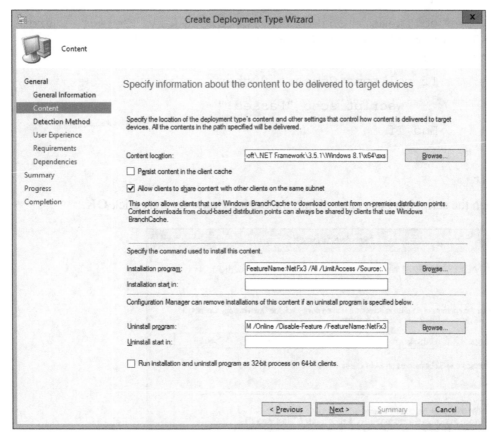

When working with script-based deployment types, no content is required, which allows you to execute any command on a remote client.

17. On the **Detection Method** page, select the **Use a custom script to detect the presence of this deployment type** option and click **Edit**.

18. In the **Script Editor**, set **Script type** to **VBScript**. Then enter the following script, or click **Open** and specify the **Framework_3.5.1_DetectionMethod_Win8.1x64.vbs** script from **D:\Setup\Scripts**.

```
strComputer = "."

Set objWMIService = GetObject("winmgmts:" _

    & "{impersonationLevel=impersonate}!\\" & strComputer &
"\root\cimv2")

Set oss = objWMIService.ExecQuery("Select * from
Win32_OperatingSystem")

for each os in oss
```

```
     if Left(os.version,3) = "6.3" AND os.OperatingSystemSKU
< 7  then
     Set colItems = objWMIService.ExecQuery("Select * from
Win32_OptionalFeature WHERE installstate='1' AND
Name='NetFx3'")
         If colItems.Count > 0 then
             wscript.echo "Passed!"
         End If
     End if
Next
```

19. When the script has been entered into the **Script Contents** area, click **OK**.

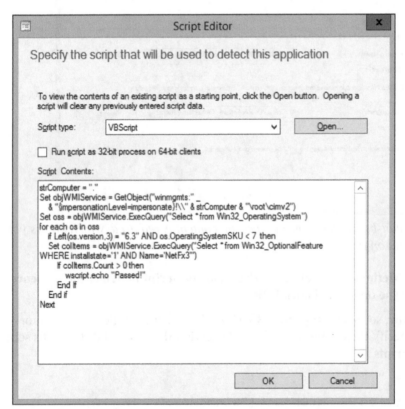

Although Configuration Manager supports PowerShell and Jscript, VBScript is the most robust option because it works on most platforms and you don't need to think about execution policies that PowerShell requires.

20. Back on the **Detection Method** page, click **Next**.

21. On the **User Experience** page, change **Installation behavior** to **Install for system** and **Logon requirement** to **Whether or not a user is logged on**, and then click **Next**.

22. On the **Requirements** page, click **Add**.

23. In the **Create Requirement** dialog box, change **Condition** to **Operating System**, select **All Windows 8.1 (64-bit)** beneath **Windows 8.1**, and click **OK**.

24. Back on the **Requirements** page, click **Summary**.

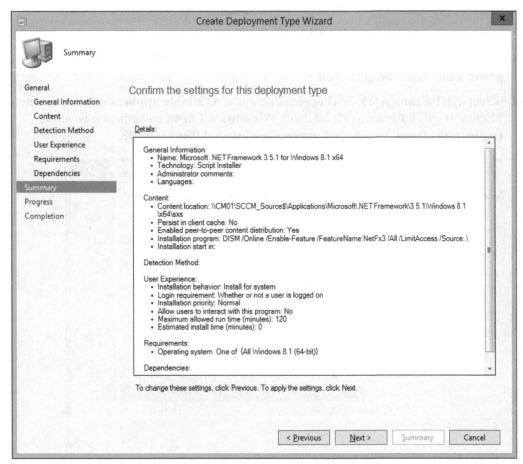

From the Summary page, you can click the titles on the left-hand side if you notice that you've missed a configuration.

25. Review the information on the **Summary** page, and then click **Next**.

26. When the **Completion** page appears, click **Close** to end the **Create Deployment Type Wizard**.

27. Back in the **Create Application Wizard**, click **Summary**.

28. Review the information on the **Summary** page, and then click **Next**.

29. When the **Completion** page appears, click **Close** to end the wizard.

Note: The actual setup of the dependency starts now. It can be done during the creation of a deployment type, as well.

---

30. Back at the **Applications** workspace, select the **TweetDeck** application and click **Properties** on the ribbon.

31. In the **Deployment Types** tab, select the **MSI** deployment type and click **Edit**.

32. In the **Dependencies** tab, click **Add**.

33. In the **Add Dependency** dialog box, enter **.NET Framework 3.5.1** in the **Dependency group name** field and click **Add**.

34. Select **.NET Framework 3.5.1** application in the **Available applications** list; select **Microsoft .NET Framework 3.5.1 for Windows 8.1 x64** deployment type in the **Deployment types for selected application** list; and then click **OK**.

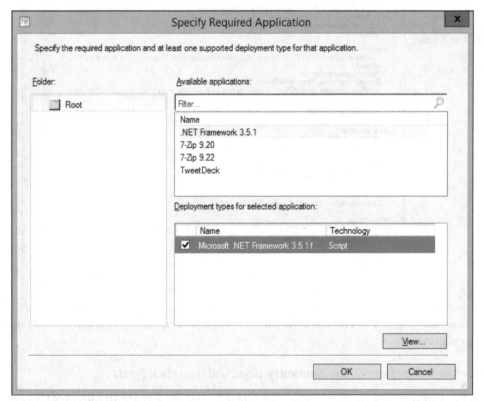

Adding the application dependency.

35. Back in the **Add Dependency** dialog box, click **OK**.

Real World Note: It is possible to add many different applications and deployment types in each dependency group. Only one deployment type/application will be installed even if Auto Install is selected on multiple dependencies. The agent will evaluate them in the priority order starting at 1.

This is often applicable with applications with dependencies to Java and other middleware applications that often update. Then it is possible to auto install only the latest version but still allow older versions.

36. In the **TweetDeck – Windows Install (*.msi file) Properties** dialog box, click **OK** twice.

Note: It is possible to define multiple dependencies. Each separate software program that is required must be entered within a separate dependency group; otherwise, only one software program will be installed.

37. Right-click **TweetDeck** in the application list, and select **View Relationships** and **Dependency** to view the newly created dependency.

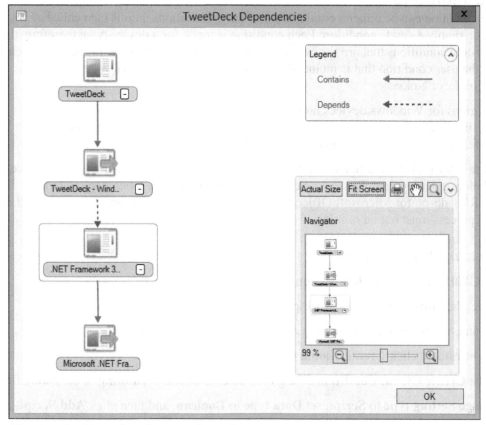

The visualization of application dependencies is a great resource when you are creating documentation as you easily can expand or collapse nodes and use the zoom functionality to show exactly what you want.

Requirements

Dependencies and requirements differentiate from each other in that dependencies are other applications that must be present in order to install an application, whereas requirements are basically global conditions that must be true before the Configuration Manager client will continue to download and install an application.

A requirements can be of three different categories, Device, User or Custom, where the last one doesn't come out of the box. Two of the most common usages for requirements are to limit the versions of the operating system that the application can be installed on and to limit the installation to apply only to devices that are set to be the user's primary device.

> **Real World Note**: Even though requirements are an excellent way for the administrator to control what gets installed where, there is a limited form of feedback to the end user when he or she tries to install an application where no deployment type is applicable due to requirements constraints. It is therefore important to give adequate training and information to end users.

Global Conditions

Each global condition can be either a combination of other conditions, and is then called an *expression*, or simply a single condition. Each condition is made for a device type; therefore, there can be no custom conditions that are for users. An exception to this rule are expressions, which can include the user condition that is included out of the box. Device types can be Windows, Windows Mobile, or Nokia.

Global conditions for Windows devices hold by far the most comprehensive subset of possibilities. Each global condition is made up by a setting type that for Windows devices can be a set of 10 different things, such as a registry key, WQL query, or script.

A common case for global conditions is to use a WQL query to check whether a specific process is running before a deployment. For example, such a scenario could be when deploying the Microsoft CRM add-on for Microsoft Office Outlook. During the installation of the add-on, the Outlook.exe process must not be running.

Add a Custom Global Condition

1. On **CM01**, start the **ConfigMgr console**.

2. Select the **Software Library** workspace.

3. Expand **Application Management** and click **Global Conditions**.

4. On the ribbon, click **Create Global Condition.**

5. In the **Create Global Condition** dialog box, enter **Outlook is running** in the **Name** field.

6. Change **Setting type** to **Script**, set **Data type** to **Boolean**, and then click **Add Script**.

7. In the **Edit Discovery Script** dialog box, change **Script language** to **VBScript**.

8. Enter the following script and click **OK** (you can also open the OutlookIsRunning.vbs script included in the book sample files in the editor).

```
On Error Resume Next
strComputer = "."
Set objWMIService = GetObject("winmgmts:\\" & strComputer & "\root\cimv2")
Set colItems = objWMIService.ExecQuery("Select * from Win32_Process Where Name = 'outlook.exe'",,48)
If colItems.Count > 0 Then
    wscript.echo 0
Else
    wscript.echo 1
End If
```

9. Back in the **Create Global Conditions** dialog box, click **OK** to complete the creation of the global condition.

The newly created global condition can now be added to an application as a requirement of type Custom.

Supersedence

One big challenge back in Configuration Manager 2007 was when a new version of an application was released. A wide-spread solution was to create a collection with a query rule that included all computers with the old version of the product and then target an advertisement to that collection. For all computers that only needed the new version, a different collection had to be used.

With the introduction of the application model, there is now support for superseded applications. During the definition of a superseded product, there is a step to specify how to handle the superseded product. One must then choose whether the old version should be uninstalled or left to be dealt with by the installation feature of the new version, as some installation programs, such as Microsoft Office, handle that.

Set Up Application Supersedence

To complete this guide, you must have completed the steps in the "Create an Application" and "Add an Additional Deployment Type" sections earlier in this chapter for both version 9.20 and 9.22 of the 7-Zip application.

1. On **CM01**, start the **ConfigMgr console** if it is not already started.

2. Select the **Software Library** workspace.

3. Expand **Application Management** and click **Applications**.

4. Select the **7-Zip 9.22** application and click **Properties** on the ribbon.

5. In the **Supersedence** tab, click **Add**.

6. In the **Specify Supersedence Relationship** dialog box, click **Browse**, and then select the **7-Zip 9.20** application in the **Choose Application** dialog box and click **OK**.

7. Back in the **Specify Supersedence Relationship** dialog box, select the corresponding architectural edition of the **7-Zip 9.22** application, select the **Uninstall** check box for each edition, and then click **OK**.

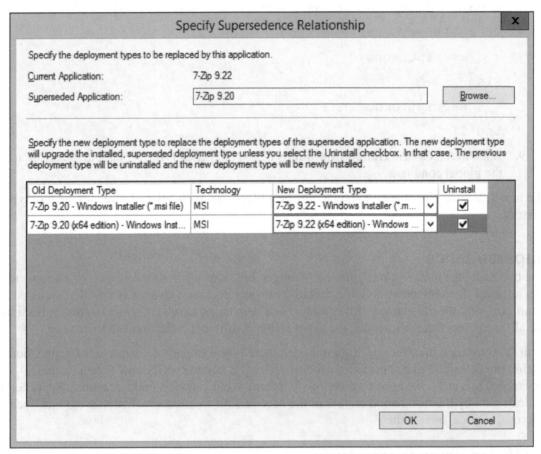

Selecting the Uninstall check box will run the uninstall program specified in the old deployment type before running the installation program in the new deployment type. For installers that automatically handle the uninstall of old versions, there is no real need to select this unless there are reboots needed between the uninstall and installation.

8. When back in the **7-Zip 9.22 Properties** dialog box, you can specify additional applications to supersede; however, in this case, go ahead and click **OK** to close the dialog box and save the changes.

> **Real World Note**: Configuration Manager does not automatically upgrade already deployed versions of the application until the new application is deployed to devices or users. Creating different collections and deploying the old and the new versions of the application to each collection allows different departments, for example, to run the upgrade at different times.

Deploying Applications

A deployment can be made *available* or *required*. The difference is quite obvious in that a required application is forced by the administrator, much like a group policy, whereas the available application is optional for the end user, or device for that matter, to install.

In a perfect environment, all applications would be installed without a fuss, but that's not the world we live in. Therefore, troubleshooting application deployment is quite common for a Configuration Manager operator. When dealing with deployment in the application model, there are three crucial log files:

- AppEnforce.log
- AppIntentEval.log
- AppDiscovery.log

These log files are located in the C:\Windows\CCM\Logs folder and are best read using the CMTrace tool.

Deploy an Application

Perform the following steps to deploy an application:

1. On **CM01**, start the **ConfigMgr console**.

2. Select the **Assets and Compliance** workspace.

3. Expand **Device Collections** and select the **Software Distribution** folder.

4. Click **Create Device Collection** on the ribbon.

5. Enter **Igor Pavlov 7-Zip** in the **Name** field, select the **All Systems** collection as the **Limiting collection** using the **Browse** button, and then click **Next**.

6. Click **Add Rule / Direct Rule** on the **Membership Rules** page.

7. In the **Create Direct Membership Rule Wizard**, click **Next**.

8. Enter **PC0002** in the **Value** field to deploy the application to the previously deployed Windows 8.1 machine, and then click **Next**.

9. Select the resource on the **Select Resources** page and click **Summary**.

10. On the **Summary** page, click **Next**.

11. On the **Completion** page, click **Close**.

12. Back at the **Create Device Collection Wizard**, click **Summary**.

13. On the **Summary** page, review the details and click **Next**.

14. When the **Completion** page appears, click **Close.**

15. Select the **Software Library** workspace.

16. Expand **Application Management** and click **Applications**.

17. Select the **7-Zip 9.22** application and click **Deploy** on the ribbon.

18. In the **Deploy Software Wizard**, click the **Browse** button next to **Collection**.

19. Change from **User Collections** to **Device Collections**; then click the **Software Distribution** folder, select the newly created **Igor Pavlov 7-Zip** collection, and click **OK**.

20. Back in the **Deploy Software Wizard**, click **Next**.

21. On the **Content** page, click **Add** and select **Distribution Point**.

22. In the **Add Distribution Point** dialog box, select **CM01.CORP.VIAMONSTRA.COM** and click **OK**.

23. Back on the **Content** page, click **Next**.

24. Change **Purpose** to **Required** and click **Summary**.

25. Review the information on the **Summary** page and then click **Next**.

26. When the **Completion** page appears, click **Close**.

Review Deployment Status

1. On **PC0002**, log on as **VIAMONSTRA\Administrator**.

2. Copy **CMTrace** from **\\CM01\SMS_P01\tools** to **C:\Windows\System32** and run it; when it prompts you, allow it to be the default program to view log files.

3. Navigate to **C:\Windows\CCM\Logs** on the client.

4. Open **AppIntentEval.log** using **CMTrace**.

Note: If none of the App* log files can be found in the log folder, trigger an update of the Machine Policy within the Configuration Manager Agent found in the Control Panel.

---

5. When the entry with the deployment type is found, open the **AppEnforce.log**.

When you can read the information in the preceding log file, you also can start the application, as well, because it has been installed.

Revision History

Each time a change is performed on an application, or deployment type, Configuration Manager creates a new revision of that application. Every revision of that application is kept so that it is easy to revert a change that might have be made in error. To remove an application, there cannot be any revisions of other applications that are dependent on the application that is subject to removal. It can therefore be necessary to delete old revisions of applications that are no longer in use. Before allowing you to remove an application, however, Configuration Manager makes sure that such a dependency does not exist.

View, Revert to, and Delete Revisions

1. On **CM01**, start the **ConfigMgr console** if it is not already started.

2. Select the **Software Library** workspace.

3. Expand **Application Management** and click **Applications**.

4. Select the **7-Zip 9.22** application and click **Revision History** on the ribbon.

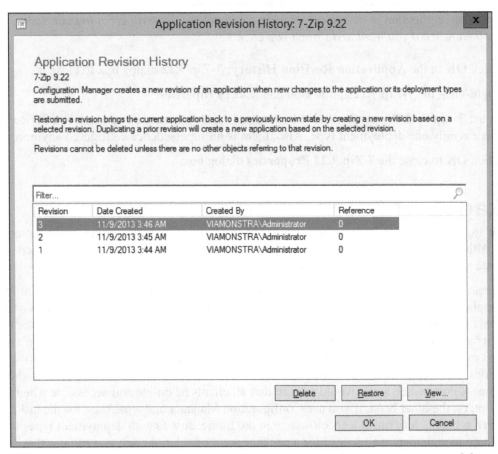

When you have an old revision with a reference to an application you want to delete, you can select the revision and click Delete to remove it so you are able to delete the other application.

5. In the **Application Revision History: 7-Zip 9.22** dialog box, select the **Revision 1** and click **Restore**.

6. Click **Yes** in the confirmation dialog box. You now get a new revision of the 7-Zip 9.22 application.

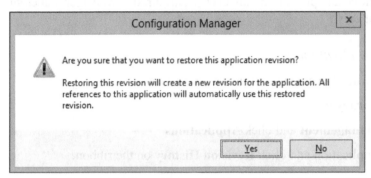

Restoring an application to an earlier revision could potentially have great impact, so make sure you know what you want to do when you click Yes.

7. Click **OK** in the **Application Revision History: 7-Zip 9.22** dialog box to close it.

8. Right-click the **7-Zip 9.22** application and select **Properties**.

9. In the **7-Zip 9.22 Properties** dialog box, select the **Deployment Types** tab and notice that there is only one deployment type. Also, there is no supersedence configured anymore.

10. Click **OK** to close the **7-Zip 9.22 Properties** dialog box.

Packages

Before the application model, only packages could be used to deploy software in Configuration Manager. Although still there for legacy and migration reasons, there also are scenarios when packages are still preferred over applications.

Such a scenario is when there is no requirement to check that the application is installed or not to have the application state based, e.g. when no detection method is preferred. An example is when you just want to copy data to all SCCM clients but allow the end user to move, delete, or alter the files after it has been copied, or when you simply want to run a command on clients and don't care how it went more than the exit code that the command or script returned. You might want to delete all files within a specific folder such as the C:\Windows\Temp folder on all clients in the organization. A PowerShell script would require that all clients be online and accessible when you run the script; on the other hand, if you use Configuration Manager and a package for the task, you can even schedule it to run at a specific time in the future. Just as with deployment types in the application model, there isn't a need for a package source folder, though you can use that, as well.

Real World Note: There are known issues when installing applications as part of a task sequence during OSD, so, in such cases, packages are the way to go. For installation of software that is needed only during OSD, there is no need to use the more complex application model. Such software can be driver software like fingerprint reader software or Bluetooth software.

Chapter 5

Software Updates

Keeping your Windows client up to date in terms of security updates and other important updates is essential to providing a secure, stable, and optimized client experience for your end users. As Microsoft no longer provides service packs containing hundreds of fixes, it is even more important to have a solid environment for keeping your clients up to date.

Configuration Manager vs. Windows Server Update Services

Many corporations are using Windows Server Update Services (WSUS), even though they often are using Configuration Manager. One of the most common questions we receive regarding software updates in Configuration Manager vs. stand-alone WSUS is what are the differences and advantages of using Configuration Manager to do the patching instead of WSUS?

Benefits of Using Configuration Manager for Software Updating

Actually, there are quite few reasons to do the patching using Configuration Manager instead of stand-alone WSUS.

- **Offline servicing**. In Configuration Manager, you can do offline servicing, which basically means that you can apply a number of security updates and other updates and inject them right into your installation image with a few clicks.

- **One infrastructure and one client**. One significant benefit of using Configuration Manager to do the patching is that you do not need to maintain a separate infrastructure for your WSUS servers, and the updates are distributed using the distribution points you already have in place for your clients. Furthermore, you will see no collisions when installing patches and applications, as they both are handled using the same installation agent.

- **Maintenance windows and scheduling**. Something that is not possible using traditional WSUS updating is to schedule when updates should be installed. This is definitely possible when updating through Configuration Manager.

- **User experience**. With the good old patching done via WSUS, users do not really get much of a choice other than to postpone the installation for up to some number of hours. Configuration Manager and Software Center provide a better user experience and can let the users decide when to install certain things and not interrupt daily work, thus keeping the users productive.

Configuration Manager

With the preceding benefits, ViaMonstra is of course using Configuration Manager to manage and distribute new security updates that are released by Microsoft at least once per month.

Software Update Point

The Software Update Point role in Configuration Manager is the role that handles the software updates. It integrates with WSUS, and therefore WSUS must be installed on the software update point before installing the Software Update Point role.

> **Note**: To complete the step-by-step guides for software updates, you must have an Internet connection in the virtual machine. Again, if you need help getting the Internet to work in the virtual machine, please see Johan Arwidmark's guide on how to set up virtual routers in the lab environment at http://tinyurl.com/cln7fd2.

Prepare by Installing WSUS

1. On **CM01**, log on as **VIAMONSTRA\Administrator** and start **Server Manager**.

2. Click **Manage**, and then choose **Add Roles and Features**.

3. On the **Before you begin** page, click **Next**.

4. On the **Select installation type** page, click **Next**.

5. On the **Select destination server** page, make sure **CM01.corp.viamonstra.com** is selected, and click **Next**.

6. On the **Select server roles** page, select **Windows Server Update Services**, choose **Add features** when a prompt to install additional features appears, and then click **Next**.

7. On the **Select features** page, click **Next**.

8. On the **Windows Server Update Services** page, click **Next**.

9. On the **Select role services** page, clear the **WID Database** check box, select the **Database** check box, and then click **Next**.

10. On the **Content location selection** page, enter **D:\WSUS** in the **Store updates in the following location** text box and click **Next**.

11. On the **Database Instance Selection** page, enter **CM01** and click the **Check connection** button. Make sure that the text **Successfully connected to server** shows and then click **Next**.

12. On the **Confirm installation selections** page, click **Install**.

13. On the **Installation progress** page, wait for the installation to finish and then click **Close**.

14. Now in **Server Manager**, click **WSUS** in the menu to the left.

15. Note the yellow bar that reads **Configuration required for Windows Server Update Services on CM01** and click the **More** link.

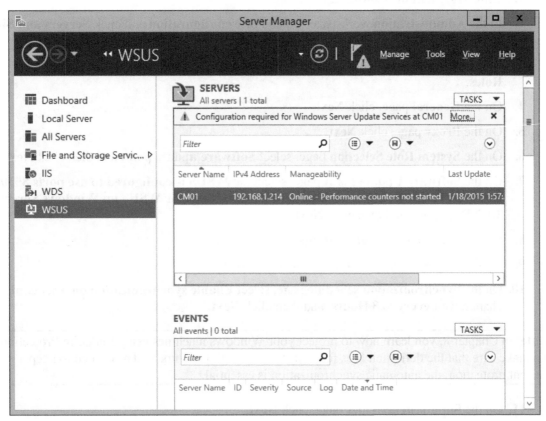

You must perform the post-configuration of Windows Server Update Services after installing the WSUS role.

16. Click the **Launch Post-Installation tasks** link to start the post-configuration.

Note: Click the link once and leave it. The work has started in the background, though it might appear that nothing actually happens when you click the link. You will be notified in the user interface when the configuration is complete.

17. When the configuration is complete, which will take a minute or two (watch the Stage column in the top pane, and the status in the bottom pane), close the **All Server Task Details** window.

Install and Configure the Software Update Point

1. On **CM01**, start the **ConfigMgr console**.

2. In the **Administration** workspace, expand **Site configuration** and click **Servers and Site System Roles**.

3. Right-click the **CM01.corp.viamonstra.com** site server and choose **Add Site System Roles**.

4. On the **General** page, click **Next**.

5. On the **Proxy** page, click **Next**.

6. On the **System Role Selection** page, select **Software update point** and then click **Next**.

7. On the **Software Update Point** page, select the **WSUS is configured to use ports 8530 and 8531 for client communications (default settings for WSUS on Windows Server 2012 R2)** option and then click **Next**.

8. On the **Proxy and account settings** page, click **Next**.

9. On the **Synchronization source** page, click **Next**.

10. On the **Synchronization schedule** page, select **Enable synchronization on a schedule**, change **Run every** to **8 Hours**, and then click **Next**.

Note: In Chapter 8, you learn how to protect your Windows machines using Endpoint Protection. To make sure that the definition files for Endpoint Protection are updated as needed to keep a current protection, the automatic synchronization is essential.

---

11. On the **Supersedence rules** page, click **Next**.

12. On the **Classifications** page, in addition to the default selections, also select **Critical Updates** and **Definition Updates**, and then click **Next**.

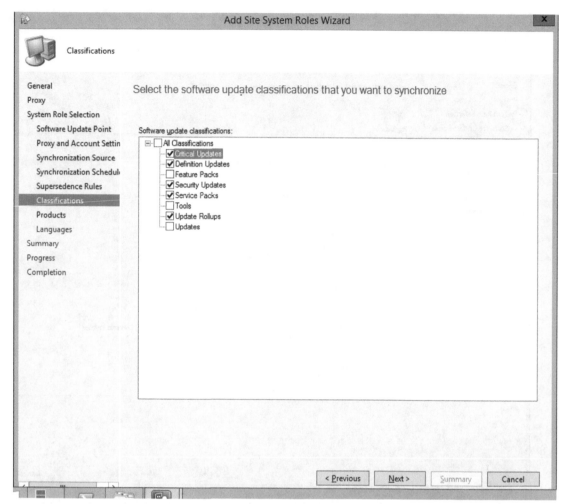

Once again as you are soon to deploy System Center Endpoint Protection for your client machines, you will have to obtain the definition updates for the antimalware software to be up to date and maintain a good level of protection.

13. On the **Products** page, select the **All Products** check box and then click it again to clear the box. Click **Next**.

Note: This gets rid of all predefined selections so that you can choose exactly what you want to synchronize. You will choose the products later, after you have updated the catalog to include updates for the latest versions of Windows.

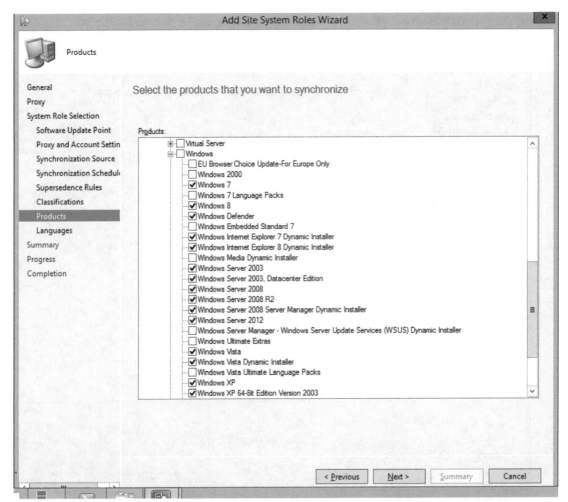

This is what the default selection looks like. Surely you can find several problems with this picture. One is that you do most likely not want to synchronize updates for Windows Vista and hopefully not Windows XP anymore (remember XP is not supported as of April 2014). Another problem with this picture is that you do not see the category for Windows 8.1 and Windows Server 2012 R2 until you do the initial synchronization.

14. On the **Languages** page, clear all language check boxes except for **English** and click **Next**.

15. On the **Summary** page, click **Next**.

16. On the **Completion** page, click **Close**.

Synchronize with Windows Update (Initial Sync)

Initial synchronization is done to make sure that you get the most recent catalog files from Microsoft, that is so you can get new products to choose from when selecting which updates to synchronize from Microsoft. For example, you must do that to obtain updates for Microsoft's latest versions of Windows 8.1 and Windows Server 2012 R2.

1. On **CM01**, start the **ConfigMgr console**.

2. Click the **Software Library** in the left menu.

3. Expand **Software Updates**, click **All Software Updates**, and then click the **Synchronize Software Updates** button on the ribbon. When asked whether you really want to run a synchronization, answer **Yes**.

Note: Now wait few minutes for it to do the initial synchronization with Microsoft's Windows Update servers. You can check the status of the synchronization in the SMS_WSUS_SYNC_MANAGER log in the Monitoring section under Component Status. You will see a message with ID 6702 when the synchronization is done. You also can open the wsyncmgr.log directly, which is found in the Logs directory of your Configuration Manager installation folder.

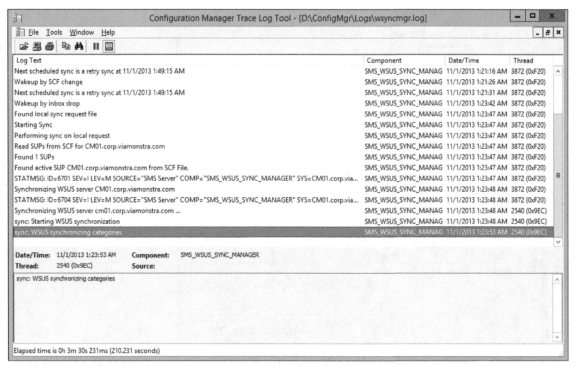

The wsyncmgr.log tells you exactly what is going on and notifies you when the synchronization is complete. It takes several minutes to complete, so be patient.

Choose Products to Synchronize

Now that the synchronization has been done, the list of products has been updated so that you can select the most recent versions of Microsoft software for which to fetch software updates.

1. On **CM01**, start the **ConfigMgr console**.

2. In the **Administration** workspace, expand **Site Configuration** and click **Sites**.

3. Right-click the site named **P01 – ViaMonstra Headquarters Primary Site** and choose **Configure Site Components / Software Update Point**.

4. Click the **Products** tab.

5. Scroll down to the **Forefront** section, select **Forefront Endpoint Protection 2010**. Then scroll down to the **Windows** section, select **Windows 8.1**, and click **OK**.

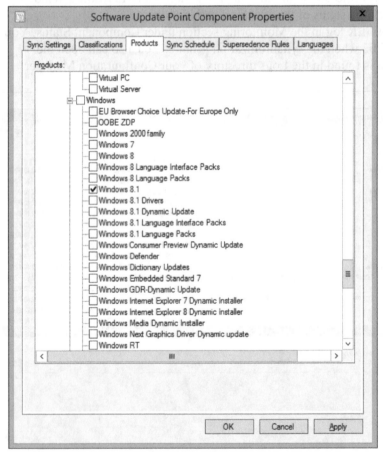

Now that you have synchronized with Microsoft Update Services, you can see new products such as Windows 8.1.

6. In the **Software Library** workspace, expand **Software Updates** and click **All Software Updates**.

7. Click the **Synchronize Software Updates** button on the ribbon. When asked to run synchronization, answer **Yes**.

> **Note**: It takes several minutes for the sync to initialize and figure out which updates are available for the selected product(s). Once again, you can follow the progress by looking in the wsyncmgr.log log file, which is located in the Logs directory of your Configuration Manager installation folder.

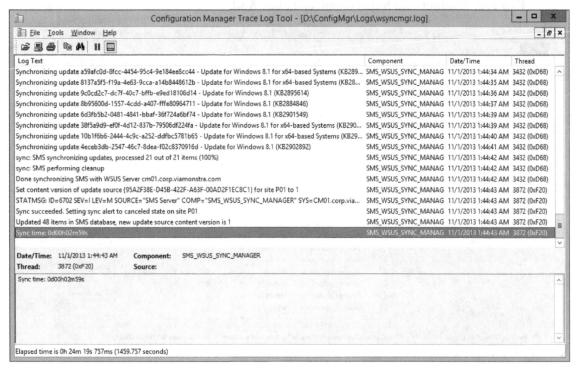

In the wsyncmgr.log, you can see the updates synchronizing and when done you can proceed to actually working with the updates, i.e. deploying them to your client machines.

Working with the Software Updates

Now that you are all set up with the updates and the updates are coming into the Software Updates node in the ConfigMgr console, it is high time to start actually working with the updates, gathering them into groups, downloading them, and then distributing them to your clients.

Software Update Groups

1. On **CM01**, in the **ConfigMgr console**, go to **Software Library**, expand **Software Updates**, and click **All Software Updates**.

2. Refresh the view of **All Software Updates** by clicking the **refresh button** to the right, in the address bar.

3. To the right of the Search input field, click **Add Criteria**; scroll down to and select **Expired**, **Product**, and **Superseded**; and click **Add**.

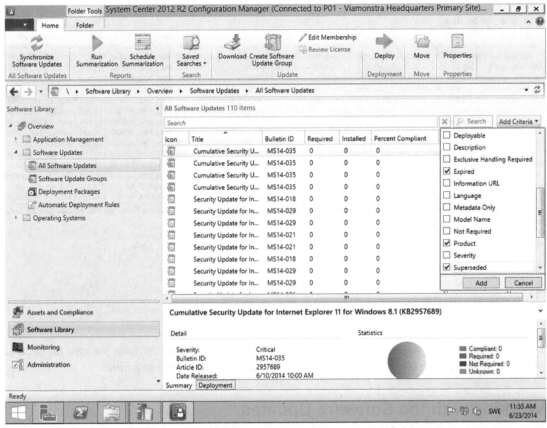

You can filter the updates using a great number of attributes.

4. In the orange bar that appears and says "**AND Product**," click the link for **Active Directory Rights Management Services Client 2.0**, scroll down to **Windows 8.1**, and click it.

5. Change **Expired** from **Yes** to **No**, and then change **Superseded** to **No**. This will filter out irrelevant updates.

6. Click the **Search** button to the right of the **Search** input field to list all updates targeted for Windows 8.1.

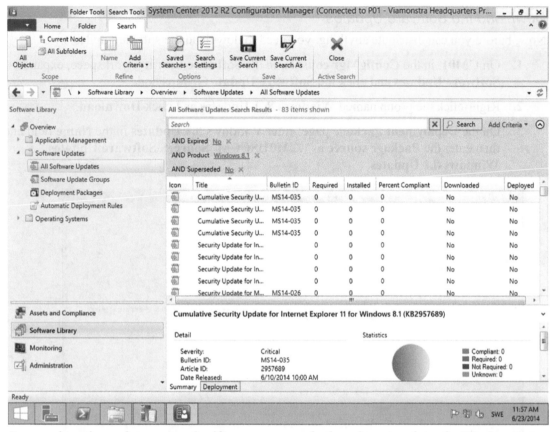

By searching for updates using the filters, you see only the relevant updates for Windows 8.1.

7. Simplify searching in the future by clicking **Save Current Search As** on the ribbon, enter the name **Windows 8.1 Updates** and click **OK**.

Note: When saving a search in ConfigMgr 2012 R2, the current search filter is cleared.

8. To filter the updates again, in the ribbon, select **Saved Searches / Manage Searches for Current Node**, select **Windows 8.1 Updates**, and click **OK**.

9. Select all updates that have now been filtered out by clicking one of the updates in the list and then pressing **Ctrl + A**.

10. Right-click any update and choose **Create Software Update Group**.

11. In the **Create Software Update Group** dialog box, enter **Windows 8_1 Updates** as the **Name** and **All updates applicable to Windows 8.1** as the **Description**, and then click **Create**.

Note: Now all selected updates are added to the Windows 8_1 group of updates. Note that you cannot use dots in the Name field, which is why you are using an underscore instead.

Download the Software Updates

Now, before you can distribute anything, you need to download the software updates:

1. On **CM01**, in the **ConfigMgr console**, in the **Software Library** workspace, expand **Software Updates** and click the **Software Update Groups** node.

2. Right-click the group named **Windows 8_1 Updates** and click **Download**.

3. On the **Deployment Package** page, enter **Windows 8.1 Updates** in the **Name** field and then enter the **Package source** as **\\CM01\SCCM_Source$\Software Updates\ Windows 8.1 Updates**.

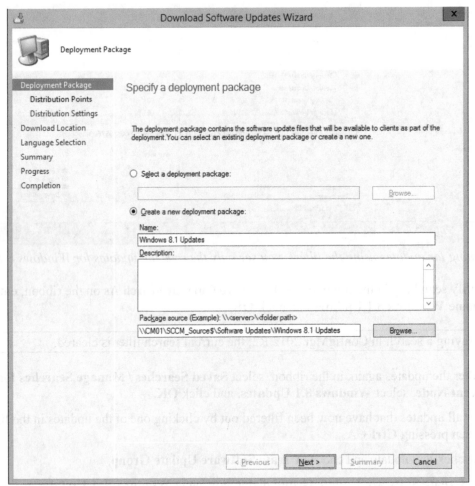

Now you are configuring a deployment package for our Windows 8.1 Updates.

4. On the **Distribution Points** page, click **Add** and then **Distribution Point**. Complete the
    following:

    In the **Add Distribution Points** dialog box, select the distribution point
    CM01.CORP.VIAMONSTRA.COM, and then click **OK** followed by **Next**.

5. On the **Distribution Settings** page, accept the default settings and click **Next**.

6. On the **Download Location** page, accept the default settings and click **Next**.

7. On the **Language Selection** page, accept the default settings and click **Next**.

8. On the **Summary** page, click **Next**.

Note: Now the actual files are downloaded to the source folder you specified. This certainly takes
some time depending on your Internet connection speed.

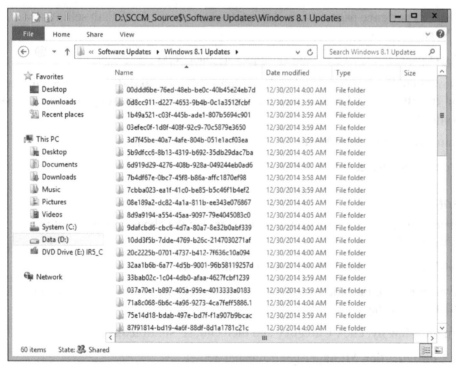

*When the updates are downloaded, they are stored in separate folders in the software updates
package source folder.*

9. On the **Completion** page, click **Close**.

Deploy the Updates to the Clients

Last but not least, it is time to actually deploy the updates to the client machines:

1. On **CM01**, in the **ConfigMgr console**, in the **Software Library** workspace, expand **Software Updates** and click the **Software Update Groups** node.

2. Right-click the software update group named **Windows 8_1 Updates** and click **Deploy**.

3. On the **General** page, click the **Browse** button and complete the following:

    In the **Select Collection** dialog box, choose the collection **All Windows 8.1 Systems** and then click **OK** followed by **Next**.

4. On the **Deployment Settings** page, accept the default settings and click **Next**.

5. On the **Scheduling** page, under **Software available time**, select **As soon as possible** and then click **Next**.

6. On the **User Experience** page, review the options and accept the default settings by clicking **Next**.

7. On the **Alert** page, accept the default settings and click **Next**.

8. On the **Download Settings** page, select **Download software updates from distribution point and install**. This makes sure that your clients get the important updates regardless of their connection. Click **Next**.

9. On the **Summary** page, click **Next**.

10. On the **Completion** page, click **Close**.

Patch the Client

Now that the updates are published, you need to make sure that the clients are aware of the updates and actually install them:

1. On **PC0002**, log on as **VIAMONSTRA\Administrator**.

2. Start to type **control panel** and open the **Control Panel** when listed in the search results. Complete the following:

    In the **View by**, click **Category** and then choose **Small icons**.

3. Open the **Configuration Manager** control panel applet.

    a. Click the **Actions** tab, select **Software Updates Scan Cycle**, and click **Run Now**. In the dialog box that appears, click **OK**. Wait a couple of minutes for the scan to take place.

> **Note**: The action going on at this point in time can be found in the log file WUAHandler.log in the folder C:\Windows\CCM\Logs. Have a peek in this file if you want to know for certain when you can proceed with the next step in this guide.

    b. After waiting for a few minutes, click **Software Updates Deployment Evaluation Cycle** and click **Run Now**. You are notified instantly of available changes. Click the notification to start Software Center.

4. In Software Center, you see all available updates that are applicable to this particular machine and can go ahead and install the updates.

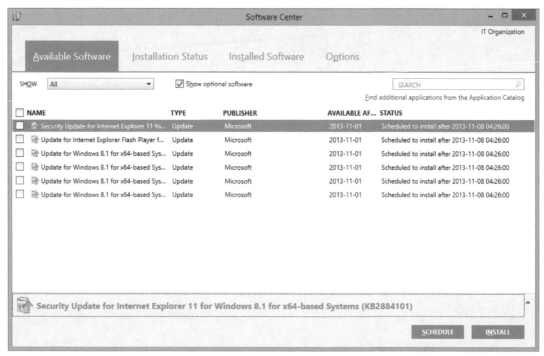

Software Center lists all applicable updates for your client machine, and the user can choose to install them right away or schedule it for a more convenient time.

Servicing Images Offline

Although it is possible to service images offline in Configuration Manager, we currently do *not* recommend this solution for production use as there are problems with updates that will break your image (updates requiring multiple reboots). Instead we recommend building a reference image where the updates are installed online in a controlled fashion. For additional information on how to create reference images, check the following link on Microsoft TechNet: http://technet.microsoft.com/en-us/library/dn744290.aspx.

Chapter 6

User Profiles and Data

User profiles and data always have and always will be sensitive issues. They are simply important for keeping a good user experience, as well as providing means for users to work with their data and documents regardless of where they are. For the first time in many years, you now have some really nice improvements to what you can do with user profiles with the introduction of User Experience Virtualization (UE-V). UE-V takes setting roaming to a whole new level. Also, there are new possibilities for accessing the data in the cloud or users accessing their data from their own devices, thanks to a new Windows feature called *Work Folders*. This chapter also contains a part about backing up your clients using Data Protection Manager 2012 R2.

Folder Redirection and Offline Files

Folder Redirection is a really good thing in terms of dealing with user data. We implement it in all our deployment projects if it is not already in place. What is so beautiful about Folder Redirection is that you can redirect your Document folder, the desktop, Favorites folder for Internet Explorer, and more to a network drive, which means you can always log in to another machine and get the same data and settings on that machine. Along with offline files, all this data also is made available offline, providing a way for your users to work outside the office without a connection to the actual file server.

Typically and historically, deploying folder redirection has been done using group policies applied to the users. By instead managing these settings in Configuration Manager, you can deploy folder redirection and also get instant feedback and actually inventory and see where folder redirection has been applied.

Offline Files

When you activate Folder Redirection, it by default enables Offline Files. This adds the benefit of keeping all those redirected files available offline when a user is not connected to the file server resource on the internal network, which is perfect for your mobile users. They always have the data they need, and changes are synchronized when a connection to the file server is restored, either through a remote access connection or when on the internal network.

If you have used, as we have, Folder Redirection with Offline Files in Windows XP, you will see extreme changes in how it works in more modern versions of Windows, that is, Windows 7 and later. It's seamless for the user in all scenarios, and the synchronization is done in the background rather than at logoff time as is the case in Windows XP.

> **Note**: Actually, Offline Files was totally rewritten for Windows Vista; the feature was improved further in Windows 7 and received additional improvements in Windows 8 and 8.1.

Setting Up Folder Redirection with Offline Files

Configuring Folder Redirection is done in two steps: making sure there is a file share available to house the folder structure and data, and performing a group policy configuration or a configuration item using Configuration Manager. We also add a third step to configure Always Offline mode which comes in handy in some scenarios.

Before proceeding, as we mentioned, Folder Redirection also can be configured now using Configuration Manager and not solely by group policies. However, in practice, they have one thing in common. Both set the necessary registry keys under HKEY_CURRENT_USER\Software\Microsoft\Windows\CurrentVersion\Explorer in Shell Folders and User Shell Folders.

> **Note**: If you already have Folder Redirection in place in your existing enterprise environment, you can skip ahead to the "Work Folders" section later in this chapter. Work Folders also can pose as the modern variant of folder redirection where you keep one folder in sync on all your devices. Once again, more on Work Folders later in this chapter.

Create the Folder Structure on the File Server

1. On **FS01**, log on as **VIAMONSTRA\Administrator**.

2. Using **File Explorer**, create a folder named **Shares** in the root of the **D**: drive.

> **Real World Note**: Don't use the C: drive to store data. Always keep this on a separate volume from the operating system volume.

3. In the **Shares** folder, create a new folder named **UserData**. Right-click the **UserData** folder and select **Properties** / **Security** / **Advanced**.

4. Click the **Disable inheritance** button, and in the **Block Inheritance** dialog box, select **Remove all inherited permissions from this object**.

5. Click **Add** and then click the **Select a principal** link. In the **Enter the object name to select** input area, type **SYSTEM** and click **OK**. Enter the following permissions for SYSTEM and then click **OK**:

   o   Applies to: **This folder subfolders and files.**

   o   Basic permissions: **Full control**

6. Repeat step 5 to set the following permissions for **FS01\Administrators, CREATOR OWNER**, and **Authenticated Users**:

   o   FS01/Administrators: **Full control** in **This folder, subfolders and files**.

   o   CREATOR OWNER: **Full control** in **Subfolder and files only**.

o   Authenticated Users: **This folder only**:

- **Traverse folder / execute file**

- **List folder / read data**

- **Read attributes**

- **Read extended attributes**

- **Create folders / append data.**

Note: When editing special permissions, you must click the Show advanced permissions link in the Permission Entry for UserData window to be able to set the preceding special permissions.

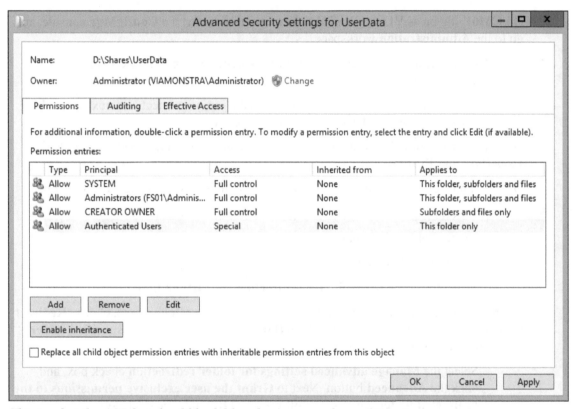

This is what the ACL list should look like when you are done editing it.

7.   When you are done, click **OK**.

8.   Without closing the **UserData Properties** dialog box, in the **Sharing** tab, select **Advanced Sharing**.

9.   Select the **Share this folder** check box and click the **Permissions** button.

10. Remove **Everyone** and add the **Authenticated Users** group with **Full control**. Click **OK** three times.

Configure Folder Redirection and Offline Files Using Configuration Manager

Starting with System Configuration Manager 2012 SP1, you can configure Folder Redirection and Offline Files in Configuration Manager instead of traditional group policies. Before the Folder Redirection settings can be applied to your users, you must configure the client settings to allow for user data and profiles. Let's get started with using Configuration Manager 2012 R2 to manage your users' folder redirection.

Note: Configuring Folder Redirection and Offline Files in Configuration Manager 2012 R2 can be applied only to Windows 8 and Windows 8.1 machines. If you are still using Windows 7, you must configure Folder Redirection using group policies (see the section "Configure Folder Redirection and Offline Files Using Group Policies" a bit later in this chapter).

1. On **CM01**, log on as **VIAMONSTRA\Administrator**, start the **ConfigMgr console**, and go to the **Administration** workspace.

2. Click **Client Settings**; then right-click **Default Client Settings**, choose **Properties**, and complete the following:

   > Click **Compliance Settings**, and then make sure you select **Yes** next to **Enable User Data and Profiles**. Click **OK** when done.

3. Go to the **Assets and Compliance** workspace, expand **Compliance Settings**, and click **User Data and Profiles**.

4. On the ribbon, click the **Create User Data and Profiles Configuration Item** button.

5. On the **General** page, enter the following information and click **Next**:

   o Name: **Folder Redirection**.

   o Description: **Folder redirection for all users**.

   o Select the check boxes **Folder redirection** and **Offline files**.

6. On the **Folder Redirection** page, under **Action** and next to **Documents**, choose **Redirect to remote**, and enter the path \\FS01\UserData in the **Redirect to the specified folder** field. Then complete the following:

   > Select the **Manage advanced settings for folder redirection** check box, and click the **Advanced** button. Next to **Grant the user exclusive permissions to the redirected folder**, choose **No** followed by **OK**, and then click **Next**.

Note: The default options set the owner of the files to the user. That means you as the administrator will not be able to access the files without changing the owner and replacing the ACLs. In some cases this is wanted, whereas in others it is not. In particular, when you do not want administrators to access the contents of the user folders, you should use the default setting.

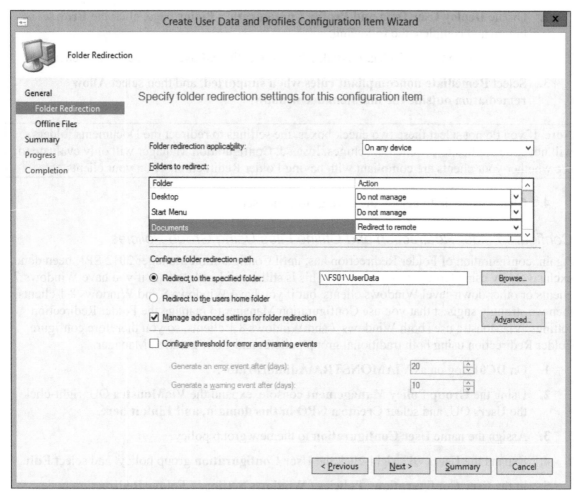

Configuring Folder Redirection using Configuration Manager is a one-stop place to configure it, and you have some benefit of choosing the configuration for which devices the folder redirection should be applied to, as well.

7. On the **Offline Files** page, note all options without changing any settings and then click **Next**.

8. On the **Summary** page, click **Next**.

9. On the **Completion** page, click **Close**.

Deploy Folder Redirection and Offline Files Using Configuration Manager

Now that the configuration item is created, you need to deploy it to some users so that it will be applied to the specified users.

1. Now right-click the item named **Folder Redirection** and choose **Deploy**.

2. On the **Deploy User Data and Profile Configuration Policy** page, click the **Browse** button and complete the following:

   In the Select Collection dialog box, select the **All users** collection and click **OK**.

3. Select **Remediate noncompliant rules when supported**, and then select **Allow remediation outside the maintenance window**.

Note: If you do not select these two check boxes, the settings to redirect the Documents folders will never be applied to the client machines. Instead, Configuration Manager will only evaluate to see whether your clients are compliant with having Folder Redirection set on your clients.

4. Click **OK** again to deploy the settings to your users.

Configure Folder Redirection and Offline Files Using Group Policies

Again, configuration of Folder Redirection has, until Configuration Manager 2012 SP1, been done exclusively by using Group Policy settings. This is still a valid path to take if you have Windows 7 clients or other down-level Windows clients, but if you have Windows 8 and Windows 8.1 clients, then we strongly suggest that you use Configuration Manager to manage the Folder Redirection settings. ViaMonstra uses both Windows 7 and Windows 8.1 clients, so you therefore configure Folder Redirection using both traditional group policies and Configuration Manager.

1. On **DC01**, log on as **VIAMONSTRA\Administrator**.

2. Using the **Group Policy Management** console, expand the **ViaMonstra** OU, right-click the **Users** OU, and select **Create a GPO in this domain, and Link it here**.

3. Assign the name **User Configuration** to the new group policy.

4. Expand the **Users** OU, right-click the **User Configuration** group policy, and select **Edit**.

5. In the **User Configuration / Policies / Windows Settings / Folder Redirection** node, right-click **Documents** and select **Properties**.

6. In the **Setting** drop-down list, select **Basic – Redirect everyone's folder to the same location**.

7. In the **Root path** text field, enter **\\FS01\UserData**. In the **Settings** tab, clear the **Grant the user exclusive rights to Documents** check box and click **OK**. In the Warning dialog box that appears, click **Yes**. Close the **Group Policy Management Editor**, but leave the **Group Policy Management** console open.

Note: The default options set the owner of the files to the user. That means you as the administrator will not be able to access the files without changing the owner and replacing the ACLs. In some cases this is wanted, whereas in others it is not. In particular, when you do not want administrators to access the contents of the user folders, you should use the default setting.

Classic configuration of Folder Redirection using group policies.

Create a WMI Filter to Keep This Configuration for Windows 7 Only

Because Windows 7 machines cannot use the new Configuration Manager User Data and Profiles configuration item, the configuration on PC0001 will use the Group Policy configuration, whereas PC0002 will use the Configuration Manager configuration. To make sure that the group policy does not apply to PC0002, you need to make sure that the Folder Redirection GPO applies only to Windows 7.

1. On **DC01**, in the **Group Policy Management** console, in the left pane, right-click **WMI Filters** and select **New**.

2. In the **Name** field, enter **Windows 7** and then click **Add**.

3. In the **Query** text area, enter the following:

    ```
    SELECT * FROM Win32_OperatingSystem WHERE Version LIKE
    "6.1%" AND ProductType ="1"
    ```

4. Click **OK** and ignore the warning; then click **Save**.

5. In the **ViaMonstra / Users** OU, select the **User Configuration** GPO.

6. Make sure that the **Scope** tab is the active one, and at the very bottom of the page, click the drop-down list under **WMI Filtering**.

7. Choose **Windows 7**, and when asked **Would you like to change the WMI filter to Windows 7?**, click **Yes**.

Note: Although you do not verify that the WMI filter is working as expected in this guide, you can check this by running logging in to a client as a user in the ViaMonstra / Users OU, run gpresult /h C:\Windows\Temp\GPResult.html and looking in the resulting HTML file to verify that the WMI filter evaluation has been performed.

Verify That Folder Redirection Is in Effect

Now is the time to verify that Folder Redirection works as expected.

1. On **PC0001**, log in as **Don** in the **VIAMONSTRA** domain.

2. Open **Windows Explorer** (named liked that in Windows 7) expand **Documents**, and click **My Documents**.

3. Right-click anywhere in the empty white area to the left and select **New / Text Document**.

4. As the file name, enter **PC0001** (creates the PC0001.txt file).

5. Open the text file with **Notepad** and enter the text **This was created on PC0001**; save the file and close **Notepad**.

6. Log off **PC0001**, and on **FS01**, verify that the **PC0001.txt** file is in the **D:\Shares\UserData\Don\Documents** folder. If it is not, log on to **PC0001** and log off one more time to make sure the policy is in effect.

7. On **PC0002**, log in as **Don** in the **VIAMONSTRA** domain.

8. Right-click the **start button**, type in and select **Control Panel**; then click **Category**, choose **Small icons**, and open the **Configuration Manager** control panel applet.

9. Click the **Actions** tab, select **User Policy Retrieval & Evaluation Cycle**, and click **Run Now**. In the dialog box that appears, click **OK** and then wait one minute so that the policy can be refreshed.

10. Click the **Configurations** tab, select the configuration item **Folder Redirection** (click Refresh if it's not listed), and click the **Evaluate** button. When notified, log off of **PC0002**.

11. On **PC0002**, log in again as **Don** in the **VIAMONSTRA** domain.

12. Open **File Explorer**, and verify that the text file **PC0001.txt** exists in the **Documents** folder and that the contents of the file match the text you entered in the file on PC0001.

Real World Note: If you redirect your folders to a Distributed File System (DFS) path, Windows Search does not honor this type of link. That means it will not be able to index your folders if you are not using Offline Files (for instance, on stationary machines). The same behavior existed in Windows 7 and has not been fixed for Windows Search in Windows 8 or Windows 8.1.

View Compliance Status in Configuration Manager

The great thing about using User Data and Profiles via Configuration Manager is that you get compliance status, which means you can monitor whether users have Folder Redirection applied.

1. On **CM01**, log on as **VIAMONSTRA\Administrator** and start the **ConfigMgr console**.

2. Select the **Monitoring** workspace, and click **Deployments**.

3. Right-click **Folder Redirection** and choose **View Status**. Now you see which users are compliant with using Folder Redirection, which are not, and where there are errors. Thereby you can proactively fix any errors encountered.

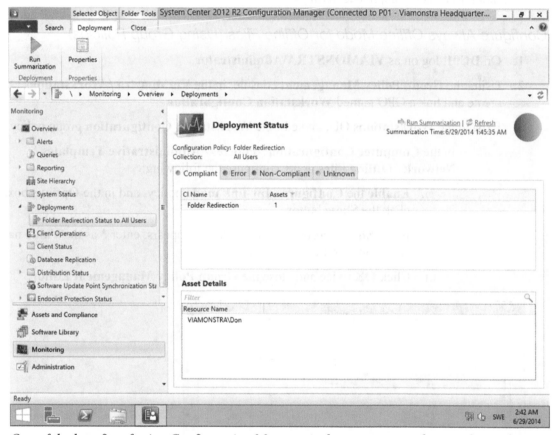

One of the benefits of using Configuration Manager is that you can see the compliance for your users in terms of whether Folder Redirection is applied or not.

Always Offline Mode

There are not many new features introduced for Offline Files with Windows 8 and 8.1 except for stability and performance improvements. One major difference, however, is Always Offline mode, which makes you run in offline mode even when you are online to get improved performance when working with cached files. The synchronization of files back to the server is then performed at an interval of every two hours or by a value that you configure.

If you configure Folder Redirection using Configuration Manager, it overrides any settings for Offline Files that you set using group policies. Therefore, to apply Always Offline mode for Offline Files using Configuration Manager, you need to apply it using the configuration item in Configuration Manager Compliance Settings.

Configure Always Offline Mode for Offline Files (Using Group Policies)

1. On **DC01**, log on as **VIAMONSTRA\Administrator**.

2. Using the **Group Policy Management** console, in the **ViaMonstra / Workstations** OU, create and link a GPO named **Workstation Configuration**.

3. Expand the **Workstations** OU, and edit the **Workstation Configuration** group policy:

   In the **Computer Configuration / Policies / Administrative Templates / Network / Offline Files** node, configure the following:

   i.   **Enable** the **Configure slow-link mode** policy, and in the **Options** box, click the **Show** button.

   ii. In the **Show Contents** dialog box that appears, enter * as the **Value name** and **Latency=1** as the **Value**.

   iii. Click **OK** twice and close the **Group Policy Management Editor**.

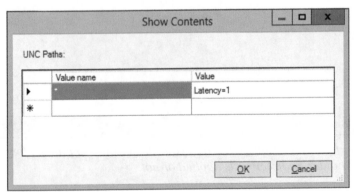

This is what the configuration in the group policy should look like.

Configure Always Offline Mode for Offline Files (Using Configuration Manager)

1. On **CM01**, log on as **VIAMONSTRA\Administrator**.

2. Select the **Assets and Compliance** workspace, expand **Compliance Settings**, and click **User Data and Profiles**.

3. Right-click the configuration item **Folder Redirection** and choose **Properties**.

4. Click the **Offline Files** tab, and then click the **Advanced** button and complete the following:

    a. Click the **Add** button.

    b. In the **Path** text box, type in **\\FS01\UserData**.

    c. In the **Latency threshold (milliseconds)** text box, type in **1**.

    d. Click **OK** three times.

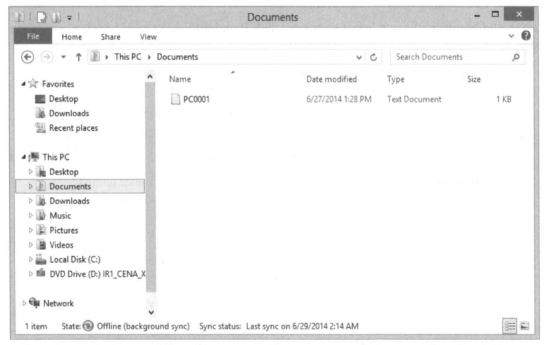

When Always Offline mode has been activated, you can note in the status bar that Offline Files is offline in background sync mode.

User Experience Virtualization

With UE-V, Microsoft introduces what could be called a light version of roaming user profiles. At the same time, it solves all challenges related to roaming user profiles and enables you to roam settings for Windows and Office and whatever other settings you define for your environment and applications.

> **Note**: UE-V is included in Microsoft Desktop Optimization Pack (MDOP). MDOP is available only to those with this addition to their volume license agreements. UE-V version 1.0 was released in November 2012 and has received one service pack since then, followed by the new major release of version 2.0 in late 2013.

Basics of UE-V

UE-V basically saves settings in the shape of files or registry settings for Windows and applications and saves them in a network location such as the user's home directory or a directory which you designate. So when users log in from another computer, the settings are read from the network share and applied to their user profiles and applications.

UE-V version 2.0 enables roaming even more settings for primarily Office by default but also for modern apps in Windows 8 and 8.1. One of the major changes since version 1.0 is that UE-V 2.0 no longer requires you to use Offline Files. Instead scheduled tasks are used to roam settings at the default interval of every 30 minutes and as defined by several built-in triggers, but more on that later.

You should be aware of a number of things in UE-V in order to understand how it works when roaming settings:

- **Agent**. To be able to roam settings between client computers as well as servers, you install an agent that needs to be run on each machine that will roam settings.

- **Templates**. The template files in XML format describe which settings are roamed.

- **Triggers**. There are various triggers which decide when the roaming takes place, for instance, when an application starts and closes and when you lock and unlock a machine.

- **Settings packages**. The UE-V settings are stored in a hidden folder named SettingsPackages in the home directory or another directory that you specify.

Templates

Which settings will be saved and roamed between the machines is determined by templates in XML format. Predefined templates are shipped with UE-V for roaming settings for:

- Windows 7; Windows 8 and Windows 8.1; and Windows Server 2008 R2, Windows Server 2012, and Windows Server 2012 R2.

  o Windows Accessories (Notepad, WordPad, and Calculator)

  o Desktop background and theme settings.

  o Start menu and taskbar settings, folder options, and more user settings. This is not activated by default, however.

  o Internet Explorer 8, 9, 10, and 11 settings, including Favorites.

  o All Office 2007 and 2010 applications. Office 2013 support is available from TechNet Gallery for UE-V templates at http://bit.ly/1kvugdY.

  o Lync client.

Real World Note: One of the most frequently asked questions we have received about UE-V is whether it roams the Outlook email signature. The answer is yes, sort of. It roams it, but the user has to set it in the Signatures option in Outlook to be able to use it. Also, for it to work with localized Office versions, i.e. any Outlook language version other than English, requires alteration of the templates. For instance, in our native language Swedish, the folder "signatures" is called "signature" and the templates must be updated accordingly. For more information on Outlook email signature roaming with UE-V, have a look at http://www.theexperienceblog.com/2013/09/24/roaming-outlook-email-signatures-with-ue-v/.

Generating Your Own Templates

You can easily create your own templates to roam particular settings in Windows or an application. Shipped with UE-V is the UE-V Template Generator which guides you through the process of creating your own templates.

Microsoft also provides a gallery where others can publish templates that you can use instead of reinventing the wheel. Look at http://go.microsoft.com/fwlink/?LinkID=246589.

Real World Note: Those of you familiar with USMT (User State Migration Tool) will be familiar with the templates. Although the XML templates for USMT and UE-V differ, the principle is the same. The templates are preferably stored on a network location which makes it a lot easier to manage and update them. Using the UE-V ADMX group policy templates, you can define where that location is so that the UE-V agent can fetch the template information from there.

Triggers

Unlike roaming user profiles that are read and saved at logon and logoff, UE-V uses various triggers to determine when settings are roamed.

- **Application start and close**. When a user closes Word, for instance, the settings for Word are saved to the designated network share (via a local cache). When the user opens Word the next time or on another machine, the settings from the local cache are read and applied to the application as it starts.

- **Locking a machine**. When a user locks a machine, Windows settings are saved to the network location via the local cache.

- **Logon or logoff**. Some settings, such as region and language, Start screen, and taskbar settings, are saved and applied only at logon and logoff.

Company Settings Center

New in UE-V 2.0 is a graphical user interface available for the end users. From there users can see exactly which settings are being roamed for which applications, as well as manually trigger a synchronization.

Setting Up UE-V

You learn here how to set up UE-V from start to finish. Please note that to complete this lab, you do need access to the MDOP package which is not freely available.

Note: MDOP can be found and evaluated on Microsoft TechNet or MSDN for anyone who has a subscription to either of these.

Prepare Settings for a User Account for Roaming Settings Using UE-V

In this step, you make sure that the user Don has a home directory set on his user account in Active Directory, as that setting is used by default by UE-V for storing the roamed settings.

1. On **DC01**, log on as **VIAMONSTRA\Administrator**.

2. Using **Active Directory Users and Computers**, in the **ViaMonstra / Users** OU, right-click **Don** and select **Properties**.

3. In the **Profile** tab, in the **Home folder** area, select **Connect** and then select **H:**; in the **To** text box, type **\\FS01\UserData\Don** and then click **OK**. In the **Active Directory Domain Services** warning dialog box, click **Yes**.

Configuring the Don user account.

Install the Agent on PC0001 and PC0002

Note that if you do not have access to MDOP, you do not have the necessary tools to proceed with this guide. Typically you would use a distribution engine, such as application deployment in Configuration Manager, to deploy the UE-V agent, but for this demonstration you rely on the manual installation.

Note: The UE-V 2.0 Agent requires PowerShell 3.0, part of Windows Management Framework 3.0, but that is already installed on PC0001 via the hydration setup described in Appendix A.

1. On **PC0001**, log on as **VIAMONSTRA\Administrator**.

2. Mount the **MDOP 2014** ISO file that you have downloaded in the virtual machine.

3. Using **Windows Explorer**, double-click the drive letter to which you mounted the ISO file to open the MDOP splash screen.

4. Then click **User Experience Virtualization**, followed by clicking **UE-V 2.0 Agent**.

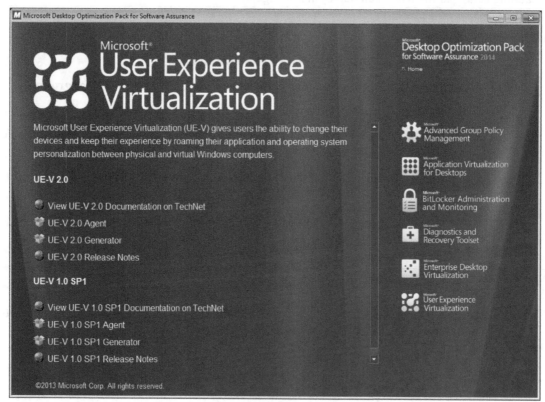

UE-V and a few other tools are available in MDOP, which add to the value of the Windows client and make the end user's life easier, as well as the IT folks' day-to-day work smoother.

5. On the **Welcome to the Microsoft User Experience Virtualization Agent Setup Wizard** page, click **Next**.

6. On the **End-User License Agreement** page, select **I accept the terms in the License Agreement** and click **Next**.

7. On the **Microsoft Update** page, select **Do not use Microsoft Update** and click **Next**.

8. On the **Customer Experience Improvement Program** page, select **Do not join the program at this time** and click **Next**.

9. On the **Begin Installation** page, click **Install**.

10. When the installation is complete, click **Finish** and then click **Restart**.

11. On **PC0002**, repeat the preceding steps to install the Microsoft User Experience Virtualization Agent on that machine, as well.

Note: By default, the agent looks in Active Directory to see whether the user has a home share set. If there is a home share designated, it will be used; otherwise, you need to specify another location to which to save the settings packages, for instance using the provided group policy templates or by adding setup parameters when deploying the agent.

Verify that UE-V Works

1. On **PC0001**, log in as **Don** in the **VIAMONSTRA** domain.

2. Right-click the **Desktop**, choose **Personalize**, and then click **Desktop Background**.

    a. In **Picture Location**, choose **Windows Desktop Backgrounds**.

    b. Click the **Clear all** button, and then select a **desktop background** of your choice and click **Save changes**. Close the Personalization control panel.

    c. Lock **PC0001** by clicking the **start button**, followed by the arrow next to **Shut down**, and then **Lock**.

3. On **PC0002**, log in as **Don** in the **VIAMONSTRA** domain.

4. Verify that the desktop background is now the same as the one you set on **PC0001**.

Note: It may take a little while until the background changes.

5. As a last step, open the **Control Panel** on **PC0002**; then open **Company Settings Center** and note for which applications you can roam settings.

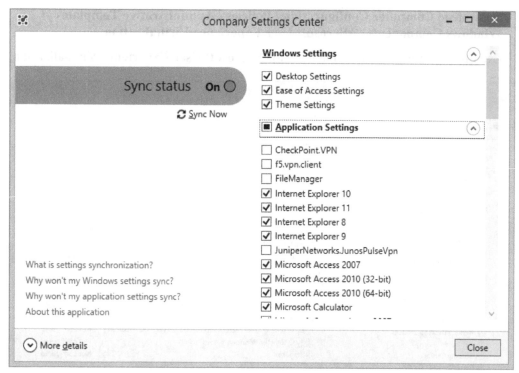

Remember that you can create your own templates or download templates from TechNet Gallery to add more roaming settings to Windows and applications.

Group Policy Templates for Managing UE-V

To centrally manage UE-V, there are Group Policy templates available that you add to your central store to make them available to anyone managing and editing Group Policy objects in your environment. The Group Policy templates are not included in the MDOP ISO and must be downloaded separately from http://www.microsoft.com/en-us/download/details.aspx?id=41183.

Add the Group Policy Templates for UE-V

Start by downloading the MDOP ADMX templates from the preceding link and then extracted the contents of the downloaded EXE to a folder on DC01. The templates are copied to the central store so that everyone can manage the UE-V settings that need to be configured.

1. On **DC01**, log on as **VIAMONSTRA\Administrator**.

2. Copy the contents from the **UE-V2.0** directory, where you extracted the MDOP ADMX files, to the following folder:

   C:\Windows\SYSVOL\domain\Policies\PolicyDefinitions.

   Note that you can exclude the language folders for the languages you do not need.

3. Start the **Group Policy Management** console, and edit **Workstation Configuration** under the **ViaMonstra / Workstations** OU.

4. Navigate to **Computer Configuration / Policies / Administrative Templates / Windows Components / Microsoft User Experience Virtualization**.

5. Explore the settings found in the node for **Microsoft User Experience Virtualization**.

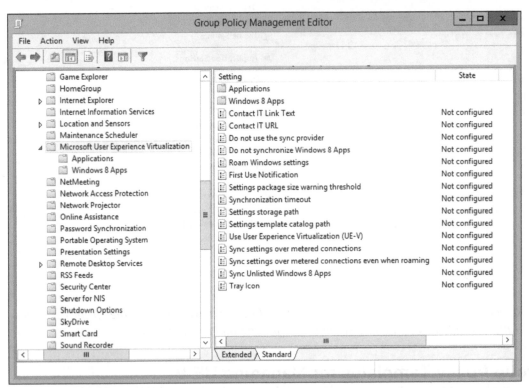

In the UE-V GPO settings, you can set the template catalog path to a central location, for instance, which is a strong recommendation in an enterprise scenario.

State Migration Point

Replacing a Windows client is a deployment scenario that in most deployment solutions means that the user needs to save whatever he or she want to keep from the existing machine and then bring that back on the new machine. That includes settings for Windows, applications, and data. It actually takes quite some time to get up and running after a computer replacement. UE-V and Folder Redirection, as discussed earlier in this chapter, can definitely make this situation better, and, even better, preserve not only the entire user profile but also the relevant documents and data stored on the client disk.

The replacement scenario is really something that is not available in any other deployment solution, at least not a Microsoft deployment solution, but with Configuration Manager this can be automated to provide a good user experience while minimizing the IT department's efforts.

Activating the state migration point, which is a separate role in Configuration Manager, is not only useful for users getting their machines replaced, it also can be used, for instance, when moving from a traditional workstation or laptop to a mobile device such as a tablet. The connection between the existing device and the new device is done in the ConfigMgr console to connect the two computer names.

You then target a task sequence to collect the data and settings from the existing machine. When you deploy the new OSD task sequence, it will figure out that there is a state migration available on the state migration point and apply it to the new machine.

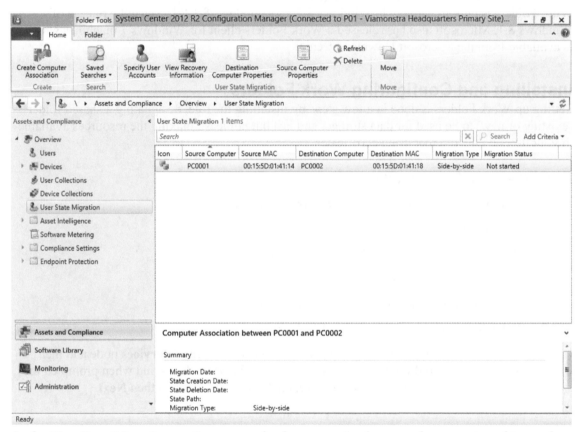

In the User State Migration section, you make the connection between the current machine and the new machine replacing the current one.

Work Folders

New in Windows Server 2012 R2 is a feature called *Work Folders*. This feature lets your users access their enterprise data from personal devices, while still enabling the IT department to control the data and ensuring the data does not get in the wrong hands in case the device is lost or stolen. It also might be a good replacement for Folder Redirection, as there are some changes in the sync engine that makes Work Folders more reliable compared to Folder Redirection when used with Offline Files.

Work Folders are stored in the enterprise network on file servers running Windows Server 2012 R2. Also, the data on the devices can be encrypted, and you as an IT administrator have the power to remotely wipe the data in the event that the device is lost or stolen. Key for making it work from the user's personal devices are Active Directory Federation Services (ADFS).

Work Folders Clients and Apps

Work Folders is built in natively in Windows 8.1 and Windows 8.1 RT. Since the release of Windows 8.1, Microsoft also has released a Work Folders client for Windows 7 machines which is available from the Microsoft Download Center.

Installing and Configuring Work Folders

Setting up Work Folders is done in a few steps by installing the role, designating a shared folder (existing or new) to be used for data storage, and last but not least, making the resources available to your users on the Internet using certificates.

Install the Work Folders Role

1. On **FS01**, log on as **VIAMONSTRA\Administrator**.

2. Start **Server Manager**.

3. Click the **Manage** button, followed by **Add Roles and Features**.

4. On the **Before you begin** page, click **Next**.

5. On the **Select installation type** page, click **Next**.

6. On the **Select server destination**, click **Next**.

7. On the **Select server roles** page, expand the **File and Storage Services** node and then expand the **File and iSCSI Services** node. Select **Work Folders** and when prompted to add the feature **IIS Hostable Web Core**, click **Add features** and then **Next**.

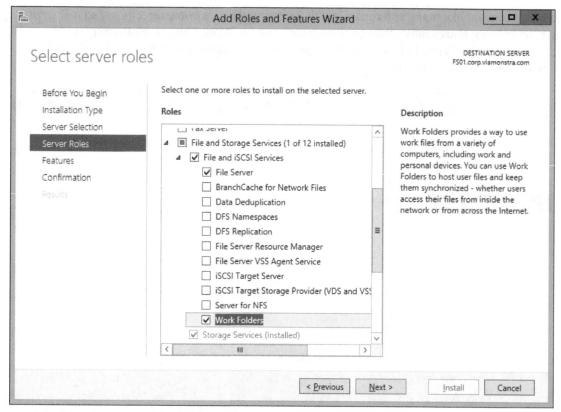

Work Folders is a part of the File and Storage Services role.

8. On the **Select features** page, click **Next**.

9. On the **Confirm installation selections** page, click **Install** and wait for the components to install.

10. On the **Installation progress** page, when the installation is complete, click **Close**.

11. Restart **FS01** (or make sure the Windows Sync Share service is started).

Create the Sync Share

In this guide, you create the share where the Work Folders data will be stored for your users.

1. On **FS01**, using **Server Manager**, click **File and Storage Services** in the left menu.

2. Click **Work Folders**.

3. Click the **Tasks** button and choose **New Sync Share**.

4. On the **Before you begin** page, click **Next**.

5. On the **Select the server and path** page, select the **Select by file share** option to choose the existing shared folder **UserData**. Then click **Next**.

Note: ViaMonstra, like many enterprises out there, currently uses home directories, so it is terrific to use the existing shares rather than creating a new one for Work Folders. Not setting up additional shares for Work Folders usually helps keep user experience at the very best level by not having multiple locations in which to store data.

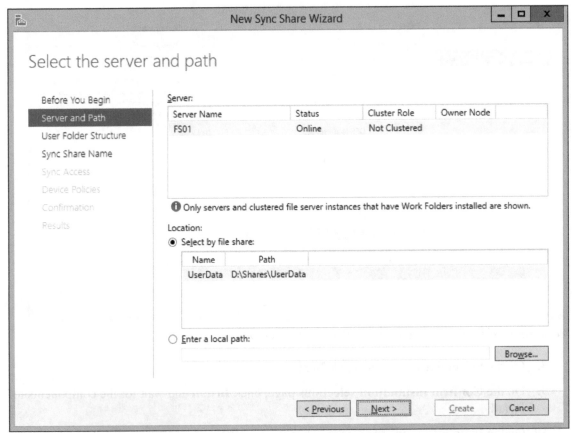

Choosing an existing share fits very well in most organizations, as they already have this in place. That is the case for ViaMonstra.

6. On the **Specify the structure for users folders** page, select the **Sync only the following subfolder** check box. Enter **Documents** in the input area and click **Next**.

Note: For Work Folders to work with your existing home directories, as well as Folder Redirection, you choose the default option not to use UPN, i.e. alias@domain.com. To make only the Documents folder available, you enter that one, leaving other redirected folders, such as AppData and Desktop, intact.

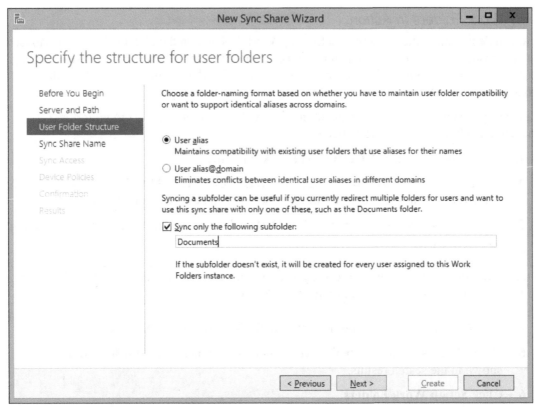

Keeping the alias in legacy mode and making sure only the Documents folder is available, let's Work Folders hook into your existing Folder Redirection environment.

7. On the **Enter the sync share name** page, accept the default name, and click **Next**.

8. On the **Grant sync access to groups** page, click the **Add** button and complete the following:

   a. Enter **domain users**, click **Check Names**, and then click **OK**.

   b. Clear the **Disable inherited permissions and grant user exclusive access to their files** check box, and then click **Next**.

9. On the **Specify device policies** page, select **Encrypt Work Folders**, clear the **Automatically lock screen, and require a password** check box, and then click **Next**.

> **Note**: If you leave the Automatically lock screen setting and require a password checked, the user setting up Work Folders needs to be a local administrator on the machine. In enterprises, this is rarely the case, and this is intended to enforce additional security policies on personal devices.

10. On the **Confirm selections** page, click **Create**.

11. On the **View results** page, click **Close**.

Verify Work Folders in Action

Now you demonstrate the concept of setting up Work Folders on the client side. At ViaMonstra, you demonstrate this by using a domain-connected machine. In the real world, however, you would make this available on the Internet to any user with a device, making Work Folders available for connection from a personal device.

In an enterprise environment, you can automatically deploy Work Folders to your domain connected machines using group policies.

1. On **PC0002**, log in as **VIAMONSTRA\Administrator**.

2. Using the **Registry Editor**, navigate to **HKEY_LOCAL_MACHINE\SOFTWARE\ Microsoft\Windows\CurrentVersion** and create a new key named **WorkFolders**.

3. In the **WorkFolders** key, create a **DWORD** value named **AllowUnsecureConnection** and set the value to **1**.

> **Note**: As you do this for testing purposes, you do not have a valid certificate to use. Therefore, you must turn off the certificate requirement on PC0002.

4. On **PC0002**, log off, and log in as **Don** in the **VIAMONSTRA** domain.

5. On the **Start screen**, start typing **work folders**, and then click **Work Folders** when shown in the search results.

6. Click **Set up Work Folders**.

7. Click **Enter a Work Folders URL instead**.

8. Enter **http://fs01.corp.viamonstra.com** and click **Next**.

9. On the **Introducing Work Folders** page, click **Next**.

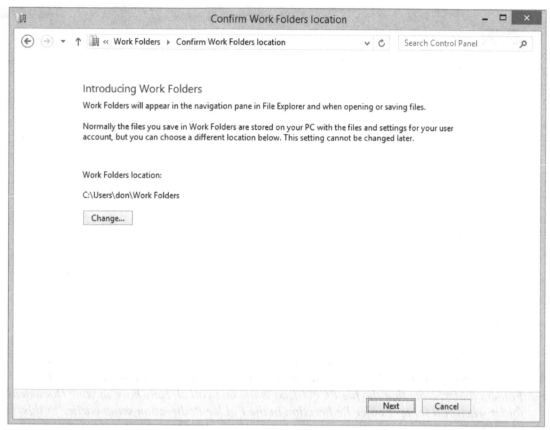

On the Introducing Work Folders page, the user can choose where the Work Folders are stored.

10. On the **Security Policies** page, select **I accept these policies on my PC**, click **Set up Work Folders**, and then click **Close**. Two windows appear, one being the actual Work Folders folder and the other the Work Folder control panel.

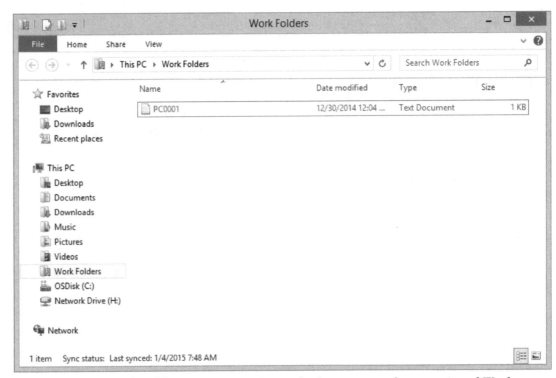

After setting up Work Folders, you can see instantly the contents of your assigned Work Folders folder. Note that the file PC0001.txt is the one you already have in your Documents folder when you set up Folder Redirection in the Folder Redirection setup earlier in this chapter.

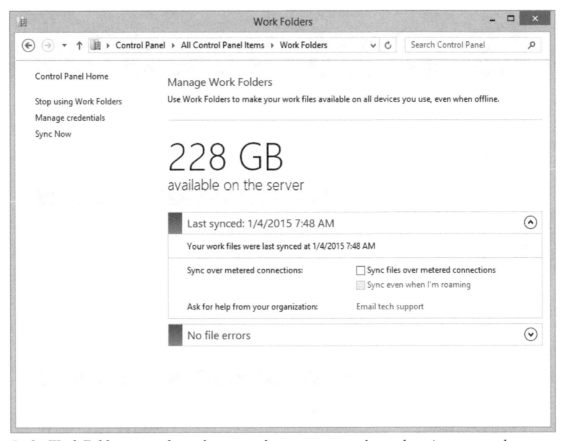

In the Work Folders control panel, you see the sync status and can also trigger manual synchronizations if necessary.

Manage Work Folders from the Server Side

To manage and see the status of Work Folders on the server, you do this in the Work Folders section in Server Manager:

1. On **FS01**, log on as **VIAMONSTRA\Administrator**.

2. Start **Server Manager**.

3. Click **File and Storage Services** and then **Work Folders**.

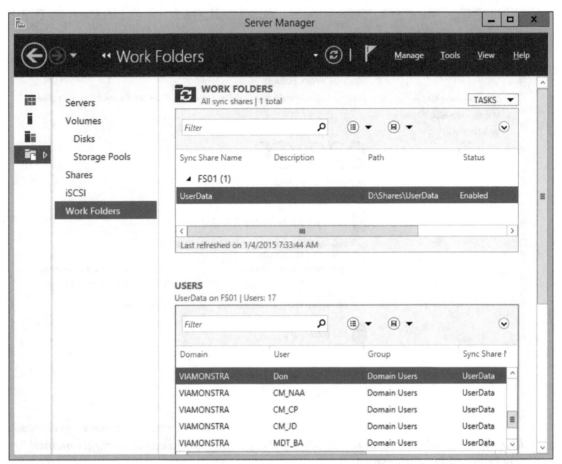

*In the Work Folders section of Server Manager, you see all Work Folders users and the
overall status of the Work Folders server storage space and shares.*

4. Right-click **Don** in the **Users** list pane and choose **Properties** to see the current
    information on Don's Work Folders and the devices connected to Work Folders.

The Work Folders properties for Don show which devices the user has connected to Work Folders, and you also see whether there are errors in synchronizing.

Workplace Join

With Workplace Join, any user of your corporation can add their personal device partly to your domain. The benefits of this is to access applications or resources in your internal network and also providing single sign-on for the users of those resources.

Also, device management using Microsoft Intune can be activated to manage the devices, configuration-wise and for publishing or pushing apps to those devices. At the time of writing this book, the operating systems that support Workplace Join are Windows 8.1, Windows 8.1 RT, Windows 7, and iOS.

A requirement for using Workplace Join is to install Active Directory Federation Services, a role in Windows Server 2012 R2, that handles the device registration. It also requires a valid certificate that is trusted by the devices that are to be workplace joined.

To join a Windows 8.1 or Windows 8.1 RT device with this feature, you go to PC Settings / Network and choose Workplace. By entering your email address, you can either join it to the workplace or just enable device management.

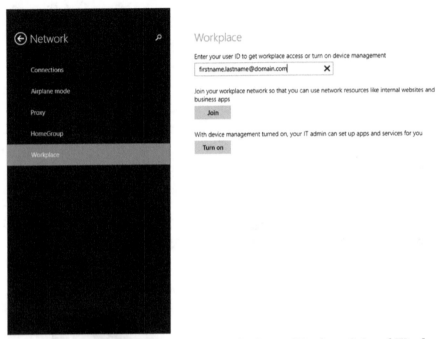

The ability to workplace join a device is built into Windows 8.1 and Windows RT 8.1. Your users simply have to enter their email addresses to be able to join their devices to the workplace.

OneDrive for Business

Microsoft offers two online storage services. One is OneDrive for personal use, and the second is OneDrive for Business, which is intended for business use. Note that previously OneDrive was named SkyDrive, but due to name conflicts Microsoft had to change the name, which became OneDrive.

Differences Between OneDrive and OneDrive For Business

Except for the difference that OneDrive is for personal use, OneDrive for Business is included with either Office 365 or SharePoint 2013. Note that Microsoft in these services and products refers it as "OneDrive" although it actually is OneDrive for Business. With OneDrive for Business, you can collaborate on the same documents with other users of your organization, i.e. multiple users can edit a document simultaneously.

By default, OneDrive for Business as a part of Office 365 gives each user 1TB storage, and when hosted on premises as a part of the SharePoint Server 2013, you as an administrator freely define the amount of storage available to your end users.

OneDrive for Business Client

In both Windows 7 and Windows 8, OneDrive must be installed as either a client on Windows 7 machines or as a client or modern app in Windows 8. Starting with Windows 8.1, Microsoft has integrated support for OneDrive into the operating system, which means you can access OneDrive instantly if you connect your login account to a Microsoft Account. However, this applies only to personal storage via your personal Microsoft Account.

There is also a OneDrive for Business version, and it has a separate client that provides features other than those with the regular OneDrive client used for personal use. The OneDrive for Business client must be installed separately, but please note that if you are running Office 2013 Professional Plus or the Office 365 versions of Office 2013 intended for business use, you already have the OneDrive for Business client installed.

Note: The OneDrive for Business client in various languages, for both x86 and x64, can be found at http://support.microsoft.com/kb/2903984/en-us.

Evaluating OneDrive for Business

ViaMonstra is evaluating Office 365 and OneDrive for Business, which is included in the Office 365 subscription. Specifically, the company has signed up for a trial Office 365 Midsize Business account to perform the evaluation, primarily of OneDrive for Business.

Note: You can sign up for Office 365 at http://www.office365.com and evaluate Office 365 for 30 days without any charges.

After signing up and distributing and installing the OneDrive for Business client, you can start the evaluation. Although you can access the storage using the web interface, having the client on the users' devices is recommended.

Steps for Evaluating OneDrive for Business

To start evaluating OneDrive for Business, these are the basic steps that must be performed:

1. Sign up for an Office 365 trial account at **http://www.office365.com**.

2. Download the **OneDrive for Business** client (unless you are using Office 2013 Professional Plus, as in that case you already have it).

3. Sign in to your **Office 365** account by going to **http://www.office365.com**.

4. Go to your **OneDrive** in the top menu in Office 365 web interface.

5. Click the **Sync** button in the top right corner to start synchronizing this folder with your client machine.

159

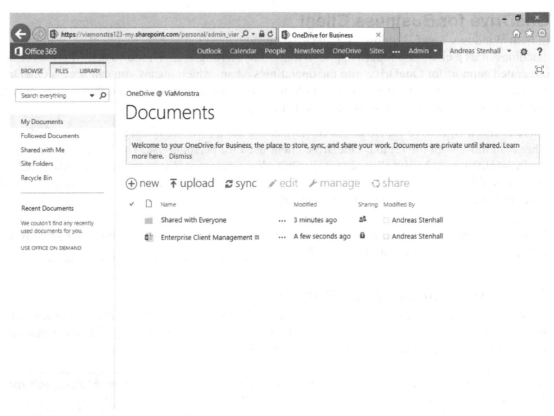

In all document libraries in Office 365, you can see the Sync button, which you use to connect that document library and make it available offline on your machine.

6.   Work with the **OneDrive for Business** files in **File Explorer** on your machine.

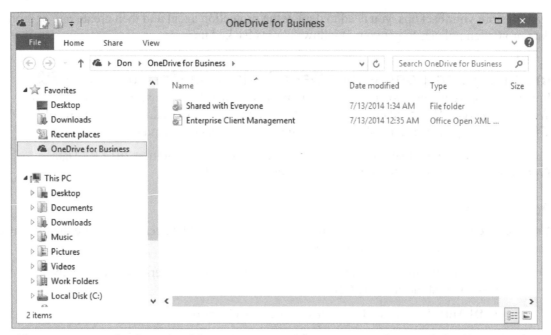

After connecting the document library to your machine, start working with the files as with any other file storage solution.

Data Protection Manager 2012 R2

If you cannot rely solely on replication methods, such as Folder Redirection or cloud-based storage, you can certainly use System Center 2012 R2 Data Protection Manager (DPM) to back up your data from Windows clients.

The DPM client is called *protection agent*. Backups in DPM are done by creating a data protection policy that the protection agent reads and applies on the Windows client. Data is then backed up at chosen interval for predefined folders. Optionally, the user also can select additional folders to back up, except for the ones you specify via the central data protection policies.

> **Note**: Data Protection Manager is based on the old Windows feature *shadow copies*, which has been around for 10 years or so. It takes delta snapshots at block level of the disk and the files that you back up. Shadow copies also was behind the Windows 7 *previous versions* feature, ever popular among IT professionals. Microsoft decided that previous versions wasn't used by anyone, so it was removed from Windows 8 and replaced it with a tool to do backups called *File History*. The benefit with previous versions was that it could be used to recover user data in case of an accidental deletion, and it frequently proved itself to be a great solution. However, File History is not an enterprise solution, and users must setup the backups themselves, which is not a good solution.

To get up and running with DPM, you need a lot of disk storage, or you also can sign up for storing the backups in Windows Azure, the Microsoft cloud. When you have decided where you want to store your backups, you need to deploy the protection agent and then create one or more data protection policies to get your Windows clients backed up.

Installing and Configuring Data Protection Manager 2012 R2

In these steps, we assume you have a virtual machine named DPM01 with a default setup of Windows Server 2012 Standard edition installed on a single 72 GB partition and 4 GB of RAM. The machine is joined as a member server to the VIAMONSTRA domain.

These steps also require that you have downloaded System Configuration 2012 R2 Data Protection Manager and SQL Server 2012 Standard with SP1.

Add an Extra Disk

You use an empty disk to store the backups in Data Protection Manager. To achieve that, you need an additional disk in your virtual machine.

1. In the virtualization tool that you use, add an extra disk (preferably dynamically expanding) at the size **100 GB**.

2. On **DPM01**, log on as **VIAMONSTRA\Administrator**.

3. Using **Disk Management**, **Server Manager** or **PowerShell**, configure the disk you added to be online, but don't create any volumes on it.

Install .NET Framework 3.5.1

1. On **DPM01**, mount the **Windows Server 2012 R2 ISO**, and note which drive letter has been assigned as it is used in the next step. If it is not E:, as in the step 2 example, please replace E: with the drive letter of your mounted ISO.

2. Start an **elevated command prompt** (run as administrator), and run the following command:

```
Dism.exe /Online /Enable-Feature /All /FeatureName:NetFX3
/Source:E:\sources\sxs
```

Install the SQL Database

1. On **DPM01**, mount the **SQL Server 2012 Standard with SP1 ISO**, and note which drive letter has been assigned as it is used in the next step.

2. Open **File Explorer** and double-click the **E:** drive to launch the SQL Setup.

3. Click **Installation** in the left menu and then **New SQL Server stand-alone installation or add features to an existing installation**.

4. On the **Setup Support Rules** page, click **OK**.

5. Wait for the **Product Key** page to appear, select either **Specify a free edition** and select **Evaluation** or use your real product key if you have the license, and then click **Next**.

6. On the **License Terms** page, select **I accept the license terms** and click **Next**.

7. On the **Product Updates** page, click **Next** (ignore the warnings if you don't have Internet access).

8. On the **Setup Install Files** page, wait for the install to finish, and then on the **Setup Support Rules** page, click **Next**.

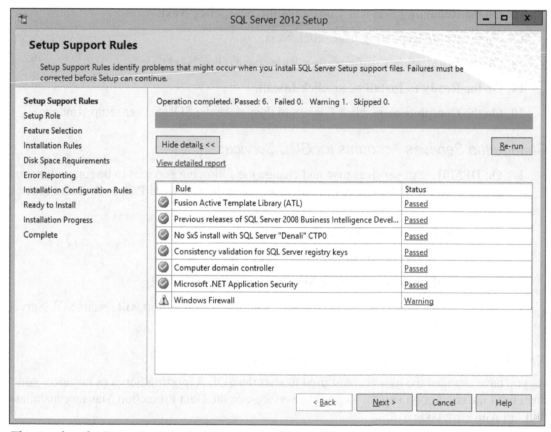

This is what the Setup Support Rules page should look like.

9. On the **Setup Role** page, accept the default settings and click **Next**.

10. On the **Feature Selection** page, select the following components and click **Next**:

    o   **Database Engine**

    o   **Reporting Services – Native**

    o   **Management Tools** (both **Basic** and **Complete**)

11. On the **Installation Rules** page, click **Next**.

12. On the **Instance Configuration** page, change the **Instance root directory** to **D:\MSSQL**, but leave the **Instance ID** as it is and click **Next**.

13. On the **Disk Space Requirements** page, click **Next**.

14. On the **Server Configuration** page, click **Next**.

15. On the **Database Engine Configuration** page, click **Add Current User**. Also add the **DPM01\Administrators** group, by clicking **Add** (will be renamed to BUILTIN\Administrators after being added). Then click **Next**

16. On the **Reporting Services Configuration** page, click **Next**.

17. On the **Error Reporting** page, click **Next**.

18. On the **Installation Configuration Rules** page, click **Next**.

19. On the **Ready to Install** page, click **Install**.

20. On the **Complete** page, click **Close** and then close the SQL Server setup window.

Change the Services Accounts for SQL Services

1. On **DPM01**, start **services.msc** and change the following services to be run with the user account **VIAMONSTRA\Administrator**, using the password **P@ssw0rd**, and then click **Next**:

    o **SQL Server (MSSQLSERVER)**

    o **SQL Server Agent (MSSQLSERVER)**

    o **SQL Server Reporting Services (MSSQLSERVER)**

2. Restart the **SQL Server (MSSQLSERVER)** service only (you will restart SQL Server Reporting Services in the next section) .

Reset SQL Reporting Services Encryption Key

As you have changed the user account used to start the SQL Reporting Services instance, you must reset the encryption key for Reporting Services, or the Data Protection Manager installation will fail with error code 812.

1. On **DPM01**, start the **Reporting Services Configuration Manager** console, and when it has started, click **Connect**.

2. In the left menu, select **Encryption Keys**.

3. Click the **Delete** button and choose **Yes** when prompted.

4. When that is done, start **services.msc** and restart **SQL Server Reporting Services (MSSQLSERVER)**. Close the Reporting Services Configuration Manager console and the Services console.

Note: The encryption key reset is done only for the purposes of this guide and demonstration. Be careful if and when working with SQL Reporting Services in your production environment.

Install Data Protection Manager

1. On **DPM01**, mount the **System Center 2012 R2 Data Protection Manager ISO**, and note which drive letter has been assigned as it is used in the next step.

2. Open **File Explorer**, go to the **E**: drive (or the drive where you mounted the ISO file), open the **SCDPM** folder, and run **setup.exe**.

3. Under the **Install** section, click **Data Protection Manager** to start the installation.

4. On the **Microsoft Software License Terms** page, select **I accept the license terms and conditions** and click **OK**.

5. On the **Welcome** page, click **Next**.

6. On the **Prerequisites** page, in the **Instance of SQL Server** field, enter **DPM01**; then press the **Tab** key to enable the **Check and Install** button, and click the **Check and Install** button.

Note: If required, for example after installing the SISFilter, restart DPM01 and restart the installation again until the Prerequisites page does not show any red crosses.

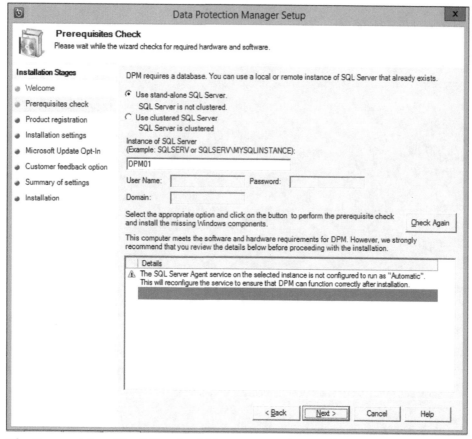

The Prerequisites Check list should be empty or show only warnings that we are aware of.

7. On the **Product Registration** page, enter the product key (this requires an active MSDN or TechNet subscription) and click **Next**. Use the "System Center 2012 R2" product key.

Note: There is also an evaluation version of System Center 2012 R2 Data Protection Manager available that you can download. Unlike the other System Center 2012 R2 products, where the evaluation version is built-in, System Center 2012 R2 Data Protection Manager has a separate media for the evaluation version.

---

8. On the **Installation Settings** page, accept the default settings and click **Next**.

9. On the **Microsoft Update Opt-in** page, select **I do not want to use Microsoft Update** and click **Next**.

10. On the **Customer Experience Improvement Program** page, select **No, remind me later** and click **Next**.

11. On the **Summary of Settings** page, click **Install**.

12. On the **Installation** page, click **Close**.

Configure Disks in DPM

Now you add a disk that will be used by DPM for storing the backed up data. Note that you must have added a separate disk and made sure it is online before you can add it for use in DPM.

1. On **DPM01**, start the **Microsoft System Center 2012 R2 Data Protection Manager** console.

2. In the left menu, select the **Management** workspace, and then in the left pane, click **Disks**.

3. Click **Add** on the ribbon.

4. Select **Disk 1**, and then click **Add** followed by **OK**. If asked to convert the basic disk to a dynamic disk, answer **Yes**.

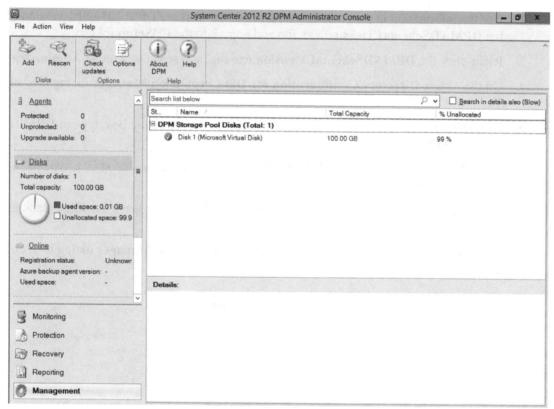

One disk added for storing backups from Windows clients.

Prepare Active Directory for End-User Recovery

Extending the Active Directory schema is necessary to make end-user recovery available to your end users, i.e. so they can restore files from backups by themselves.

> **Note**: At the time of writing of this book, there is a bug in the schema extension executable in System Center 2012 R2 Data Protection Manager that makes it crash. Until there is a hotfix released for this problem, Microsoft's recommendation is to use the DPMADSchemaExtension.exe utility from the %Program Files%\Microsoft System Center 2012\DPM\DPM\End User Recovery directory of a machine that has Data Protection Manager 2012 SP1 installed.

1. On **DC01**, log on as **VIAMONSTRA\Administrator**.

2. Use the information in the preceding note to get the working DPM 2012 SP1 version of the **DPMADSchemaExtension.exe** file and copy it to the **C:\Setup** folder:

3. Right-click the **DPMADSchemaExtension.exe** file, and select to **Run as Administrator**.

4. On the **Active Directory Configuration for Data Protection Manager** dialog box, click **Yes**.

5. In the **Enter Data Protection Manager Computer Name** dialog box, type in **DPM01** and click **OK**.

6. In the **Enter Data Protection Manager Server Domain Name** dialog box, type in **corp.viamonstra.com** and click **OK**.

7. In the **Enter Protected Computer Domain Name** dialog box, leave the value blank and click **OK**.

8. In the **Active Directory Configuration for Data Protection Manager** dialog box, click **OK**.

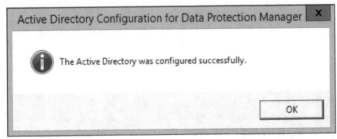

Successfully extending the Active Directory schema.

Enable End-User Recovery

Once the Active Directory schema is extended, you can enable End-user recovery.

1. On **DPM01**, log on as **VIAMONSTRA\Administrator**.

2. Start the **System Center 2012 R2 Data Protection Manager** console.

3. In the **Recovery** workspace, click the **End-user recovery** button on the ribbon.

4. On the **End-user Recovery** tab, select the **Enable end-user recovery**, and when notified about the settings being applied, click **OK** and then **OK** once again.

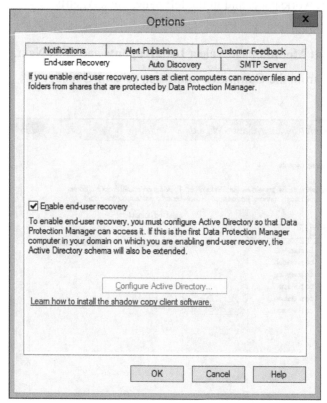

Only after you have configured Active Directory, i.e. extended the schema, are you able to select the check box to enable end-user recovery.

Install the DPM Protection Agent on PC0002

1. On **PC0002**, log on as **VIAMONSTRA\Administrator**, and enable DPM 2012 R2 agent push from **DPM01** by opening an **elevated Command prompt** and type the following command (the command is wrapped):

```
netsh advfirewall firewall add rule name="Allow DPM Remote
Agent Push" dir=in action=allow service=any enable=yes
profile=any remoteip=192.168.1.219
```

2. On **DPM01**, start the **Microsoft System Center 2012 R2 Data Protection Manager console,** select the **Management** workspace, and in the left pane, click **Agents**.

3. Click the **Install** button on the ribbon.

4. On the **Select Agent Deployment Method** page, select **Install agents** and click **Next**.

5. On the **Select Computers** page, from the **Computer name** list, select **PC0002**, click **Add**, and then click **Next**.

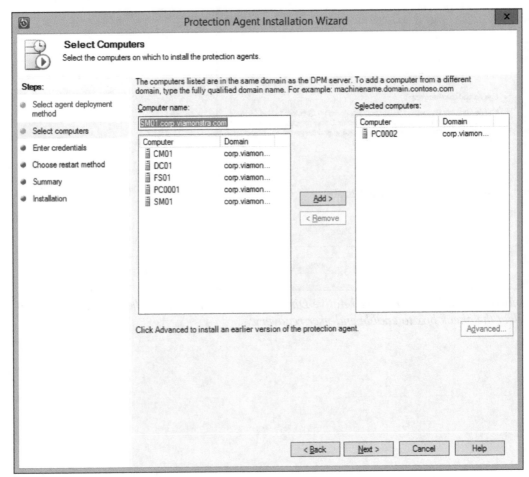

Deploying the protection agent from the DPM console.

6. On the **Enter Credentials** page, enter the following values and click **Next**:

    o   User name: **Administrator**

    o   Password: **P@ssw0rd**

7. On the **Choose Restart Method** page, select **Yes. Restart the selected computers after installing the protection agent (if required)**, and then click **Next**.

8. On the **Summary** page, click **Install**. Wait for the installation to finish and for PC0002 to restart (if needed) before continuing. Then click **Close**.

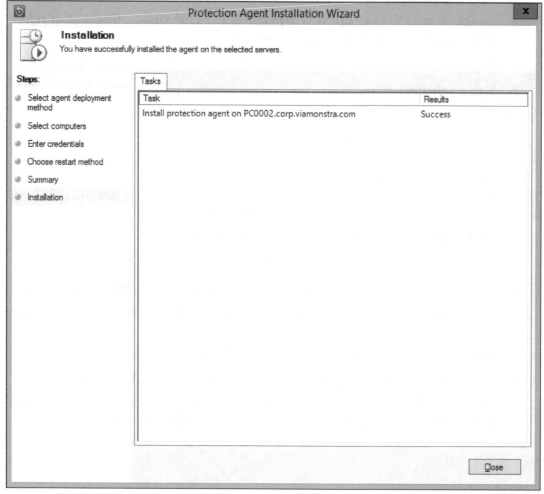

Agent successfully installed on PC0002.

Prepare the Client for End User Recovery

Before starting to backup clients, you need to perform some configuration on the client.

Real World Note: By default DPM assumes that you are a local administrator. As that is hardly ever the case in a real-world scenario, you must define a registry value with each user on the client machine. If you do not do this, your users cannot restore files by themselves using the DPM client.

---

1. On **PC0002**, log on as **VIAMONSTRA\Administrator**.

2. Start **regedit.exe**.

3. Browse to **HKEY_LOCAL_MACHINE\SOFTWARE\Microsoft\Microsoft Data Protection Manager\Agent\ClientProtection**.

4. Right-click anywhere in the empty area to the right and create a new **String Value**.

5. Name it **ClientOwners**.

6. Enter the value **VIAMONSTRA\Don** and click **OK**.

7. Close **regedit** and restart **PC0002**.

Configure the Protection Group

The Protection Group is a configuration item that defines what to back up, how often, and so forth. This configuration is done in groups on the DPM server.

1. On **DPM01**, log on as **VIAMONSTRA\Administrator**.

2. Start the **Microsoft System Center 2012 R2 Data Protection Manager** console.

3. In the left menu, click the **Protection** workspace, and then click **New** on the ribbon.

4. On the **Welcome to the New Protection Group Wizard** page, read through the text and click **Next**.

5. On the **Select Protection Group Type** page, select **Clients** and click **Next**.

6. On the **Select Group Members** page, select **PC0002**, click **Add**, and then click **Next**.

7. On the **Specify Inclusions and Exclusions** page, in the **Enter the Folder Path** section, select **Desktop** from the drop-down list; then set the **Rule** to **Include** and click **Next**.

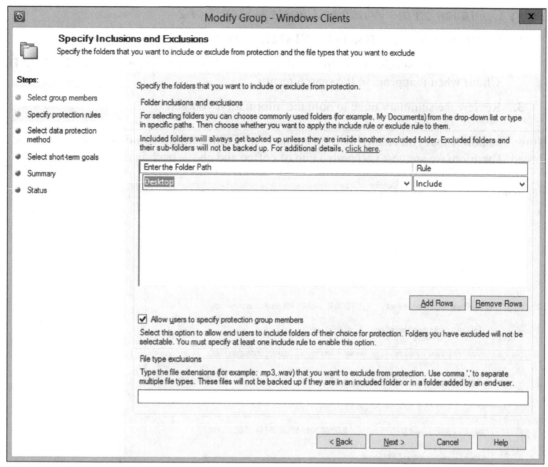

You can choose to include or exclude any folders, or even choose to back up the entire system disk of Windows clients.

8. On the **Select Data Protection Method** page, set the **Protection group name** to **Windows Clients** and click **Next**.

9. On the **Specify Short-Term Goals** page, review the settings and click **Next**.

10. On the **Allocate Storage** page, set **Data per computer** to **1GB** and click **Next**.

11. On the **Summary** page, click **Create Group**.

12. On the **Status** page, once the protection group is created, click **Close**.

Verify Operation on the Windows Clients – Step 1 of 2

1. On **PC0002**, log in as **Don** in the **VIAMONSTRA** domain.

2. From the **Start screen**, type **dpm** and then start **Microsoft System Center 2012 R2 DPM Client** when it appears in the search results.

3. Review the summary page to note the information you get.

Note: The policy that you created will be applied on PC0002 within 15 minutes and cannot be forced. Therefore we suggest you grab a cup of coffee and check back in a few minutes.

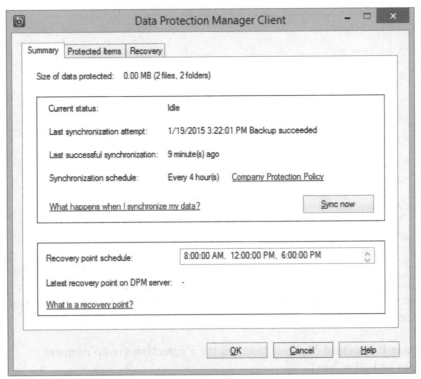

The Summary tab of the DPM client lists some basic information about the amount of data backed up, the last recovery point, and more.

4. Click the **Protected Items** tab and make sure that the **Users / Don / Desktop** folder is selected and therefore will be backed up.

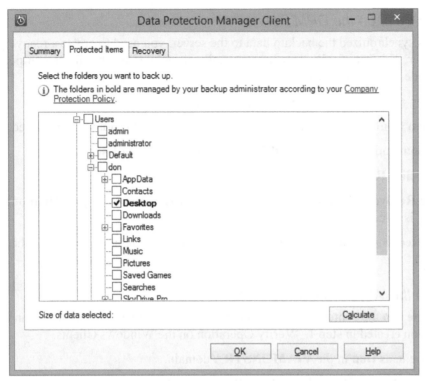

As displayed, only the Desktop is selected for backup and that is what you set centrally. Your user can (if allowed) choose additional folders to be included in the backup.

5. Minimize the **Data Protection Manager Client** dialog box.

6. Right-click anywhere on the **Desktop** and choose **New / Text Document**. Name the new file **Text file**.

7. Open the text file in **Notepad**, enter **This is very important information**, save the file, and close **Notepad**.

8. Restore the **Data Protection Manager Client** dialog box that you minimized previously, and in the **Summary** tab, click the **Sync now** button. Wait until the synchronization has finished.

Note: Sometimes the GUI is not refreshed properly, so if nothing happens for a minute, close the Data Protection Manager Client and open it again from the Start screen or from the notification area to verify that the synchronization has been performed successfully.

Create a Recovery Point on the DPM Server

Now that the client has synchronized the backup data to the server, you need to create a recovery point on the DPM server. This is typically done automatically at set intervals, but for the purposes of this step-by-step guide, you create one manually.

1. On **DPM01**, log on as **VIAMONSTRA\Administrator**.

2. Start the **System Center Data Protection Manager** console if it is not already started.

3. In the **Protection** workspace, select **pc0002.corp.viamonstra.com\User data**.

4. On the ribbon, click **Recovery Point**.

5. On the **Create Recovery Point** page, make sure that **Create a recovery point without synchronizing** is selected and click **OK**.

6. In the **Create Recovery Point** dialog box, wait for the recovery point to finish and then click **Close**.

Verify Operation on the Windows Clients – Step 2 of 2

In this step, you simulate that the contents of a document have been accidentally deleted, or in this case, the text file that you created in step 1, "Verify Operation on the Windows Clients."

1. On **PC0002**, log in as **Don** in the **VIAMONSTRA** domain.

2. Once again, open the text file on the desktop. Remove all the contents from it, save the file, and close Notepad.

3. To restore the contents of the file, start the **Data Protection Manager Client**.

4. Click the **Recovery** tab.

5. Click the search glass icon to the right of the listing **DPM01.corp.viamonstra.com**.

6. Expand **Computer: PC0002.corp.viamonstra.com**.

7. It will list the recovery point. Click **Open** next to it. This will bring up File Explorer, listing the contents of that particular recovery point, and you can browse to the Desktop of don. From there you can restore the file to any location you want by simply copying it back to the Desktop, for instance.

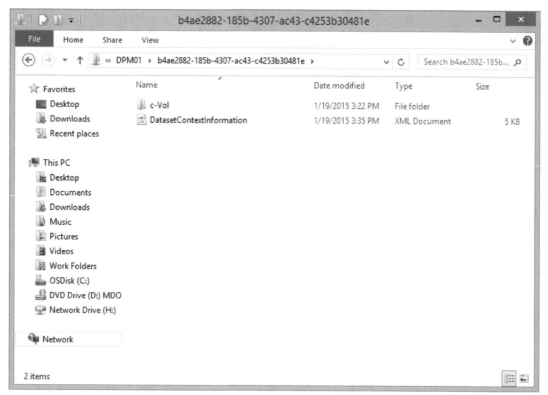

When you open a recovery point, it will list all the contents from that point in time on the volume. ACLs on files are honored so that a user cannot access other users' content.

Chapter 7

Device Management Using Microsoft Intune

Mobile device management in terms of managing Windows RT devices, i.e. Windows on ARM tablets, is done using Microsoft Intune. Using Microsoft Intune, you also can manage other types of devices such as iOS and Android devices. Microsoft Intune is a Microsoft cloud service which means it can be used in cloud-only mode. However, by connecting Microsoft Intune to your Configuration Manager system, you can get additional features and manage all your devices from the same console regardless of whether it is a traditional PC or a mobile device running iOS, Windows RT, or Android.

Stand-alone Microsoft Intune vs. Intune Connected to Configuration Manager

When using Microsoft Intune, you have the option of using the stand-alone version of Microsoft Intune or Intune combined with System Center Configuration Manager in what is called Unified Device Management or the Hybrid Intune deployment. The stand-alone version of Intune is a totally web-based interface and completely separated from any other management solution. You also can use Microsoft Intune and integrate it into Configuration Manager, and that has many benefits. The most significant benefits when integrating Intune into Configuration Manager are that you use one tool to manage all your devices regardless of the type of device and you get much more control over the devices that you manage in terms of what settings can be configured on the mobile devices.

Connecting Microsoft Intune to Configuration Manager

Connecting Microsoft Intune to your Configuration Manager system is not very hard, although it involves quite a few steps to make it happen and work. Basically, you connect your Microsoft Intune subscription to Configuration Manager, set up a synchronization so that users from your local Active Directory are synced to Microsoft Intune, providing the means for your end users to enroll their devices, let it be Windows Phone, Windows RT, iOS devices, or Android devices.

> **Real World Note**: Among the advantages of using Microsoft Intune connected to Configuration Manager instead of the stand-alone Microsoft Intune web interface is the additional control that you have over configuration settings, the ability to see user-installed apps (i.e. software inventory), and many more details. Using Configuration Manager, you can choose to set a device to Company owned, and that gives you the additional possibilities for managing your devices.

Adding Your Own Domain to Microsoft Intune

To enroll Windows devices such as Windows RT, you first have to add your public domain name in Microsoft Intune and verify it by creating a TXT entry in your DNS zone. Secondly, you need to add a DNS name entry (CNAME) for enterpriseenrollment.domain.com, which points to enterpriseenrollment.manage.microsoft.com. This is used when activating Device Management and Workplace Join.

> **Real World Note**: As we will demonstrate in the following guides, however, you can use the built-in onmicrosoft.com account to enroll devices based on iOS, as that enrollment procedure does not rely on the enterpriseenrollment domain alias.

In the following examples, ViaMonstra has signed up for an Intune trial account with the domain viamonstra123.onmicrosoft.com.

Create a Microsoft Intune Account

Before doing anything else, you need to sign up for a trial account of Microsoft Intune. ViaMonstra is evaluating Intune to see whether that is the way to go when managing their mobile devices. ViaMonstra is signing up for a 30-day free trial and will connect Microsoft Intune to its Configuration Manager system.

> **Note**: As of November 2014, Microsoft rebranded Intune from Windows Intune to Microsoft Intune. However, the branding and replacement of Windows Intune in the graphical user interface is a work in progress, and therefore you will see some references to Windows Intune in the following step-by-step guides and in the screenshots.

1.   Start by browsing to **windowsintune.com** and sign up for a free trial.

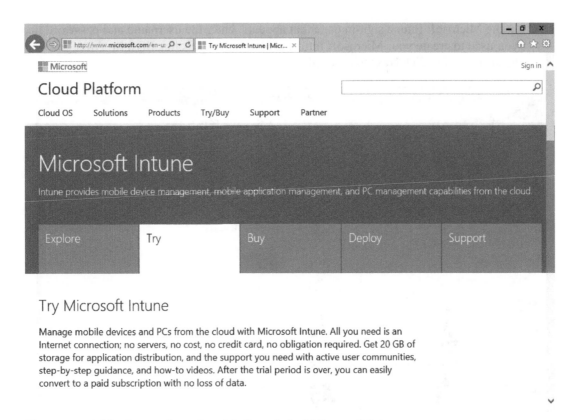

You can quickly sign up for a free 30-day trial of Microsoft Intune.

Connect Microsoft Intune to Configuration Manager

Now you connect Microsoft Intune to Configuration Manager:

1. On **CM01**, log on as **VIAMONSTRA\Administrator**.

2. Start the **ConfigMgr console**.

3. In **Administration** workspace, expand **Cloud Services**, and click **Windows Intune Subscriptions**.

4. On the ribbon, click the **Add Windows Intune Subscription** button.

5. On the **Introduction** page, click **Next**.

6. On the **Subscription** page, click the **Sign In** button and complete the following:

    a. In the **Set the Mobile Device Management Authority** dialog box, select the **I understand that after I complete the sign-in process, the mobile device management authority is permanently set to Configuration Manager and cannot be changed** check box.

    b. Click **OK**.

181

7. In the Microsoft Intune sign-in page that appears, enter the username and password that you used to create your Microsoft Intune trial account and click **Sign in**. After you've been signed in, click **Next** to proceed.

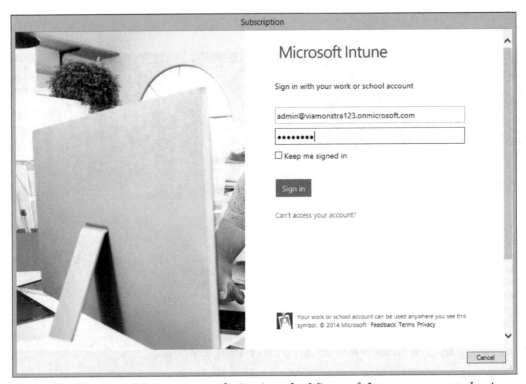

In the Configuration Manager wizard, sign into the Microsoft Intune account to begin connecting Configuration Manager to Microsoft Intune.

8. On the **General** page, click the **Browse** button and complete the following:

   a. In the **Select Collection** dialog box, choose the **Collection** named **All Users** and click **OK**.

Real World Note: In the real world, you would typically not let all users be enrolled using Microsoft Intune. Instead, you would create a collection and then designate Microsoft Intune users to that collection.

   b. In **Company Name**, enter **ViaMonstra Inc**.

   c. In the **Configuration Manager site code** drop-down list, choose the site code **P01**, and then click **Next**.

9. On the **Platforms** page, click **Next**. You configure this later on.

10. On the **Company Contact Information** page, click **Next**.

11. On the **Company Logo** page, click **Next**.

12. On the **Summary** page, click **Next**.

13. On the **Completion** page, review the information, and then click **Close**.

Install the Windows Intune Connector Role

After adding the Microsoft Intune Subscription to Configuration Manage, you also need to install the Windows Intune Connector role to Configuration Manager. This role is in charge of synchronizing data with Microsoft Intune.

1. On **CM01**, start the **ConfigMgr console** if it is not already started.

2. In the **Administration** workspace, expand **Site Configuration**, and click **Servers and Site System Roles**.

3. Right-click the **Site system** named **CM01.corp.viamonstra.com** and choose **Add Site System Roles**.

4. On the **General** page, click **Next**.

5. On the **Proxy** page, click **Next**.

6. On the **System Role Selections** page, choose **Windows Intune Connector** and then click **Next**.

7. On the **Summary** page, click **Next**.

8. On the **Completion** page, click **Close**.

Configure UPNs for Your Users

Before synchronizing user accounts to Microsoft Intune, which you set up shortly, you need to make sure that the UPNs of our users are consistent with Microsoft Intune configuration. This means that you must add your public domain name (as noted earlier in this chapter) to Microsoft Intune and then make sure that you have this domain set as a UPN for your user accounts in Active Directory. ViaMonstra will not add its public domain name at this stage of evaluating Microsoft Intune and will use the onmicrosoft.com-assigned domain name.

1. On **DC01**, log on as **VIAMONSTRA\Administrator**.

2. Start the **Active Directory Domains and Trusts** console.

3. Right-click the node **Active Directory Domains and Trusts [DC01.corp.viamonstra.com]** and choose **Properties**.

4. In the **Alternative UPN suffixes** input area, type the domain name of your trial Microsoft Intune account (something like companyname.onmicrosoft.com), click **Add**, and then click **OK**.

Real World Note: In the real world, you would need to add a public domain name here. To enroll Windows RT devices, you must add your public domain name first to Microsoft Intune using https://account.manage.microsoft.com and then add the corresponding UPN to your Active Directory if you do not already have the UPNs in place.

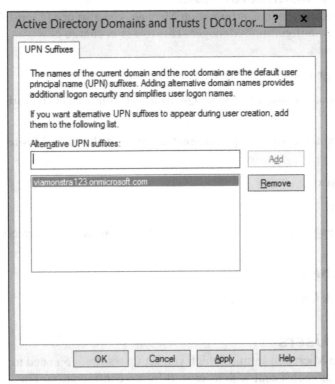

In our example, you are using viamonstra123.onmicrosoft.com as a UPN suffix, but change this to whatever domain name you have registered in Microsoft Intune.

5.   Close the **Active Directory Domains and Trusts** console

Set UPN for Your Test User

To finish the UPN configuration, you need to set the UPN for the user you are going use to test enrolling a device in Microsoft Intune.

1.   On **DC01**, start the **Active Directory Users and Computers** console.

2.   Expand **corp.viamonstra.com**, and then expand the **ViaMonstra / Users** OU.

3.   Right-click **Don** and choose **Properties**.

4.   Click the **Account** tab.

5.   In the User logon name text box, type in **don**. Then in the drop-down list, select the UPN suffix that you added in the preceding guide and then click **OK**.

By changing the UPN of Don you make sure that Don's user account will be synced properly to Microsoft Intune.

Set Up DirSync to Synchronize Users Accounts to Intune

Now you will set up DirSync, a tool that synchronizes user accounts and also passwords from your local Active Directory to Microsoft Intune so that your users can use their existing user accounts to enroll their mobile devices in Intune and Configuration Manager.

1. On **DC01**, log on as **VIAMONSTRA\Administrator**.

2. Start **Server Manager**, select **Local Server** on the left side.

3. On the **Local Server** page, click **On** next to **IE Enhanced Security Configuration** on the right side.

4. In the **Internet Explorer Enhanced Security Configuration** window, set the IE ESC setting to **Off** for both **Administrators** and **Users**, and then click **OK**.

Note: Setting the Internet Explorer Enhanced Security Configuration to Off for Administrators isn't recommended in a production environment; however, it makes life a lot easier throughout this book.

5.   Using **Internet Explorer**, sign in to **https://account.manage.microsoft.com** using the admin account you created previously in this chapter when signing up for the Microsoft Intune trial account.

Real World Note: Once again, in a real-world scenario you would add your own domain information to Microsoft Intune. This way when you sync users to Intune they keep their UPN and are able to use it when enrolling the device. For the demonstration purposes of ViaMonstra, you add the UPN manually to one test account in your local Active Directory.

6.   Click the **Users** link in the left menu.

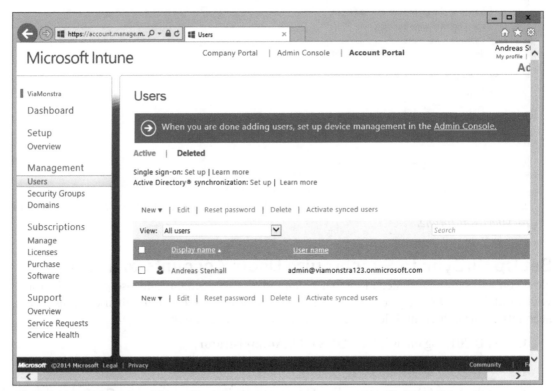

In the Microsoft Intune Admin Console, you can activate user synchronization to sync users from your local Active Directory to the Microsoft Intune account.

7.   Click the **Set up** link to the right of **Active Directory® synchronization**.

8.   Under the headline **Activate Active Directory synchronization**, click the **Activate** button. When prompted whether you really want to activate directory synchronization, click **Activate** again.

Real World Note: If the page just reloads when you click the Activate button, you must add the domain account.manage.microsoft.com to the Trusted Sites list of Internet Explorer.

9. Under the headline **Install and configure the Directory Synchronization tool**, select the **64-bit version** and then click **Download** to download DirSync.

Real World Note: Yes, you will install the DirSync on the domain controller, which is a new feature as of DirSync released in October 2013. However, for real-world scenarios, we recommend that you set up a separate server for handling directory synchronization. Never use DirSync on a domain controller in a production environment.

10. When DirSync has downloaded, go to the location where you downloaded **dirsync.exe**, and to start the installation, right-click **dirsync.exe** and choose **Run as Administrator**.

11. On the **Welcome** page, click **Next**.

12. On the **Microsoft Software License Terms** page, select **I accept** and click **Next**.

13. On the **Select Installation Folder** page, accept the default settings, and click **Next**.

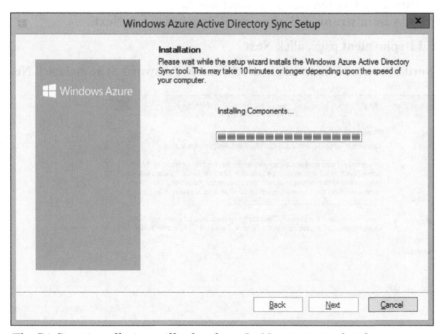

The DirSync installation will take about 5- 10 minutes to finish.

14. On the **Installation** page, when the install has finished, click **Next**.

15. On the **Finished** page, clear the **Start Configuration Wizard now** check box and click **Finish**.

16. Log off **DC01** and then log in again as **VIAMONSTRA\Administrator**.

Note: You cannot start the configuration until you log out and log in again. This is a known limitation when installing DirSync on a domain controller, again something that under real-world circumstances you would not do in a production environment.

17. Start **Directory Sync Configuration** from the **Start screen** by right-clicking it and choosing **Run as Administrator**.

18. On the **Welcome** page, click **Next**.

19. On the **Windows Azure Active Directory Credentials** page, enter the username and password of the account that you signed up for the trial account for Microsoft Intune, and then click **Next**.

20. On the **Active Directory Credentials** page, enter username **VIAMONSTRA\Administrator** and password **P@ssw0rd**. Click **Next**.

21. On the **Hybrid Deployment** page, click **Next**.

22. On the **Password Synchronization** page, select **Enable Password Sync** and click **Next**.

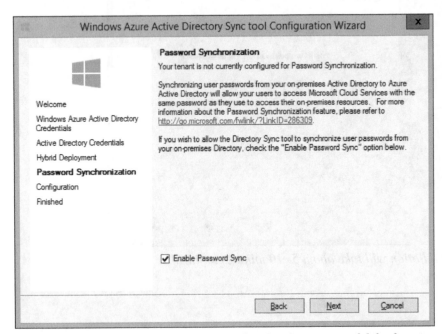

Synchronizing your local passwords to the cloud is very useful for keeping one password for your users and not mixing them up with each other.

23. On the **Configuration** page, click **Next**.

24. On the **Finished** page, click **Finish**. Click **OK** in the alert that pops up.

Configure the User in Microsoft Intune

Before the users can enroll their devices, they must be assigned to the Microsoft Intune group of users.

1. Point your web browser to **https://account.manage.microsoft.com** and log in using the credentials you used when signing up for the Microsoft Intune trial.

2. Click **Users** in the left menu.

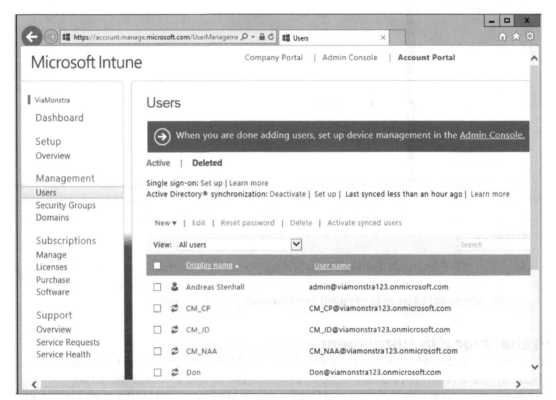

DirSync has synchronized the user accounts from your local Active Directory to the Microsoft Intune service.

3. Click the link for **Don** in the **Users** table.

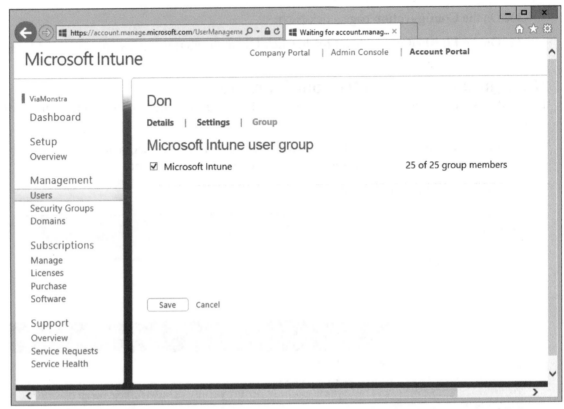

Before the user can enroll his or her device, the user must be assigned to the Microsoft Intune group.

4. Select the **Microsoft Intune** check box and then click the **Save** button. If asked to set a location, choose a location in the drop-down list and click **Save**. Don now has all properties set to be able to enroll his devices.

Prepare for iOS Enrollment

For your users to be able to enroll their iOS devices in Microsoft Intune and Configuration Manager, you need to create a certificate from Apple that is used to handle the secure communication channel with Intune and Configuration Manager. ViaMonstra does have some iOS devices and will enroll them in Intune and Configuration manager.

1. On **CM01**, log on as **VIAMONSTRA\Administrator**.

2. If it is not already started, open the **ConfigMgr console** and go to **Administration**, expand **Cloud Services**, right-click **Windows Intune Subscriptions**, and choose **Create APNs certificate request** (or click **Create APNs certificate request** on the ribbon).

3. In the **Request Apple Push Notification Service Certificate Signing Request** dialog box, click the **Browse** button. Choose **Desktop**, enter the name **APN**, click **Save**, and then

click **Download**. If prompted to log in, do so using the admin account that you created for the Intune account. When the certificate request has been downloaded, click **Close**.

4. On a machine with **Chrome** installed (or install Chrome on DC01), go to **http://go.microsoft.com/fwlink/?LinkId=264215**, which redirects you to the Apple certificate site. Log in using an Apple account.

> **Real World Note**: The Apple certificate site does not work very well in Internet Explorer. Actually Microsoft recommends using a third-party browser such as Chrome or Firefox for using Apple's certificate site.

5. Click **Create a Certificate** button, and then read and accept the terms of use. Click the **Browse** button and point to the APN file that you created on the desktop on DC01. Then choose **Upload**.

6. Choose **Download** and save the file to **Desktop** with the default filename **MDM_ Microsoft Corporation_Certificate.pem**.

7. Go back to the **ConfigMgr console**, right-click **Windows Intune Subscription** under **Cloud Services / Windows Intune Subscriptions**, and choose **Properties**.

8. Click the **iOS** tab and select **Enable iOS Enrollment**. Then click the **Browse** button and point to the **MDM_ Microsoft Corporation_Certificate.pem** file on the desktop. Click **Open** and then **OK**. You now are able to enroll any iOS device.

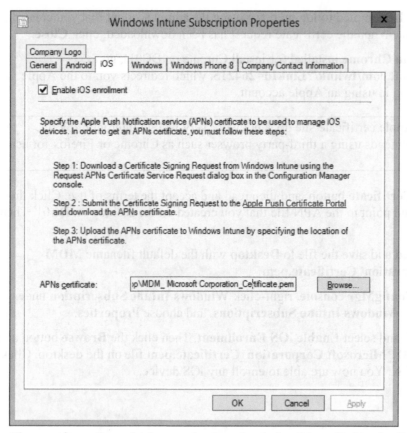

The certificate from Apple must be downloaded and installed in the Configuration Manager environment for iOS device enrollment to work.

Enroll an iOS Device to Microsoft Intune

Now it is time to enroll an iOS device in your environment.

1. With your iOS device, go to the **App Store** and install the app named **Company Portal**. Alternatively, you can use the iOS **Safari** browser to navigate to **m.manage.microsoft.com** to enroll your iOS device.

Real World Note: In addition to one being an app and the other being a webpage, there is another difference between the Company Portal app and the Company Portal web app. On iOS devices, your users will not be able to sideload apps that you have deployed from the Company Portal app. Sideloaded apps can be installed by users only from the Company Portal web app.

---

2. Sign in using **don@viamonstra123.onmicrosoft.com** and the password **P@ssw0rd**.

Note: Viamonstra123.onmicrosoft.com is the test trial account for ViaMonstra. You will have another domain name, so use that one instead.

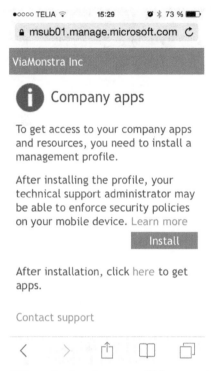

When signing in, you will have to install the management profile so that email profiles, settings, and the like can be configured and managed on your device.

3. After signing in, you need to click the Install button to add your device, which in practice installs a management profile on your iOS device. After that is done, your iOS device will show up in the ConfigMgr console after a short wait.

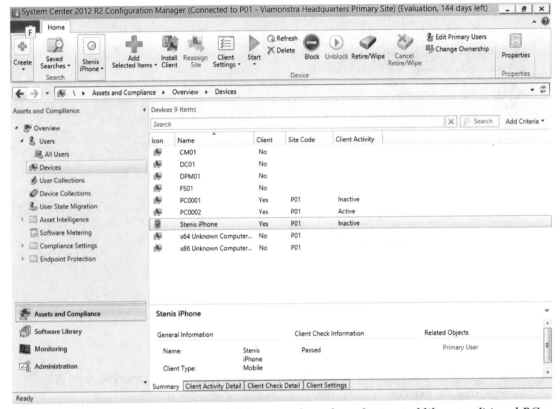

Your iOS device shows up in the ConfigMgr console and can be treated like a traditional PC. That is true device management.

Enrolling a Windows Device

To enroll a Windows device for management, as mentioned earlier in this chapter, you have to add your public domain name to Microsoft Intune and also create a CNAME DNS record for enterpriseenrollment.yourdomain.com that you point to enterpriseenrollment.manage.microsoft.com.

Enroll a Windows 8.1 or Windows 8.1 RT Device

The enrollment process of a Windows 8.1 or Windows 8.1 RT device is pretty straightforward.

1. On a **Windows 8.1** or **Windows 8.1 RT** device, press the **Windows logo key + C** to display the **Charms** menu.

2. Choose **Settings** / **Change PC settings** / **Network** / **Workplace** and turn on **Device Management**. Then authenticate with an account that is a part of the Intune users group, agree to the **Terms of Use**, and click **Turn on** to activate the device management.

Chapter 8

Security

Security in the Windows client is becoming more important as users tend to become more mobile and exposed on other networks, as well as having more mobile devices. In this chapter, you learn all about the essential enterprise security features AppLocker and BitLocker and Microsoft's malware solution Endpoint Protection. This chapter also covers User Account Control (UAC) configuration in the enterprise, and we deal with local administrator issues found in the enterprise.

AppLocker

AppLocker was a personal favorite security feature of ours when Windows 7 was launched a number of years ago, and nothing since then has changed our feelings about AppLocker. It is an extremely smart way of preventing unwanted things from being executed and run on your machines in an enterprise environment. AppLocker in Windows 8 and 8.1 works the very same way it did in Windows 7 except that it now offers support for "packaged apps," meaning Windows 8 apps that come in the Appx format or through the Store.

Basics of AppLocker

The basics of AppLocker are that you create a whitelist (so-called "allow rules") of what you want to allow to be run on a machine. These can be executable files, Windows Installer files, and scripts of various kinds. Anything that does not meet your allow rules is effectively blocked from executing or running on your client machines, providing a very good means for security and minimizing the chance of users running things they should not.

Starting with Windows 8, you can control packaged apps, but Windows 8 also introduced control over MST files (transform files for Windows Installer) in addition to rules for MSI and MSP files.

So the following file types can be controlled with AppLocker:

- **Executable**. EXE files

- **Windows Installer**. MSI, MSP, and MST files

- **Scripts**. PS1, CMD, VBS, BAT, and JS

- **DLL**. DLL and OCX

- **Packaged apps**. Appx files or installed packaged apps from the Store

> **Real World Note**: More and more applications are being installed in the user profile catalog instead of to Program Files. A few good examples of popular applications that do install without a user having administrative privileges are Google Chrome and Spotify. Using AppLocker blocks these types of applications from running (but that of course depends on the rules you create).

The Rules Are Important

AppLocker provides you with three types of rules:

- **Publisher rules**: Most third-party application vendors sign their executable files using a digital certificate, which proves that the executable originates from them and not from any other source. When creating rules, AppLocker will look to see whether there is a digital signature in the application you are trying to allow and then let you use that publisher's information to allow everything from Microsoft Corporation, for instance, to run. Using publisher rules are without a doubt your number one aim when dealing with AppLocker rules, as they require the least amount of administration.

- **Hash rules**: A hash rule means that you make a checksum of a file. The drawback of this is that whenever the file is updated or replaced, you need to re-hash and create a new rule that allows that file to be run. From an administrative standpoint, this is not very good as it results in a lot of administration.

- **Path rules**: Last but not least is the path rule. This type lets you create a rule to say, for instance, that everything in folder C:\Program Files will be allowed to run. This means that if the user can put something in there, it will be allowed to run. Using path rules is your very last option. We strongly recommend against using them, although there are scenarios in which using them is all right for specific needs, such as using the default rules.

Strategy

When dealing with AppLocker in enterprises, you need to find a balance between administration and security. Security folks tend to want the best possible results, meaning a total whitelist where you specify everything. For administrative purposes, this is not always the case because for this to work somewhat well, everything that you want to allow must be signed by a certificate publisher, yourself, or someone you trust.

Signing your in-house applications, converting scripts to PowerShell, and thereby signing those also, create a secure environment that improves security and minimizes administration when it comes to AppLocker.

> **Note**: One common misconception with AppLocker is that it will control and allow what a user can install, i.e. a standard user is thought to be able to install things if AppLocker allows it. That is false. To be able to install applications (in Program Files), you still need administrative privileges on the machine.

How to Activate AppLocker

Typically three things are required to activate AppLocker: rules, a started service (Application Identity service), and setting the enforcement mode. In a real-world scenario, we also recommend that you activate notifications to give your users additional information on why something was blocked from running and the potential means for resolving any issues they encounter.

Configure AppLocker

1. On **DC01**, log on as **VIAMONSTRA\Administrator**.

2. Using the **Group Policy Management** console, edit the **Workstation Configuration** group policy.

3. In the **Computer Configuration** / **Policies** / **Windows Settings** / **Security Settings** / **System services** node, double-click the **Application Identity** service.

4. Select the **Define this policy setting** check box, select the **Automatic** option, and then click **OK**.

5. In the same group policy, expand the **Computer Configuration** / **Policies** / **Windows Settings** / **Security Settings** / **Application Control Policies** node, and select the **AppLocker** node.

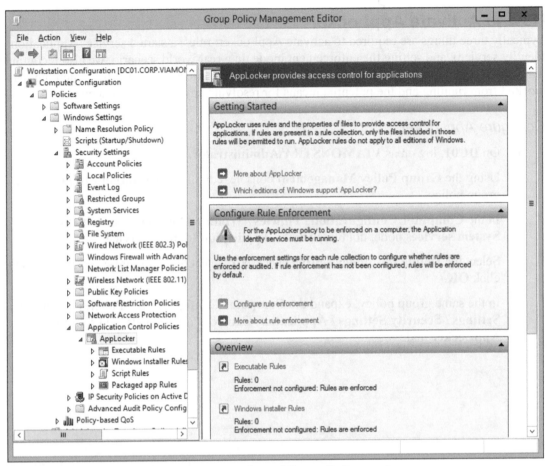

Activating AppLocker is done using a number of Group Policy settings.

6. Right-click **Executable rules** and select **Create Default Rules** (select the node first if the menu is not available).

Real World Note: The default rules allow everything in Windows to execute. Standard users can potentially copy things to the Windows\Temp folder and execute whatever they need, bypassing AppLocker.

7. Double-click **(Default Rule) All files located in the Windows folder** and select the **Exceptions** tab.

8. In the **Add exception** drop-down list, choose **Path** and click **Add**.

9. Choose **Browse folders**, browse to **C:\Windows\Temp**, and click **OK** three times.

10. Select the **AppLocker** node and click the **Configure rule enforcement** link.

11. In the **Executable rules** area, select the **Configured** check box, and in the drop-down list, select **Enforce rules**. Then click **OK**.

> **Note**: The Application Identity service now features the new Windows 8 "trigger start." This means that if the service is stopped for some reason, it will be started automatically the next time something is executed, as long as a set of AppLocker rules has been applied to the machine.

Activate the Web Page with More Support Information

1. On **DC01**, using the **Group Policy Management** console, edit the **Workstation Configuration** group policy.

2. In the **Computer Configuration** / **Policies** / **Administrative Templates** / **Windows Components** / **File Explorer** node, enable the **Set a support web page link** policy and configure the following:

   > In the **Support Web Page URL** text box, replace the prepopulated URL with **http://intranet.corp.viamonstra.com/AppLocker.html**, and click **OK**.

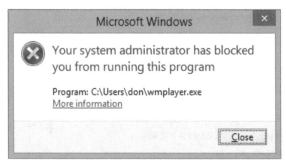

This will be displayed when something is blocked from running; when a support web page URL is entered, there is a "More information" link.

Verify AppLocker Behavior

1. On **PC0002**, log in as **Don** in the **VIAMONSTRA** domain.

2. Press the **Windows logo key** + **R**, type **gpupdate**, and press **Enter**. Wait for the group policy update to finish.

3. Press the **Windows logo key** + **R** once again and now type **eventvwr.msc** to launch **Event Viewer**.

4. In **Event Viewer**, expand **Applications and Services logs** / **Microsoft** / **Windows** / **AppLocker** / **EXE and DLL**.

5. Investigate the events found there; you should have at least one that says that an **AppLocker policy** has been applied to the system. If not, do another **gpupdate** and wait. Do not close Event Viewer.

> **Note**: Sometimes it takes a while (several minutes) for the AppLocker rules to be applied, so be patient. Event Viewer will notify you that there are new events that can be viewed by refreshing the view in Event Viewer.

6. When AppLocker policies have been applied, start **File Explorer**.

7. Go to **C:\Program Files (x86)\Windows Media Player** and open **wmplayer.exe**. Verify that the **Event Viewer** (remember to do a refresh to see all new events) shows that **Windows Media Player (wmplayer.exe)** was allowed to run.

8. Copy **wmplayer.exe** to the **C:\Users\don** folder.

9. Run **wmplayer.exe** from the **C:\Users\don** directory and note that it will not run.

10. Then look in the **Event Viewer**. You see a message that states that running Windows Media Player (wmplayer.exe) from that directory was prevented.

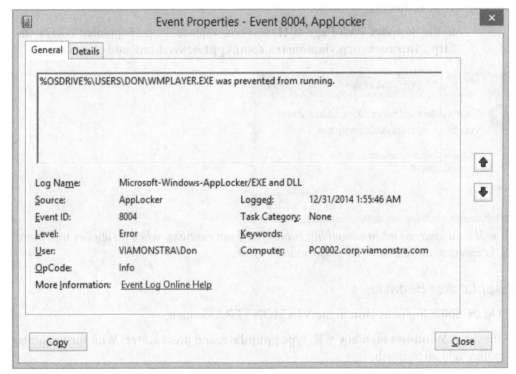

AppLocker in enforce rules mode prevented Windows Media Player from running.

Note: Before proceeding with the other labs to come, go back to DC01 and change enforcement mode from Enforce rules to Audit only in the AppLocker settings in the Workstation Configuration group policy. Do a gpupdate on PC0002 to apply the new set of policies.

Manage AppLocker for Windows Apps

AppLocker rules for modern Windows apps can be managed in two ways, either by using installed apps or by Appx packages.

Note: To perform these steps, you need to have prepared your PC0002 client with Remote Server Administration Tools for Windows 8.1, as described in Appendix B.

1. On **PC0002**, log on as **VIAMONSTRA\Administrator**.

2. Via the **Control Panel / System and Security / Administrative Tools**, start the **Group Policy Management** console, and edit the **Workstation Configuration** group policy.

3. In the **Computer Configuration** / **Policies** / **Windows Settings** / **Security Settings** / **Application Control Policies** node (expand it), double-click **AppLocker**.

4. Right-click **Packaged app Rules** and choose **Create New Rule**.

5. On the **Before You Begin** page, click **Next**.

6. On the **Permissions** page, accept the default settings and click **Next**.

7. On the **Publisher** page, click the **Select** button and complete the following:

> In the **Select applications** dialog box, scroll down and select **PC Settings**, and then click **OK** followed by **Next**.

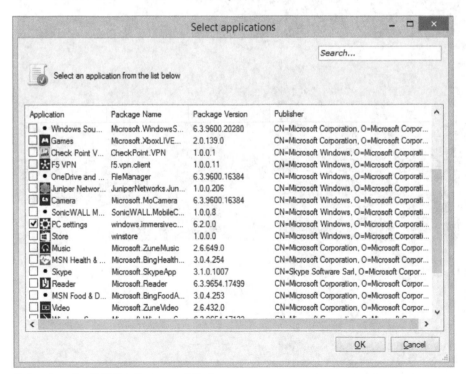

Selecting the PC Settings application.

8. On the **Exceptions** page, click **Next**.

9. On the **Name** page, in the **Description: (Optional)** text box, type in **PC Settings**, and then click **Create**.

10. Select the **AppLocker** node and click **Configure rule enforcement**.

11. In the **Packaged app Rules** area, select the **Configured** check box, and in the drop-down list, select **Enforce rules**. Then click **OK** and close the Group Policy Management console and sign out from PC0002.

Verify AppLocker for Windows 8 Apps

1. On **PC0002**, log in as **Don** in the **VIAMONSTRA** domain, and run **gpupdate** to refresh the group policy.

2. On the **Start screen**, press the **Windows logo key + C** to bring up the **Charms** menu. Choose **Settings** and then **Change PC settings**. PC settings open because you specifically allowed it to run. Click **Windows logo key + D** to return to the desktop.

3. Press the **Windows logo key** to go back to the Start screen. Click the **Mail** app. It does not start because you have specifically allowed only the PC settings app to run.

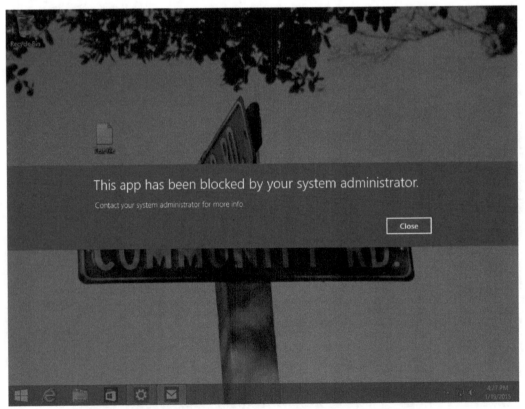

The message that displays when an app has been blocked from running.

Antimalware Software

No one (we hope) will run their Windows clients without a proper antimalware protection. Although an antivirus protection software is never close to 100% protection, it is still a basic foundation for keeping malware, maybe not so much out of your network, but at least, from spreading within the network.

Starting with Windows 8, Microsoft ships a full antivirus client with Windows, and that is Windows Defender. However, the Windows Defender that is included in Windows 8 and 8.1 is not in any terms an enterprise product and never will be. Windows Defender is shipped inbox with Windows to provide fundamental protection for all Windows machines, and the target group is consumers.

So the bottom line is that you still need some form of third-party antimalware solution if, for instance, you want to be able to receive reports when there are infections and malicious code found on the machines. You also have to be able to control your antimalware solution centrally. Those are not features that Windows Defender can provide.

System Center 2012 R2 Endpoint Protection to the Rescue

Fortunately, there are a lot of vendors when it comes to antimalware software, and Microsoft actually provides the license for its antimalware solution System Center 2012 R2 Endpoint Protection (formerly known as Forefront Endpoint Protection) as a part of the Windows device CAL (Client Access License). This means that any enterprise already has licenses to use Endpoint Protection.

One requirement for using, or should we say manage, Endpoint Protection is that you manage it via Configuration Manager, in terms of distributing the client, configuring settings, and managing the reporting part when malware is detected.

> **Real World Note**: There are a few third-party solutions out on the market that actually let you manage Endpoint Protection without using System Center Configuration Manager. One of them is from Specops Software. Although this might come in handy in smaller environments, we still recommend that you use System Center Configuration Manager because that is the supported solution to manage Endpoint Protection.

Automatically Getting Rid of Your Old Antimalware Solution

One great thing about Endpoint Protection is that it (by default, but optionally) automatically uninstalls your existing antimalware suite, at least for the most common enterprise antimalware solutions from the largest vendors on the market. The ones that can be uninstalled automatically is referenced in Microsoft TechNet Documentation at http://technet.microsoft.com/en-us/library/gg682067.aspx.

Real World Note: Some third-party antimalware solutions, such as Symantec Endpoint Protection, can be configured in its console to demand a password for an uninstall. If replacing Symantec Endpoint Protection with System Center Endpoint Protection, you must make sure that you change that password requirement for using the Symantec console to allow the uninstall to take place by the System Center Endpoint Protection installation process.

Setup Configuration Manager for Endpoint Protection

As ViaMonstra already has System Center 2012 R2 Configuration Manager in place, it will use Endpoint Protection to replace its existing antivirus software from a well-known third-party antivirus software company.

Configure the Endpoint Protection Role

Before even starting out with Endpoint Protection, you have to install the Endpoint Protection role on the Configuration Manager primary site server.

1. On **CM01**, log on as **VIAMONSTRA\Administrator**.

2. Start the **ConfigMgr console**.

3. In the **Administration** workspace, expand **Site Configuration**, and click **Servers and Site System Roles**.

4. Right-click the **Site System** named **CM01.corp.viamonstra.com** and choose **Add Site System Roles**.

5. On the **General** page, click **Next**.

6. On the **Proxy** page, click **Next**.

7. On the **System Role Selection** page, select **Endpoint Protection point**. When informed about the patching, or definition files, click **OK** and then click **Next**.

8. On the **Endpoint Protection** page, select **I accept the Endpoint Protection license terms** and click **Next**.

9. On the **Microsoft Active Protection Services** page, select **Do not join MAPS** and click **Next**.

10. On the **Summary** page, click **Next**.

11. On the **Completion** page, click **Close**.

Configure WSUS to Download and Deploy Definition Files Automatically

Definition files for System Center Endpoint Protection are released several times a day, and we are quite sure that you do not want to handle these manually, as that would be very time consuming. To approve the definitions files automatically for install on your Windows clients, you activate something called Automatic Deployment Rules in Software Updates.

1. On **CM01**, using the **ConfigMgr console**, in the **Software Library** workspace, expand **Software Updates**, and click **Automatic Deployment Rules**.

2. Click the **Create Automatic Deployment Rule** button on the ribbon.

3. On the **General** page, enter the name **Endpoint Protection Definition Files**, click the **Browse** button, and complete the following:

    In the **Select Collection** dialog box, choose the collection named **All Windows 8.1 Systems** and click **OK**; then click **Next**.

4. On the **Deployment Settings** page, accept the default settings, and click **Next**.

5. On the **Software Updates** page, in the **Properties filters**, scroll down to find **Update Classification**, select the check box in front of **Update Classification**, and complete the following:

    a. In the **Search criteria** pane, click the link **items to find**.

    b. In the **Search Criteria** dialog box, select **Definition Updates** and click **OK**, followed by **Next**.

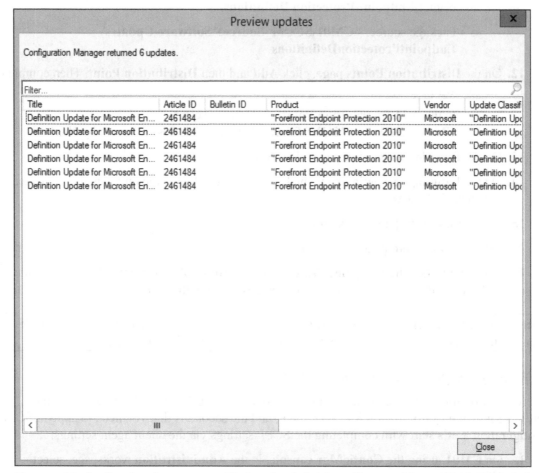

You can hit the Preview button to verify that the definitions files would actually be included with your current selection.

6. On the **Evaluation Schedule** page, select **Run the rule on a schedule**, click the **Customize** button, and complete the following:

> In the **Custom Schedule** dialog box, change **Recur every** to every **8 hours** and click **OK**, followed by **Next**.

7. On the **Deployment Schedule** page, select **As soon as possible** for **Installation deadline** and then click **Next**.

8. On the **User Experience** page, click **Next**.

9. On the **Alerts** page, click **Next**.

10. On the **Download Settings** page, select **Download software updates from distribution point and install**, and then click **Next**.

11. On the **Deployment Package** page, select **Create a new deployment package**, enter the following, and then click **Next**:

    o   Name: **Endpoint Protection Definitions**.

    o   Package source: **\\CM01\SCCM_Source$\Software Updates\ EndpointProtectionDefinitions**

12. On the **Distribution Points** page, click **Add** and then **Distribution Point**. Then complete the following:

> In the **Add Distribution Points** dialog box, select **CM01.CORP.VIAMONSTRA.COM** and click **OK**, followed by **Next**.

13. On the **Download Location** page, click **Next**.

14. On the **Language Selection** page, make sure that **English** is the only language selected and then click **Next**.

15. On the **Summary** page, click **Next**.

16. On the **Completion** page, click **Close**.

17. Now, right-click the **Endpoint Protection Definition Files** automatic deployment rule and choose **Run Now**. Answer **OK** in the message box that appears.

Note: The patch and definition files download can be verified in the PatchDownloader.log file found in the Logs directory of your Configuration Manager installation folder.

Configure the Client Settings for SCEP

There are two things you need to know about configuring SCEP. One is that you have some settings set by the Configuration Manager client, and the second is that you need to apply a SCEP configuration. Let's start with completing the SCEP settings via the client agent settings:

1. On **CM01**, using the **ConfigMgr console**, in the **Administration** workspace, select **Client Settings**.

2. Right-click **Default Client Settings** and choose **Properties**.

3. Click **Endpoint Protection** in the menu to the left, set the following values, and when done, click **OK**:

    o   **Manage Endpoint Protection client on client computers** to **Yes**.

    o   **Install Endpoint Protection client on client computers** to **No**.

Note: Although Endpoint Protection can be installed automatically, for the demonstration purposes of this book, you want to control the installation and therefore do not make it automatic.

Configure the SCEP Policy

Up next is configuring the actual Endpoint Protection settings, i.e. when and how the malware detection software is configured on the Windows client machines.

1. On **CM01**, using the **ConfigMgr console,** in the **Assets and Compliance** workspace, expand **Endpoint Protection**, and click **Antimalware Policies**.

2. Right-click **Default Client Antimalware Policy** and choose **Properties**.

3. Change **Run a daily quick scan on client computers** to **Yes**.

4. Click **Definition updates** in the left menu, click the **Set Source** button, and complete the following:

    > In the **Configure Definition Update Sources** dialog box, clear the **Updates distributed from Microsoft Update** and **Updates distributed from Microsoft Malware Protection Center** check boxes, and then click **OK** twice.

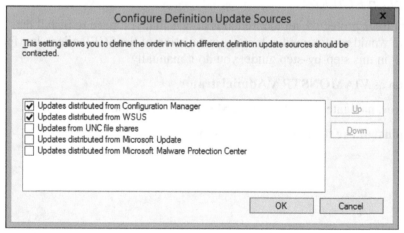

Configuring the definition update sources.

Configure Alerts for a Collection

To able to get notified whenever malware is detected, you need to configure alerts.

1. On **CM01**, using the **ConfigMgr console,** in the **Assets and Compliance** workspace, select **Device Collections**.

2. Right-click the collection named **All Windows 8.1 Systems** and choose **Properties**.

3. Click the **Alerts** tab.

4. Select the **View this collection in the Endpoint Protection dashboard** check box, and then click the **Add** button. In the **Add New Collection Alerts** dialog box, select the following check boxes and click **OK** twice:

   o **Malware is detected.**

   o **The same type malware is detected on a number of computers.**

   o **The same type malware is repeatedly detected within the specified interval on a computer.**

   o **Multiple types of malware are detected on the same computer with the specified interval.**

> **Real World Note**: Typically, in a real-world scenario, you would like to configure email alerts so that the security folks get notified instantly when malware is detected on machines. This is done in two steps: first, by configuring email notification settings for the site system, and then by creating a subscription under the Monitoring / Alerts section, both in the ConfigMgr console.

Install the SCEP Client on PC0002

So, for the Windows client to be protected, all that remains now is that you need to install the SCEP client. Typically, we would recommend automatic installation of the SCEP client, but for the demonstration of SCEP in this step-by-step guide, you do it manually.

1. On **PC0002**, log on as **VIAMONSTRA\Administrator**.

2. Using **File Explorer**, navigate to the **\\CM01\SMS_P01\Client** folder.

3. Double-click **scepinstall.exe** to launch the installation.

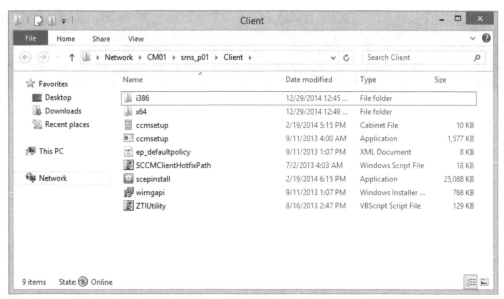

Scepinstall is a part of the Configuration Manager client installation.

Real World Note: If you are deploying the Configuration Manager client and have removed the scepinstall.exe files trying to deploy only ccmsetup.exe, it will fail because scepinstall.exe needs to be there.

4. On the **Welcome to the System Center Endpoint Protection Installation Wizard** page, click **Next**.

5. On the **System Center Endpoint Protection License Terms** page, click **I accept**.

6. On the **Join the Customer Experience Improvement Program** page, select **I do not want to join the program at this time** and click **Next**.

7. On the **Optimize security** page, click **Next**.

8. On the **Ready to install System Center Endpoint Protection** page, click **Install**.

9. On the **Completing the System Center Endpoint Protection Installation Wizard** page, clear the **Scan my computer for potential threats after getting the latest updates** check box, and then click **Finish**.

10. After the installation is completed, make sure that the definitions are being updated and that Endpoint Protection has turned green before proceeding to the next section.

Note: Before the updates can be installed, the SCEP policy that you defined in a previous step needs to be applied (either wait until the next interval or start Machine Policy Retrieval & Evaluation Cycle manually) . You can verify this in System Center Endpoint Protection by clicking the arrow to the right of Help, choosing About, and seeing that the Default Client Antimalware Policy has been applied.

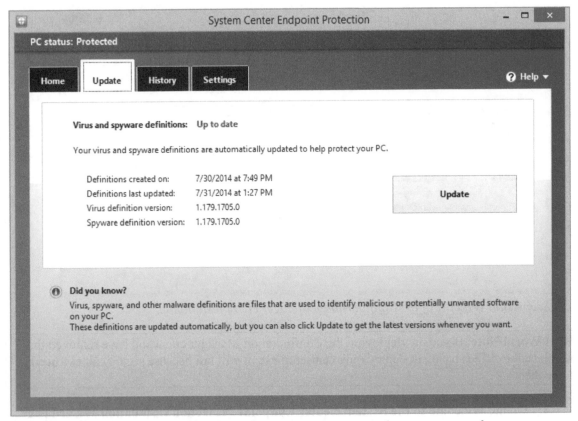

When the definition files are updated, you have protection as good as you can get from antimalware software.

Explore Monitoring and Reporting

Now that you have the Endpoint Protection client out on one client machine, you can to start monitoring and have control over your antimalware solution.

1. On **CM01**, log on as **VIAMONSTRA\Administrator**, and start the **ConfigMgr console** if it is not already started.

2. In the **Monitoring** workspace, expand **Endpoint Protection Status**, and click **System Center 2012 R2 Endpoint Protection**.

3. Explore the view and see what kind of information is in this overview pane.

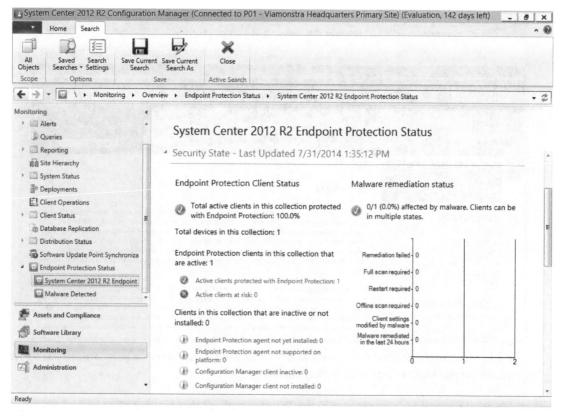

The Endpoint Protection overview page gives you a clear view of the number of infected machines and the status of definition files in terms of how long ago the clients have updated the definitions files.

Test the Antimalware Alerts and Detection

To test what actually happens when malware is detected, you can use the fake virus called Eicar, which is available from www.eicar.org. To give this proof of concept some actual data to work with, download an Eicar file from the Eicar site to trigger Endpoint Protection to generate an alert.

1. On **PC0002**, log on as **VIAMONSTRA\Administrator**.

2. Go to the Eicar web site **www.eicar.org**, and click **Anti-malware testfile** followed by **Download**.

3. Click the file **eicar.com**.

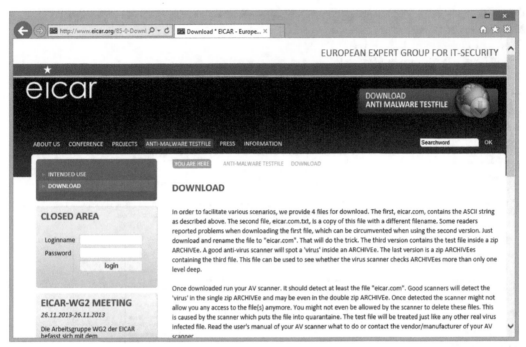

The Eicar antimalware test file is well-known and used to test antimalware solutions, as you typically do not want to test with actual malware.

4. Note the warnings you receive in the Windows client that malware has been detected and it is being cleaned out.

When malware is found, the user is notified instantly, and the alert is sent to the Configuration Manager system alerting the IT that the malware was detected.

After malware has been detected, the actions depend on your settings. Typically, Endpoint Protection cleans out the malware.

Work with the Malware Alerts and Reporting

Now that you have gotten malware on a machine, you need to verify what has happened.

1. On **CM01**, log on as **VIAMONSTRA\Administrator**, and start the **ConfigMgr console** if it is not already started.

2. In the **Monitoring** workspace, expand **Alerts**, and click **Active Alerts**. You will now see one critical alert that malware has been detected for the All Windows 8.1 Systems collection.

3. Now go down to and expand **Endpoint Protection Status** in the left menu, and click **Malware Detected**. You can see that the Eicar virus has been found.

4. Right-click the threat named **Virus:DOS/EICAR_Test_File** and choose **View infected clients**. That displays all the machines with this particular malware.

5. Click **PC0002** and then click the **Malware Detail** tab in the lower part of the console. This lists which process and the actual path of the file, providing some information on how the malware got into the system.

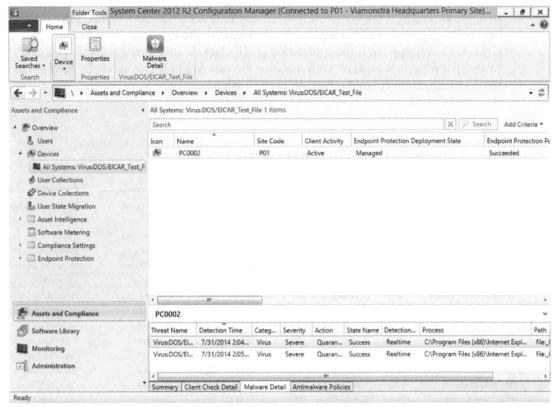

In the Malware Detail view, you get some additional information such as the process involved in the malware detection.

User Account Control

Without a doubt, UAC was the most unwanted feature introduced with Windows Vista back in the day. Although UAC still is a feature in Windows, now there isn't that much fuss about it, but what many do not know is that UAC actually provides a couple of underlying features that you will miss out on if you turn off UAC. We still see applications explicitly demanding to turn off UAC, and there are still software vendors that recommend turning off UAC. Should you turn off UAC? No, never ever!

Extra Value of Using UAC

UAC is so much more than just a dialog box wanting your permission to do things on your machine, it also provides the following:

- **Modern apps**. If you turn off UAC, you cannot use modern apps if you are running Windows 8 or Windows 8.1.

- **Application compatibility**. By default, the activated file and registry virtualization feature comes with UAC. This means that if a standard user runs a legacy application or an application that is not coded well, UAC can redirect writes to a VirtualStore instead of having the application fail in writing, for instance, to the Program Files directory. UAC virtualization is applied if the application (EXE) lacks a so-called manifest. You can easily spot what processes on your machine are running in legacy mode by having the UAC virtualization column turned on in the Task Manager.

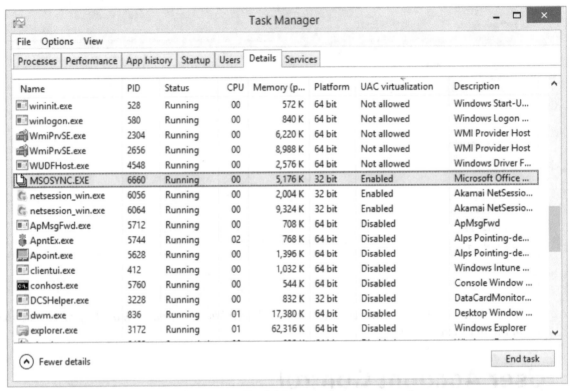

Adding the column UAC virtualization to Task Manager lets you see what processes are actually having UAC virtualization applied.

- **Internet Explorer extra security**. As long as UAC is active, Internet Explorer will run in so-called protected mode, which is sort of like running in a sandbox and provides better security.

- **Runas feature**. Whenever a UAC pops up, it allows you to elevate and enter administrator credentials. Because everything is automatic, this is a lot easier to use than "runas" was in Windows XP.

Real World Note: Too often we hear recommendations for turning off UAC just to make things work. Remember what effects turning off UAC has, and tell any provider, support technician, or developer that turning off UAC is not an option. Turning off UAC should never be considered an option.

UAC in the Enterprise

There is at least one thing to be aware of when dealing with UAC in an enterprise environment. One of the most important things to account for is remote help and support applications, i.e. ensuring that remote control works as expected.

By default, UAC prompts for elevation on something called the *secure desktop*, and that effectively blocks any remote input. This can be fixed by changing the necessary UAC settings. Note that once again we do not in any way recommend turning off UAC.

Configure UAC to Allow for Remote Support

1. On **DC01**, log on as **VIAMONSTRA\Administrator**.

2. Using the **Group Policy Management** console, edit the **Workstation Configuration** group policy.

3. In the **Computer Configuration** / **Policies** / **Windows settings** / **Security settings** / **Local policies** / **Security Options** node, configure the following:

   o Disable the **User Account Control: Switch to the secure desktop when prompting for elevation** policy.

   o Enable the **User Account Control: Allow UIAccess application to prompt for elevation without using the secure desktop** policy.

UAC File and Registry Virtualization in Action

1. On **PC0002**, log in as **Don** in the **VIAMONSTRA** domain.

2. Using the **Start screen**, start **Notepad**.

3. Right-click the **taskbar** and select **Task Manager**.

4. Click **More details** if necessary, and on the **Details** tab, right-click **notepad.exe** and select **UAC virtualization**.

5. In the **Task Manager**, click **Change virtualization**.

6. Switch back to **Notepad**, type anything in the document, and then in the **File menu**, select **Save**.

7. Name the file **UAC.txt**, and save it to **C:\Program Files**.

> **Note**: A standard user does not have write permissions to Program Files in a normally configured Windows 7, 8, or 8.1 machine.

8. Close **Notepad** when done.

9. Using **File Explorer,** navigate to **C:\Program Files**. Note that the **UAC.txt** file is not there.

10. Using **File Explorer**, navigate to **C:\Users\Don\AppData\Local\VirtualStore\Program Files**. You find the **UAC.txt** file there instead of in C:\Program Files.

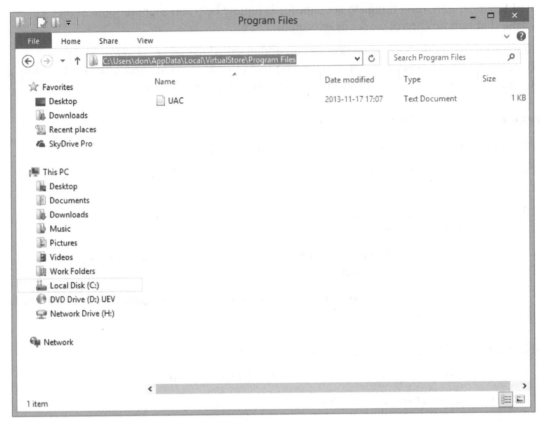

VirtualStore is the location for redirected writes.

Local Administrators

We have only one thing to say about local administrators and that is "stay away from making your users local administrators to the greatest extent possible". Two common reasons for having users as local administrators are that the applications they are using simply won't work without having local administrative privileges or the users may need to install certain drivers. From experience, we can say for sure that there are extremely few applications still out there that actually require local administrative privileges, though they do exist, unfortunately. When it comes to driver installations, you can work around that pretty well.

Real World Note: Accounts having local administrator privileges normally run as a standard user. But, if you map a network drive and then try to access it, for instance, from an elevated command prompt (using the same user account), you will not see the network mapping. See http://technet.microsoft.com/en-us/library/ee844140(v=ws.10).aspx for more information on this issue.

Applications Requiring Administrative Privileges

Typically, applications requiring local administrative privileges demand that because they write things, for instance, to C:\Program Files, or write registry settings under HKEY_LOCAL_MACHINE. A best practice for application developers is to store settings and configuration in the users AppData folder or in the user hive of the registry. In the event that you do have an application requiring administrative privileges, your number one choice would be to check with the vendor to see whether there is an updated version of the application that does not require administrative privileges.

However, if that is not an option because, for instance, the software vendor vanished, there is an option that can be of help. That is shimming the application, or creating a compatibility fix for the application to make it run as the invoking user, i.e. a standard user. That can effectively make an application that requires UAC elevation not demand UAC elevation and thereby work. Many times, there is a reason for the application's requiring administrative privileges, so you might have to loosen the ACLs on file or registry for the application to work after shimming it. A detailed guide on how to use the Application Compatibility Toolkit to create a shim is found at http://blogs.technet.com/b/askperf/archive/2010/08/27/act-suppressing-elevation-prompts-for-legacy-applications.aspx.

Driver Installations as a Standard User

Users tend to have certain needs to use various kinds of hardware, let it be 3G/4G/LTE modems to printers at home. Whenever new hardware is plugged into a modern Windows client, Windows looks in the local driver repository to see whether it can find a driver. If a matching driver is found, it is installed without requiring local administrator rights.

So, one way of having your standard users install hardware (i.e. drivers) is to inject the drivers into the local driver repository. Another way is to use group policies to enable standard users to install drivers from various classes of hardware, for instance modems and printers. More information about device installation and restrictions is found on Microsoft TechNet at http://technet.microsoft.com/en-us/library/cc731478.aspx.

Restricted Groups vs. Group Policy Preferences

Historically, getting users into groups, such as the Administrators groups on the Windows clients, is done using restricted groups in group policies. With the introduction of Group Policy Preferences, you also have the option to assign local administrators via Group Policy preferences (GPPs).

However, if you are using both restricted groups and Group Policy preferences for assigning administrators, it will not work at 100 percent because when the Group Policy settings are being applied, sometimes the GPO preferences will be overridden by the restricted groups. Our recommendation is to use one way or the other to assign users to local groups.

Real World Note: To raise security and protect the sensitive administrator accounts, domain admin accounts, and so forth, many enterprises implement smart cards for these accounts. A two-factor authentication is way better than using only username and password for authentication.

BitLocker

Full-volume encryption for disks is widely used in Windows 7 and later, and it is without a doubt the most popular and most used security feature in the modern Windows client. When using BitLocker in Windows 7, there are some challenges, but you will be glad to hear that Windows 8 solved many of them. The three most common issues with BitLocker in Windows 7 are encryption speed and two PIN code challenges. When looking at managing BitLocker in the enterprise, there are other challenges, such as actually monitoring and pulling out reports on the current BitLocker status on your machines. For that, you will use the MDOP tool Microsoft BitLocker Administration and Monitoring. We delve more into the latter later in this chapter, but let's start with some fundamental BitLocker improvements in the more modern Windows 8 and 8.1 versions of Windows.

BitLocker Now Encrypting Actual Data Only

One of the biggest drawbacks of the BitLocker implementation in previous Windows versions, such as Windows Vista and Windows 7, is that it may take several hours to encrypt a disk with BitLocker because the entire disk (or partition) is encrypted regardless of the amount of data. In Windows 8, a new feature called *Used space only* was introduced. It means that instead of encrypting an entire drive or partition, it encrypts only actual data and then encrypts additional data as it is written to the drive. We must add that performance overhead when running BitLocker is not at all noticeable; however, during encryption, time performance is noticeably slower.

In Windows 8 and later, you can still do full-volume encryption, encrypting the entire drive or partition as in previous Windows versions, but the fact that encrypting only data does not noticeably impact performance means that you can gain a lot of time.

Options for Using BitLocker in Windows

BitLocker in Windows 8 and 8.1 provides three modes for using BitLocker that were available with Windows 7 and adds two new ones. The old ones include TPM, TPM+PIN, and USB key. Using only a USB key is something we strongly recommend against, as it keeps the unlock key on a USB key drive that would always be stored with the machine. That is the equivalent of locking a door and leaving the key in the lock.

Currently, all implementations of BitLocker in any serious enterprise are done by storing the unlock key in a TPM chip, which requires hardware that has a TPM chip. The other option is to store the unlock key in the TPM chip and protect it with a PIN code. In practice, this means that the user has to enter a PIN code to be able to start a machine.

The following combinations are recommended for use with BitLocker in Windows 7 and later:

- **TPM only**. Only a TPM chip is used to house the BitLocker keys. This solution is transparent to the user and a little less secure.

- **TPM + PIN**. TPM used in conjunction with a PIN code. More secure, but it means that a user needs to remember and enter the PIN code before booting. Remote management cannot be performed.

- **Password**. A new protector that can be used for hardware that does not have a TPM chip. The user simply needs to enter a password when booting the machine. This BitLocker variant also is used when encrypting a Windows To Go workspace (USB memory stick) as the key cannot be stored in any TPM chip.

- **TPM + Network unlock (+fall back to PIN)**. The TPM is used in conjunction with network unlock when on the internal network. When outside of the corporate network, it falls back to a PIN code.

Password Protector

Until Windows 8, there was only a really bad way to use BitLocker unless you had a TPM chip, and that was to use the option of having the unlock key stored in a USB memory device. In practice, this means that to boot your machine you need to have the USB key inserted in the machine.

There is one big problem with this. What happens, for instance, if your laptop bag gets stolen? Where is the USB key to unlock the machine stored? Probably it's stored in the bag along with the machine. From a security standpoint, this is really bad.

So, starting with Windows 8, you have the option to use a password to unlock machines that lack a TPM chip. The password can be configured to allow for complexity and length via group policies.

Note: Using the password protector for BitLocker is really used only for lab and testing, and not for any serious BitLocker implementation.

Network Protector

The network protector for BitLocker is totally new and is called Network Unlock. Basically, this means that when booting, you verify, using PXE, to a Windows Deployment Services server that your machine is okay to boot, and it is then unlocked automatically. That is, it is if you are physically connected to your company network. If the machine is moved out of the office, or if the PXE service is not available, you can have it configured so that the user uses a PIN code to unlock the machine when booting it.

This effectively solves the problem with remote or nightly management of machines that have a PIN code requirement, as everything works transparently while the machine is on the internal network.

Note: To use BitLocker Network Unlock, you must have UEFI-enabled machines in native UEFI mode, something that modern Windows 8 certified machines can account for but not older machines, regardless of vendor and model.

PIN Code Change for Standard Users

As mentioned in the preceding section, remote and nightly management of machines previously was a challenge in enterprises using BitLocker with a PIN code. Another problem was that standard users could not change the PIN code. This problem is solved with BitLocker in Windows 8 if you choose to use it with a PIN code.

> **Note**: Using BitLocker with a PIN code is more secure than using it only with a TPM configuration.

Provision BitLocker in WinPE

In all deployments today, you activate BitLocker after the operating system has been installed. One of the really great benefits of Windows 8 and 8.1 is that you can enable BitLocker prior to installing Windows, provisioning BitLocker.

When you enable BitLocker on a drive, which takes only seconds, everything is encrypted on the fly when it is installed. This means little overhead and an encrypted installation the second it is finished.

> **Note**: Provisioning BitLocker in WinPE requires WinPE 4.0 minimum, which is a part of the Windows Assessment and Deployment Kit (ADK).

Windows 8.1 Activates Device Encryption Automatically

In Windows 8.1, Microsoft introduces something called Device Encryption. This is basically BitLocker, but the interesting thing is that it automatically encrypts the drives of Windows 8.1 machines if a number of prerequisites are met.

The following important information can be stated about automatic device encryption on Windows 8.1 machines:

- Prerequisites for Device Encryption is a device that supports "connected standby," has a TPM 2.0 security chip, and supports Secure Boot. To find out whether your hardware has support for connected standby, you can run the following command:

```
Powercfg.exe /availablesleepstates
```

- After Windows 8.1 installation, the encryption is then initialized, using a clear decryption key (i.e. BitLocker in suspended mode).

- If the machine is domain joined and a domain user account is used to log in to the machine, the BitLocker clear key is removed, the key is stored in the TPM chip, and the recovery key is backed up to Active Directory. The GPO setting "Do not enable BitLocker until recovery information is stored in AD DS for operating system" needs to be set for this to take place.

- If a Microsoft Account user account is used to log in to the machine, the clear key is removed and stored in TPM, and the recovery key is backed up to the user's OneDrive account.

In enterprises, this kind of behavior could very well be unwanted. However, the ability to control device encryption is possible only by setting a specific registry value, preferably during deployment time. The registry value PreventDeviceEncryption (REG_DWORD), located under HKEY_LOCAL_MACHINE\SYSTEM\CurrentControlSet\Control\BitLocker, must be set to 1 to prevent device encryption from starting automatically.

Verify Whether Device Encryption Is in Use

You can easily verify whether device encryption is applied to a device. This requires that you perform this check on a physical Windows 8.1 machine:

1. Log in to the **Windows 8.1** device.

2. Go to the **Charms** menu by pressing **Windows logo key** + **C**, or by sweeping in from the right side of the screen.

3. Choose **Settings** / **Change PC settings** / **PC and devices** and then **PC info**. If device encryption is supported and activated, you will find that information here. Otherwise, you will not see any information regarding device encryption whatsoever here.

Activating BitLocker

In the coming step-by-step guides, you install the necessary tools for BitLocker and do the necessary Group Policy configuration.

Install Tool to Verify the BitLocker Recovery Key in Active Directory

First, you start by verifying that the recovery key has been backed up to Active Directory so that if BitLocker should enter recovery mode, you can recover the drive and access the data on it. For this, you need to install the BitLocker Password Recovery Viewer:

1. On **DC01**, log on as **VIAMONSTRA\Administrator**.

2. Start **Server Manager**.

3. Click **Manage** and then **Add Roles and Features**.

4. On the **Before you begin** page, click **Next**.

5. On the **Select installation type** page, click **Next**.

6. On the **Select destination server** page, click **Next**.

7. On the **Select server roles** page, click **Next**.

8. On the **Select features** page, scroll down to **Remote Server Administration Tools** and expand it.

9. Expand **Feature Administration Tools**.

10. Expand **BitLocker Drive Encryption Administration Utilities**.

11. Select **BitLocker Password Recovery Viewer** and then click **Next**.

12. On the **Confirm installation selections** page, click **Install**. Wait a short while and then click **Close** when the installation has finished.

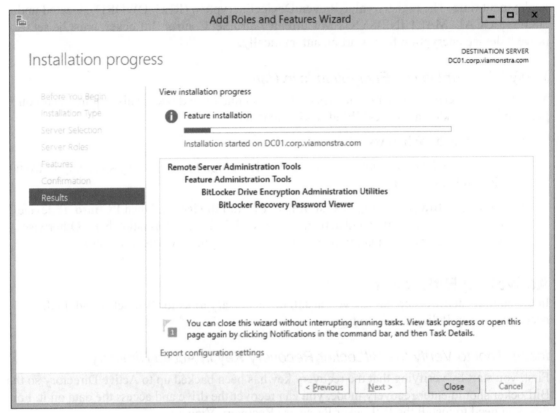

To be able to view the recovery password when or if needed, you need to have the BitLocker Recovery Password Viewer installed on at least one machine.

Set the Group Policy Settings for Using BitLocker

To activate BitLocker, you first need to configure some necessary Group Policy settings to account, for instance, for backing up the recovery key to Active Directory. To activate BitLocker for use with the new password protector key, you need to change a couple of more Group Policy settings.

1. On **DC01**, log on as **VIAMONSTRA\Administrator**.

2. Using the **Group Policy Management** console, edit the **Workstation Configuration** group policy.

3. In the **Computer Configuration / Polices / Administrative Templates / Windows Components / BitLocker Drive Encryption / Operating System Drives** node, configure the following:

> **Note**: In this procedure, you make sure that the recovery information needed to unlock the drive exists in Active Directory. The recovery password is needed if the password for unlocking BitLocker is lost or the machine has entered BitLocker recovery mode. If you do not save this information, all the data on the drive will be lost if the drive becomes locked.

   a. Enable the **Configure use of hardware-based encryption for operating system drives** policy.

   b. Enable the **Configure use of password operating system drives** policy, and for **Configure password complexity for operating system drives**, select **Require password complexity**.

   c. Enable the **Require additional authentication at startup** policy.

   d. Enable the **Choose how BitLocker-protected operating system drives can be recovered** policy, and in that policy select **Do not enable BitLocker until recovery information is stored to AD DS for operating system drives**.

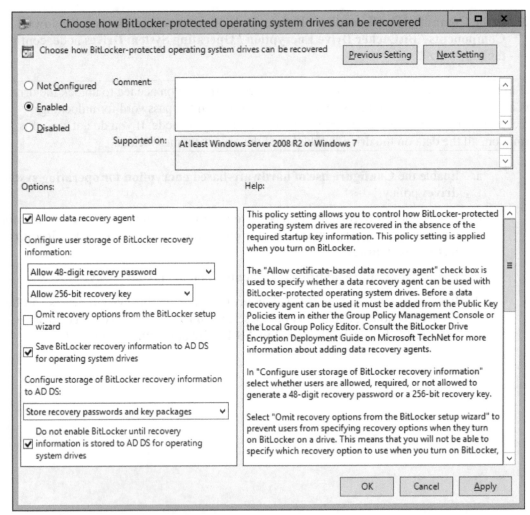

There are quite a few Group Policy options to configure for BitLocker. One of the most important ones states that the recovery key is backed up to Active Directory. That is the master key and must be saved if you at some point in time need to be able to unlock and access the encrypted data.

BitLocker on a Physical Machine

In the virtual lab environment for ViaMonstra, we cannot demonstrate the real-world use of BitLocker because, as mentioned before, that requires a TPM chip, which is not available for virtual machines using todays virtualization engines. So, to follow this guide, you need to connect a physical Windows 7, 8, or 8.1 machine to the VIAMONSTRA domain to proceed.

Note: As this step requires a physical machine, you do not have to perform the lab, but you will benefit from real-world information in the coming steps.

1. Join a physical machine (that has a TPM security chip 1.2 or later) running Windows 7, 8, or 8.1 to the **VIAMONSTRA** domain. You need to make sure that the TPM (or security chip as it is often referenced) in BIOS/UEFI is on and activated/enabled.

2. Start the **BitLocker Drive Encryption** control panel.

3. For the **Operating system drive**, click **Turn on BitLocker**. That starts the wizard that takes you through encrypting the drive.

4. On the **Choose how to unlock your drive at startup** page, choose **Let BitLocker automatically unlock my drive**.

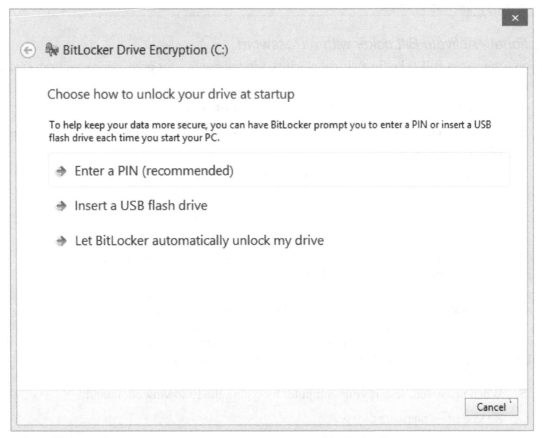

When all BitLocker prerequisites are met, you can enable BitLocker.

5. On the **How do you want to back up your recovery key** page, make sure that you save or print the key before clicking **Next** to proceed.

> **Note**: As you have previously set the Group Policy option that encryption will not be possible until the key has been backed up, you are pretty safe, but rather safe than sorry when working with BitLocker.

6. On the **Choose how much of your drive to encrypt** page, use the default options to encrypt only actual data and click **Next**.

7. On the **Are you ready to encrypt this drive** page, clear the **Run BitLocker system check** check box and click **Start encrypting**. Encryption now starts. It will take some time to finish, up to an hour or more depending on the amount of data and the speed of the hard drive.

> **Note**: You can restart a machine before it has fully encrypted the drive. To see the actual progress then, you can run fvenotify.exe to start the taskbar application that indicates whether BitLocker drive encryption is in progress.

Optional - Activate BitLocker with a Password

If you want to test BitLocker in a virtual machine (do *not* use this for production), you can enable the password protector.

1. On **PC0002**, log on as **VIAMONSTRA\Administrator**.

2. Press the **Windows logo key + R**, type **gpupdate**, and press **Enter**. Wait for the group policy update to finish.

3. Start an elevated **PowerShell prompt** (run as administrator) and run the following command:

```
Enable-BitLocker C: -PasswordProtector -Password $pw
-UsedSpaceOnly
```

4. When prompted, type the password **P@ssw0rd** and press **Enter**. Repeat entering the password once more and press **Enter** again.

> **Real World Note**: If you enable BitLocker with a password, you cannot back up the recovery keys, which means that if the information is lost, you cannot recover it if you or the user lose the drive password. Therefore, use BitLocker with a password with caution and remember that BitLocker together with a TPM chip is the recommended way to use BitLocker.

5. When prompted, restart your computer by typing the following command:

```
Restart-Computer
```

6. While PC0002 is restarting, it prompts you for a password. Enter the password you entered in step 3 to continue the boot. The encryption takes some time to finish. Watch the progress via the utility in the notification area and then take a coffee break until the encryption is done.

> **Note**: BitLocker used to be managed by using manage-bde in Windows Vista and Windows 7, but in Windows 8 and later, you also can use PowerShell cmdlets to control BitLocker. You can find more information on PowerShell in Chapter 11.

Verify the BitLocker Password

Now that the tool is installed, you can check to see whether the key has actually been backed up to Active Directory.

1. On **DC01**, start the **Active Directory Users and Computers** console.

2. Look up the computer account for the physical computer on which you enabled BitLocker, or PC0002 if you did enable BitLocker on the virtual PC0002 machine; then right-click it and choose **Properties**.

3. Click the **BitLocker Recovery** tab. Here you find the recovery key(s) for that particular machine, which is used in case you need to recover the drive or it enters recovery mode.

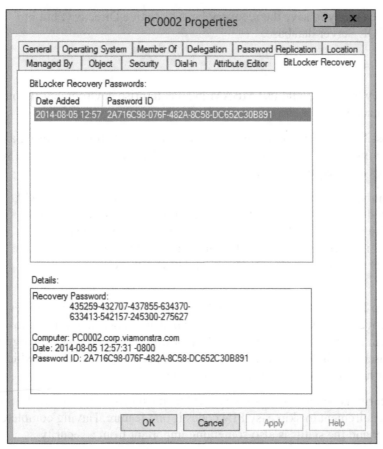

The recovery keys are backed up to Active Directory under the computer account. It keeps history if you enable and disable BitLocker multiple times during the machine's lifetime.

Enterprise Management of BitLocker

As mentioned earlier in the chapter, there are a few shortcomings when you use BitLocker without MBAM. The benefits of using MBAM are that you get full status information and reporting so you can see which machines are encrypted. In a normal BitLocker deployment, you can force the encryption during deployment, but there is no way to verify the status or enforce BitLocker encryption on machines.

One of the concerns with BitLocker is that once you hand out the recovery key to a remote user who is having problems booting the machine, you cannot reset the recovery key. That means the user may write it down because it contains 48 digits. With MBAM, the recovery key is automatically reset after you have unlocked a machine.

In the traditional BitLocker scenario, you save the recovery keys to Active Directory; but in MBAM, you save them to a SQL Server database.

Features of MBAM

There are a number of reasons why you should use MBAM in an enterprise environment if you are using BitLocker on your machines:

- **Automation**. It is possible to encrypt machines automatically with BitLocker during a new deployment or for machines already running. The MBAM agent, in combination with group policies, handles the encryption on the clients.

- **Compliance and reporting**. You can pull reports and compliance data from MBAM, which gives you a good overview on the status of machines using BitLocker. This is particularly good in the not so unlikely event that a machine is lost or stolen. From a security perspective, it is indeed very good to be able to confirm via reports that at the time when the machine was lost or stolen it actually did have BitLocker protection enabled and working.

- **Self-Service and Help Desk Portals**. When a machine enters recovery mode, the user needs the 48-digit recovery password to unlock the machine and proceed booting into Windows. The user can get the recovery password from a web site, rather than having to call helpdesk. If the user calls helpdesk, there is a custom-made Help Desk Portal which makes it very easy for helpdesk staff to retrieve the recovery keys.

- **Security**. Overall security is better when using MBAM than using a traditional BitLocker deployment. A PIN requirement to skip easy PIN codes is one feature. Having complete control over BitLocker and the status is also something important from a security standpoint.

- **System Center Configuration Manager integration**. You can integrate MBAM into System Center Configuration Manager to get reports and status on BitLocker on your clients along with all the other reports.

Preparing to Install MBAM

Although MBAM can be installed stand-alone, ViaMonstra has System Center Configuration Manager in place, so you integrate MBAM into Configuration Manager. However, there are some prerequisites that need to be done to make MBAM work optimally with Configuration Manager.

Modify and Create Necessary MOF Files

For MBAM compliance to work, you need to modify both Configuration.mof and create SMS_def.mof. Instructions on how to modify Configuration.mof can be found at http://technet.microsoft.com/en-us/library/dn645321.aspx, and the instructions to create SMS_def.mof can be found at http://technet.microsoft.com/en-us/library/dn656927.aspx. Make sure that you prepare these steps before proceeding in the following step-by-step guides.

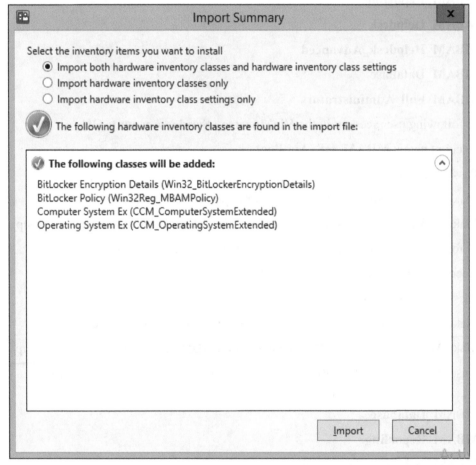

When importing the contents from SMS_def.mof, you get support for BitLocker reporting.

Create Groups and Accounts Used by MBAM

MBAM needs quite a few groups and accounts for optimal configuration in terms of access to the different components and data. Before installing and configuring MBAM, you create these groups and accounts.

1. On **DC01**, log on as **VIAMONSTRA\Administrator**.

2. Start the **Active Directory Users and Computers** console.

3. Create global security groups with the following group names in the **ViaMonstra / Security Groups** OU:

    o **MBAM_Compliance_Read**

    o **MBAM_Reporting**

    o **MBAM_Helpdesk**

    o **MBAM_Helpdesk_Advanced**

    o **MBAM_Database**

    o **MBAM_Full_Administrators**

4. Create the following user account in the **ViaMonstra / Service Accounts** OU:

    a. Account name: **MBAM_IIS_AppPool**

    b. Password: **P@ssw0rd**

    c. Make sure that only the **Password never expires** check box is selected.

    d. Make **MBAM_IIS_AppPool** a member of the **MBAM_Database** security group.

5. Create the following user account in the **ViaMonstra / Service Accounts** OU:

    a. Account name: **MBAM_Reports_RW**

    b. Password: **P@ssw0rd**

    c. Make sure that only the **Password never expires** check box is selected.

    d. Make **MBAM_Reports_RW** a member of the **MBAM_Database** security group.

6. Make the user **VIAMONSTRA\Administrator** a member of the following security groups:

    o **MBAM_Database**

    o **MBAM_Reporting**

    o **MBAM_Helpdesk_Advanced**

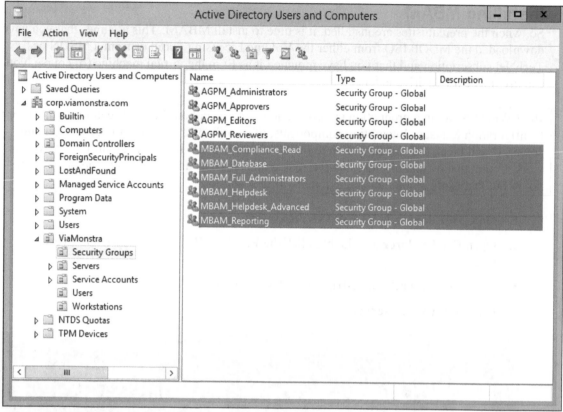

When the MBAM groups are created, it should look like this.

Install Prerequisites for MBAM Server Components

You also need to install a couple of additional components that are used by MBAM. In this guide
we assume you have download Microsoft ASP.NET MVC 4.0 Runtime from
http://www.microsoft.com/en-us/download/details.aspx?id=30683 to CM01.
 Second, make sure that you install the .NET Framework 4.5 features HTTP Activation and TCP
Activation. These feature are found under .NET Framework 4.5 Features / WCF Services in the
Add Roles and Features wizard.

1. On **CM01**, log on as **VIAMONSTRA\Administrator**.

2. Install the **Microsoft ASP.NET MVC 4.0 Runtime** using default settings.

3. Using **Server Manager**, install the .NET Framework 4.5 features **HTTP Activation** and
   TCP Activation. These feature are found under **.NET Framework 4.5 Features / WCF
   Services** in **the Add Roles and Features** wizard.

Installing MBAM

So, when the prerequisites are installed, it is time to install MBAM. This assumes that you have downloaded the MDOP ISO from either the Volume Licensing portal or from a MSDN or TechNet subscription and that you have mounted it as E: in the virtual machine (of course, you can use the next free drive letter).

> **Real World Note**: In a production environment, do not install the MBAM features (except for the Configuration Manager Integration components, of course) on a Configuration Manager site server. It will break the authentication to the distribution point. In the lab environment, we can work around that by making sure that we enable anonymous authentication to the distribution point, but that is not recommended in a real-world scenario.

1. On **CM01**, log on as **VIAMONSTRA\Administrator**.

2. Open **File Explorer** and double-click the **E:** drive. This opens the MDOP overview screen.

3. Click **BitLocker Administration and Monitoring**.

4. Click **MBAM 2.5 Server**.

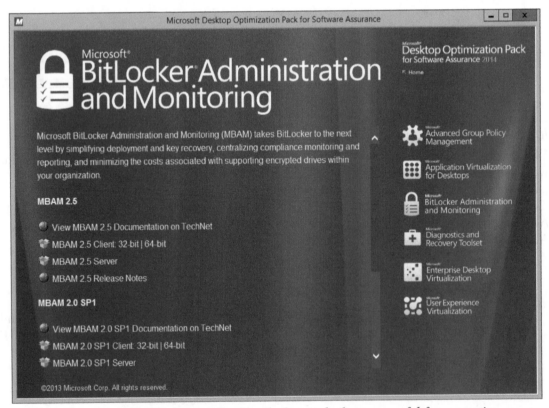

MBAM is a part of MDOP along with a lot of other tools that are useful for managing Windows clients in the enterprise.

5. On the **Welcome to the BitLocker Administration and Monitoring Setup Wizard** page, click **Next**.

6. On the **End-User License Agreement Terms** page, select **I accept the terms in the License Agreement** and click **Next**.

7. On the **Microsoft Update** page, select **Do not use Microsoft Update** and click **Next**.

8. On the **Customer Experience Improvement Program** page, select **Do not join the program at this time** and click **Next**.

9. On the **Begin the Installation** page, click **Install**. Click **Yes** on the UAC prompt.

10. When finished, click **Finish** to start the configuration.

Configure System Center Integration for MBAM

1. If not already started from the previous step-by-step guide, start **MBAM Server Configuration** by searching for it on the **Start screen**.

2. On the **Welcome to the configuration wizard for Microsoft BitLocker Administration and Monitoring** page, click **Add New Features**.

3. On the **Select Features to Add** page, select **System Center Configuration Manager Integration** and click **Next**.

4. On the **Check Prerequisites** page, click **Next**.

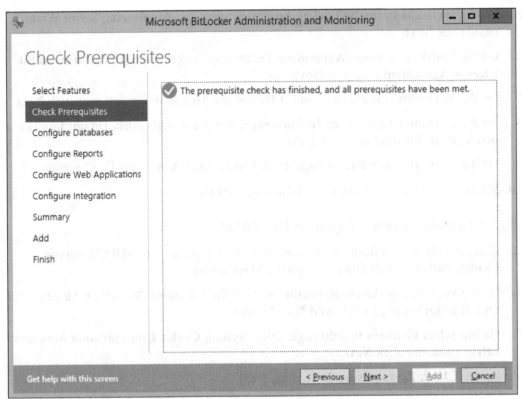

Note that the prerequisites check only checks for the installed MVC runtime and .NET features mentioned in the earlier prerequisites section. The check for MOF files or that configuration is not performed.

5. On the **Configure Integration** page, in the **SQL Server Reporting Services server:** text box, type in **CM01.corp.viamonstra.com** and click **Next**.

6. On the **Summary** page, click **Add**.

7. On the **Finish** page, click **Close**.

> **Note**: Installing the System Center Integration features add a few things into the ConfigMgr console as you will notice. For instance, there are new collections for MBAM, as well as new configuration items. Also, the compliance reports are installed, which is why the Reporting role is required to install the System Center integration features.

Configure the MBAM Database Server Components

1. On **CM01**, start **MBAM Server Configuration** by searching for it on the **Start screen**.

2. On the **Welcome to the configuration wizard for Microsoft BitLocker Administration and Monitoring** page, click **Add New Features**.

3. On the **Select Features to Add** page, select **Compliance and Audit Database** and **Recovery Database** and click **Next**.

4. On the **Check Prerequisites** page, click **Next**.

5. On the **Configure Databases** page, enter the following settings and click **Next**:

    a. For **Compliance and Audit database**:

        ▪ SQL Server name: **CM01.corp.viamonstra.com**

        ▪ Read/write access domain user or group:
           VIAMONSTRA\MBAM_Database

        ▪ Read-only access domain user or group:
           VIAMONSTRA\MBAM_Compliance_Read

    b. For **Recovery database**:

        ▪ SQL Server name: **CM01.corp.viamonstra.com**

        ▪ Read/write access domain user or group:
           VIAMONSTRA\MBAM_Database

6. On the **Summary** page, review the configuration and then click **Add**. Wait for the databases to be created.

7. On the **Finish** page, click **Close**.

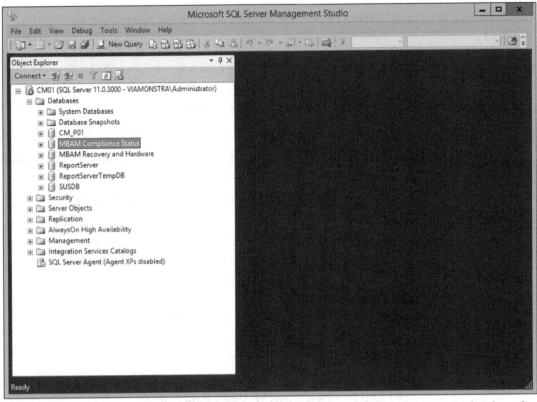

Using Microsoft SQL Server Management Studio, you can verify that the MBAM database has been created correctly.

Configure MBAM Reports

Before proceeding with configuring MBAM websites, you need to have the reports in place.

1. On **CM01**, start **MBAM Server Configuration** by searching for it on the **Start screen**.

2. On the **Welcome to the configuration wizard for Microsoft BitLocker Administration and Monitoring** page, click **Add New Features**.

3. On the **Select Features to Add** page, check **Reports** and click **Next**.

4. On the **Check Prerequisites** page, click **Next**.

5. On the **Configure Reports** page, enter the following information and then click **Next**:

    a. Reporting role domain group: **MBAM_Reporting**

    b. SQL Server name: **CM01.corp.viamonstra.com**

    c. User name: **VIAMONSTRA\MBAM_Reports_RW**

    d. Password: **P@ssw0rd**

    e. Confirm password: **P@ssw0rd**

6. On the **Summary** page, click **Add** and then wait for the report components to be installed.

7. On the **Finish** page, click **Close**.

Configure MBAM Websites

The last components on the server side that we need to configure are the websites. This includes the Help Desk Portal, as well as web services that the Windows clients use to communicate their status.

> **Note**: Typically, not all the MBAM roles should be installed on the same server as the Configuration Manager primary site server. For instance, the Help Desk and Self-Service Portals will cause problems with the Configuration Manager management point due to conflicting IIS ports. In this guide, we designate other ports than the default port 80 for demonstration purposes.

1. On **CM01**, start **MBAM Server Configuration** by searching for it on the **Start screen**.

2. On the **Welcome to the configuration wizard for Microsoft BitLocker Administration and Monitoring** page, click **Add New Features**.

3. On the **Select Features to Add** page, select **Administration and Monitoring Website** and click **Next**.

4. On the **Check Prerequisites** page, click **Next**.

5. On the **Configure Web Applications** page, configure the following information and then click **Next**:

   a. Select the check box **Do not use a certificate**.

   b. Port: **81**

   c. Web service application pool domain account: **VIAMONSTRA\MBAM_IIS_AppPool**

   d. Password: **P@ssw0rd**

   e. Confirm password: **P@ssw0rd**

   f. SQL Server name (for the compliance and audit database): **CM01.corp.viamonstra.com**

   g. SQL Server name (for the recovery database): **CM01.corp.viamonstra.com**

   h. Advanced Helpdesk role domain group: **VIAMONSTRA\MBAM_Helpdesk_Advanced**

   i. Helpdesk role domain group: **VIAMONSTRA\MBAM_Helpdesk**

   j. Select the **Use System Center Configuration Manager Integration** check box.

   k. Reporting role domain group: **VIAMONSTRA\MBAM_Reporting**

   l. SQL Server Reporting Services URL: **http://cm01/ReportServer**

6. On the **Summary** page, click **Add** and wait for the websites to be installed.

7. On the **Finish** page review the notes, and then click **Close**.

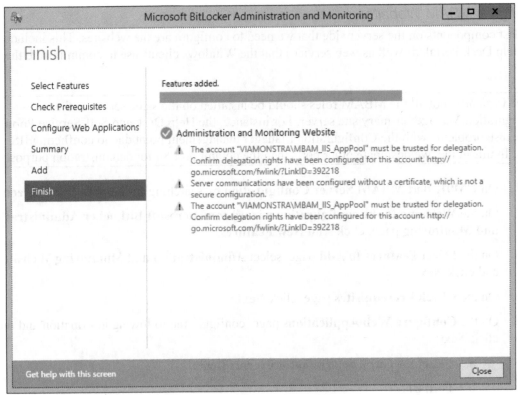

The account you just added for the application pool must be trusted for delegation.

Verify That the MBAM Components Are in Place

Now that all server components are installed and configured, it is time to actually see the result. You check this in two steps, both the Help Desk Portal and the System Center Configuration Manager integration.

1. On **CM01**, log on as **VIAMONSTRA\Administrator**, and launch the **ConfigMgr console** if it is not already started.

2. In the **Assets and Compliance** workspace, click **Device Collections**. Notice the **MBAM Supported Computers** collection which has been automatically created.

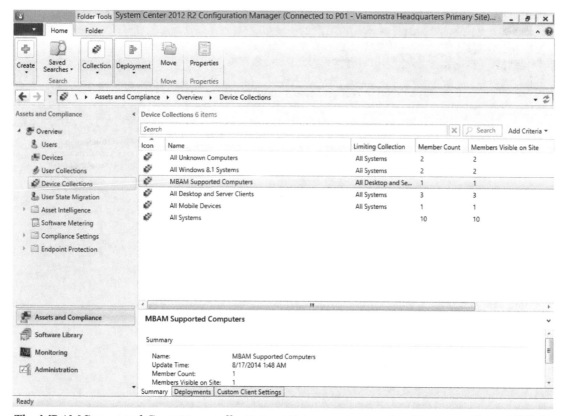

The MBAM Supported Computers collection contains computers that have an activated TPM chip which is not a virtual machine.

Note: Before the new hardware settings you configured earlier will appear in the MBAM Supported Computers collection, the client needs to receive them and perform a hardware inventory. The same applies to the MBAM reports that you use later in this chapter.

3. Expand **Compliance Settings** and click **Configuration Items**. Note the two new configuration items for MBAM.

4. Last, but not least, click the **Monitoring** tab and then expand **Reporting** / **Reports** / **MBAM**. Click the **en-us** node and note the MBAM reports that have been created.

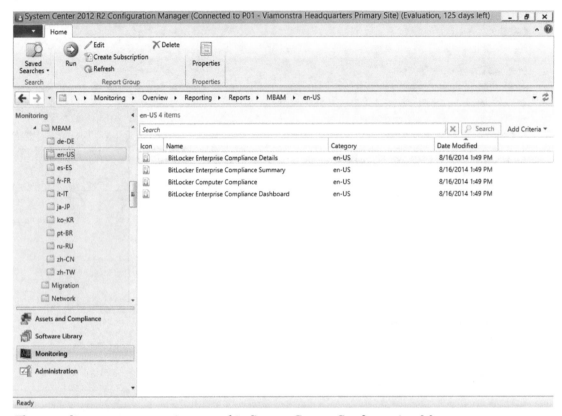

The compliance reports are integrated in System Center Configuration Manager.

5. Now start **Internet Explorer** and browse to
    http://cm01.corp.viamonstra.com:81/HelpDesk.

6. Log in with the **Administrator** account in the **VIAMONSTRA** domain.

7. Click around and see what you can do in the Help Desk Portal.

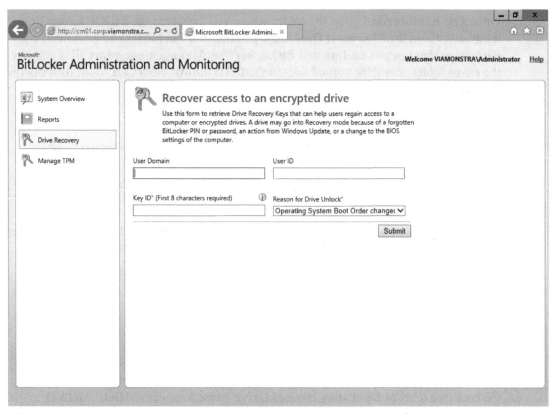

The Help Desk Portal is where you fetch the recovery keys when needed.

Make MBAM_Database SYSADMIN on the SQL Database

To successfully recover the recovery keys, you must make sure that the MBAM_Database account is the sysadmin on the SQL Server.

1. On **CM01**, start **SQL Server Management Studio**.

2. On the login page, make sure that **Database Engine**, **CM01** and **Windows Authentication** are selected and then click **Connect**.

3. Expand **Security** / **Logins** and double-click **VIAMONSTRA\MBAM_Database**.

4. Choose **Server Roles**, and then select **sysadmin**. Then click **OK** and close **SQL Server Management Studio**.

Add Group Policy Templates for MBAM

MBAM has its own settings for BitLocker. First, you must download the MDOP Group Policy templates from http://www.microsoft.com/en-us/download/details.aspx?id=41183, and second, you need to copy the GPO templates to your SYSVOL share.

1. On **DC01**, download the GPO templates from the preceding link and extract them to a location of your choice on the C: drive.

2. Open **File Explorer** and go to the folder where you extracted the MDOP Group Policy templates. From the **Microsoft Desktop Optimization Pack\MBAM 2.5** folder, copy the **BitLockerManagement.admx** and **BitLockerUserManagement.admx** files along with the **en-us** folder. Paste the copied files in the **C:\Windows\SYSVOL\domain\Policies\ PolicyDefinitions** folder.

Configure MBAM Settings via Group Policies

Now it is time to configure the group policies to for the clients to report the recovery key to MBAM.

1. On **DC01**, start the **Group Policy Management** console, and edit the **Workstation Configuration** GPO.

2. Expand **Computer Configuration / Policies / Administrative Templates / Windows Components / MDOP MBAM (BitLocker Management) / Client Management**.

3. Open the **Configure MBAM services** setting and set it to **Enabled**. Then set the following parameters after which you click **OK**:

   a. MBAM Recovery service endpoint:
      http://cm01.corp.viamonstra.com:81/MBAMRecoveryAndHardwareService/ CoreService.svc

   b. Configure MBAM Status reporting service: **Disabled**

4. Go back one level to **Operating System Drive** located beneath **MDOP MBAM (BitLocker Management)**.

5. Open the **Operating system drive encryption settings** setting and set it to **Enabled**. Then click **OK**.

> **Note**: MBAM Status reporting service endpoint does not need to be configured as we manage the compliance reports in Configuration Manager and not in the stand-alone MBAM Administration console. The setting to allow BitLocker on machines without a TPM chip is so that we can use it with MBAM on a virtual machine.

Modify the MBAM Supported Computers Collection

If you want to get the reports for a virtual machine encrypted using BitLocker you must modify the criteria for the MBAM Supported Computers collection. Typically it has all virtual machines excluded.

1. On **CM01**, open the **ConfigMgr console** if it is not already open.

2. In the **Assets and Compliance** workspace, select **Device Collections**.

3. Modify the collection **MBAM Supported Computers** by right-clicking it and choosing **Properties**.

4. Click the **Membership Rules** tab and then **Edit / Edit Query Statement / Criteria**.

5. Scroll down to **Computer System.Model is not in...** and double-click that line.

6. In the **Criterion Properties** dialog box, select the row for the virtualization platform you are using and then choose **Remove**. Then click **OK** four times.

7. Right-click the collection **MBAM Support Computers**, choose **Update Membership**, and answer **Yes** in the message box that appears. Now the virtual machine is visible.

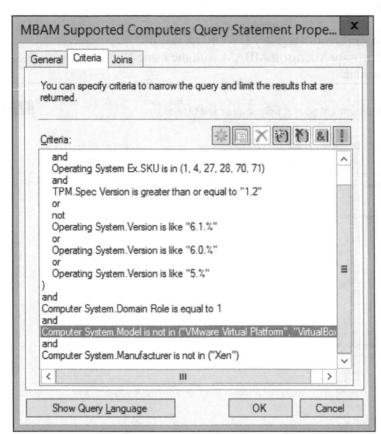

Modifying the criteria for the MBAM collection is required if you want virtual machines to appear in that particular collection.

Install the MBAM Agent on PC0002 and the Physical Machine

To install the MBAM agent, you must have access to the MDOP ISO containing the MBAM agent. You must make the content of that ISO available on PC0002 and have it available on the physical machine on which you enabled BitLocker in the "BitLocker" section of this chapter.

1. On **PC0002**, log on as **VIAMONSTRA\Administrator**.

2. Open **File Explorer** and go to the drive letter where you have mounted or placed the contents of the MDOP ISO and run **MbamClientSetup.exe** from the folder **D:\MBAM\Installers\2.5\x64**.

3. On the **License Terms** page, select **I accept** and click **Next**. The installation proceeds silently and finishes without user interaction.

4. Verify that the MBAM agent has been installed by going to the control panel and confirming that you have an icon for **BitLocker Encryption Options**.

5. Repeat the MBAM agent installation steps 1–4 on the physical machine on which you have enabled BitLocker.

Note: To speed up MBAM, you can create a registry DWORD-value in HKEY_LOCAL_MACHINE\Software\Microsoft\MBAM with the name NoStartupDelay and set it to 1. After that, restart the machine.

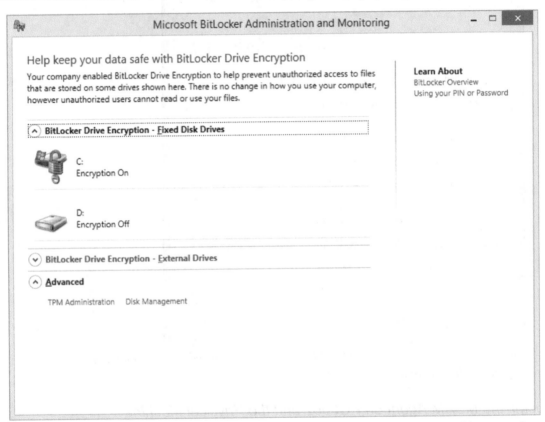

When installing the MBAM agent, a new BitLocker control panel appears, in addition to the existing one.

MBAM Compliance Reports in Configuration Manager

Now you explore the available reports:

1. On **CM01**, start the **ConfigMgr console** if it is not already started.

2. In the **Monitoring** workspace, expand **Reporting** / **Reports** / **MBAM** / **en-us**.

3. Click through the reports and see what they contain.

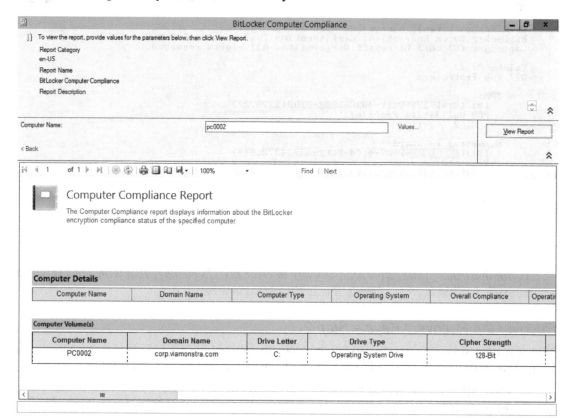

The compliance reports that are integrated in System Center Configuration Manager let you see all details on the machines, such as whether encryption is active.

Recover the Recovery Keys – Step 1

So, last but not least, you verify that you can actually recover the BitLocker recovery key if and when it's needed. First, you pick out the recovery key so that you can match it to the MBAM database recovery information.

1. On either **PC0002** or the physical machine you enabled BitLocker on, start **cmd.exe** as **Administrator**.

2. In the command prompt, enter the following command:

```
manage-bde -protectors -get c:
```

The information needed to recover the key is located in the ID section below Numerical Password. This ID is the same one that is displayed on the boot screen when BitLocker prevents Windows from starting when it has entered BitLocker recovery mode.

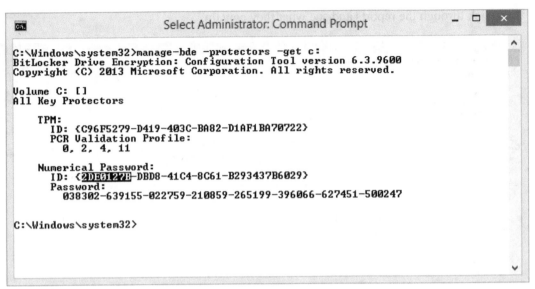

As Administrator, you see the recovery key in clear text. Remember that with MBAM, when a recovery key has been used once, it is updated to a new one.

Recover the Recovery Keys – Step 2

Now it is time to verify that you can get the recovery key out of MBAM. This is done using the Help Desk Portal, but it also could be done by the user via the Self-Service Portal.

1. On **CM01**, start **Internet Explorer** and browse to **http://cm01.corp.viamonstra.com:81/Helpdesk**.

2. Click **Drive Recovery**, enter the first eight characters of the ID retrieved in the preceding section, and click **Submit**.

3. You now are presented with the recovery key, and in a real-world scenario, you click **Done**. Before doing that, verify that the recovery key is the same as on the client from which you retrieved the ID.

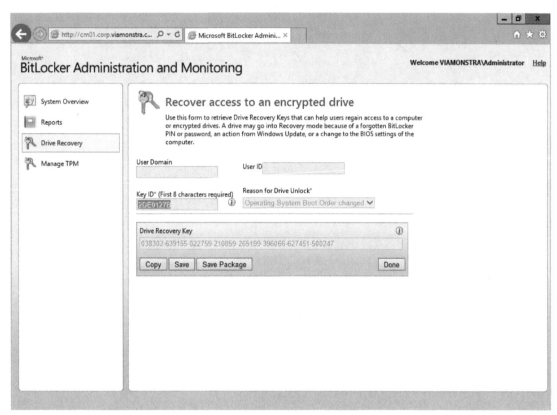

In the Help Desk Portal, you can easily retrieve the recovery keys.

Chapter 9

Remote Access and Mobility

Users are becoming more and more mobile, and as those types of users increase, we need more and better ways to support the mobility and remote access for these users. Pushing out VPN and Wi-Fi profiles is one thing you can do to ease their lives. Letting your users use Windows To Go is also a way of improving their mobile work experience.

VPN Profiles

With Windows 8.1, Microsoft worked with the major VPN vendors to provide inbox support for third-party VPN solutions. Specifically, the built-in VPN providers are Juniper Pulse, F5 Edge Point, Dell SonicWall, and Check Point VPN. These can be added manually in Windows 8.1, but using Configuration Manager gives you the option not only to distribute the VPN profiles to these types of machines, but also to deploy VPN profiles to iOS devices, as well as for Windows RT 8.1. Additionally, for iOS devices, System Center Configuration Manager can deploy Cisco AnyConnect VPN profiles.

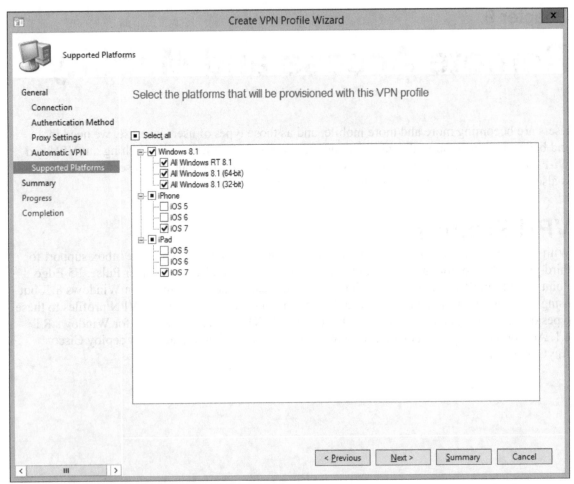

When creating a VPN profile in Configuration Manager, you can target that to specific devices, at the time of this writing, including Windows 8.1 and iOS devices.

Create a VPN Profile Using Configuration Manager

Following a simple demonstration, you create a VPN connection using Configuration Manager:

1. On **CM01**, log on as **VIAMONSTRA\Administrator**.

2. Start the **ConfigMgr console**.

3. In the **Assets and Compliance** workspace, expand **Compliance Settings** and then **Company Resource Access**, and click **VPN Profiles**.

4. On the ribbon, click **Create VPN Profile** to start the VPN profile-creating wizard.

5. On the **General** page, enter the name **ViaMonstra VPN Connection** and click **Next**.

6. In the **Connection Type** drop-down list, choose **Microsoft Automatic** and complete the following:

   Click the **Add** button, enter the Friendly name **Dummy** and the FQDN name **dummy.corp.viamonstra.com**, and then click **OK**.

7. In the **Connection specific DNS suffix** input field, enter **dummy.viamonstra.com** and then click **Next**.

8. On the **Authentication Method** page, click **Next**.

9. On the **Proxy Settings** page, click **Next**.

10. On the **Automatic VPN** page, click **Next**.

11. On the **Support Platforms** page, select **Windows 8.1** and click **Next**.

12. On the **Summary** page, click **Next**.

13. On the **Completion** page, click **Close**.

Deploy the VPN Profile to Devices

Last but not least, you deploy the VPN profiles to a collection:

1. Right-click the VPN profile named **ViaMonstra VPN Connection** and choose **Deploy**.

2. In the **Deploy VPN Profile** dialog box, click the **Browse** button next to **Collection**.

3. In the **Select Collection** dialog box, select the collection **All Users** and then click **OK** twice.

Now the VPN profile will be added to Windows 8.1 devices, and it will be found in the Network / Connection settings in PC settings.

Wi-Fi Profiles

Wi-Fi profiles in System Center Configuration Manager work pretty much the same as VPN profiles, and you can also use Configuration Manager to deploy Wi-Fi profiles to your devices. That includes Windows 8.1 and RT 8.1 devices, as well as iOS and Android devices.

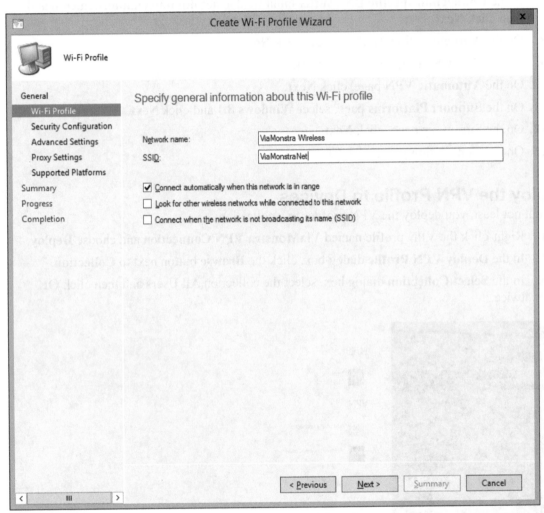

Adding and deploying Wi-Fi profiles to your client machine is easy in Configuration Manager 2012 R2.

Windows To Go

Imagine not having to bring your laptop everywhere. Imagine having your personalized installation of Windows 8.1 on a USB memory stick. That is what Windows To Go delivers. It provides the exact same experience as a traditional Windows installed on a hard drive, only this installation is done on a USB memory stick and thereby is a lot more mobile. The end user can plug the USB memory stick into virtually any computer (with limitations, discussed shortly) and boot from the USB memory stick and have their own workspace.

Using Configuration Manager, you can provision Windows To Go to your end users so that they can create their own Windows To Go workspaces.

Windows Store Now Enabled by Default

With Windows 8, the Windows Store is inactivated by default on all Windows To Go workspaces. This is because apps are tied to the physical hardware and each app is allowed to be tied to only five physical machines at a time. With Windows To Go in Windows 8.1, the Store is actually enabled by default. The reason for this is that the previous limitation of installing apps on five machines is now 81 machines. We really doubt that anyone will hit the roof of that limit.

Requirements

To start with, Windows To Go is a feature that comes with Windows 8 and 8.1 Enterprise. When it comes to hardware requirements, Windows To Go is supported only on USB 3.0 devices that are certified for Windows To Go. You cannot simply take any USB memory stick and use it with Windows To Go. That is because you need a drive that reports as a fixed drive in Windows. A typical USB memory stick reports as a removable drive and cannot be partitioned, which is required to use a Windows To Go workspace on machines running in UEFI or BIOS mode.

When Windows To Go was launched with Windows 8, not many devices were certified for Windows To Go, but the list has constantly grown since then. A list of all certified devices to use for Windows To Go is available from Microsoft TechNet at http://technet.microsoft.com/en-us/library/hh831833.aspx#wtg_hardware. As of Windows 8.1, there is now support for devices that have integrated storage as well as a smart card.

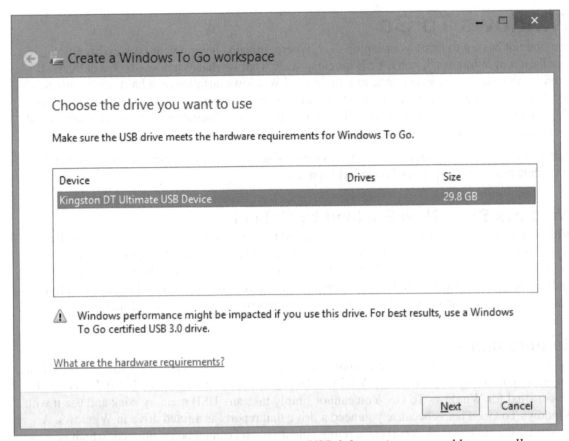

Running Windows To Go on a USB 3.0 device on a USB 2.0 port is supported because all hardware doesn't support booting using the USB 3.0 port.

Note: Windows To Go can definitely be used on USB hard disk drives for demonstration or proof of concept but not for production use.

Windows To Go is designed to work with KMS (Key Management Server) or ADBA (Active Directory Based Activation). Although Windows To Go technically works with MAK activation keys, that is not recommended because MAK keys are tied to the hardware. If a device moves around from one piece of hardware to another, there are obvious problems because your MAK keys will run out pretty fast.

Real World Note: During the Windows 8 beta stage, we (twice) did a three-hour presentation on Windows 8, running on Windows To Go. We ran demos and had three virtual machines running on a four-year old USB 2.0 5400 RPM hard drive. It became a little hot, but it worked like a charm and performance did not suffer noticeably in any way. The point is that Windows To Go works with old drives, but it works even better with certified drives that are USB 3.0. And remember that only certified devices are supported by Microsoft.

What About Security?

It is no secret that USB memory sticks are very small and tend to have feet, so they are often lost. Windows To Go on USB memory sticks is no different, and to account for lost USB memory sticks possibly containing sensitive information, you can use BitLocker with the new password protector to protect the content on the USB memory stick.

Another security feature is that by default you are not able to access the drives of host (physical) machine when using the Windows To Go workspace on that machine. It is recommended to keep it that way, but you can change that by setting a different SAN policy.

How to Create a Windows To Go Workspace

With the Windows To Go tool that is built in to Windows 8 and 8.1 Enterprise, you can create a workspace that enables you to stage your Windows To Go drives to USB devices. Using System Center 2012 Configuration Manager with Service Pack 1 and R2, it is possible to let the users provision their own Windows To Go workspaces. That is the method that ViaMonstra will be using.

In these guides, you will perform a number of steps:

Step 1: Prepare a package for BitLocker

Step 2: Prepare a task sequence.

Step 3: Deploy the task sequence.

Step 4: Create the image used when creating the Windows To Go workspace.

Step 5: Deploy Windows To Go to your users.

Step 6: Users create their own Windows To Go workspace.

Prepare a BitLocker Package for Windows To Go

In this step, you create a package in Configuration Manager that contains the BitLocker for Windows To Go tools. That ensures that BitLocker is enabled on the Windows To Go workspace when done.

1. On **CM01**, log on as **VIAMONSTRA\Administrator**.

2. In the **ConfigMgr console**, in the **Software Library** workspace, expand **Application Management**, and click **Packages**.

3. Click **Create Package** on the ribbon.

4. On the **Package** page, enter the name **BitLocker for Windows To Go**, and then select the **This package contains source files** check box. Click the **Browse** button.

5. In the **Set Source Folder** dialog box, select **Local folder on site server** and enter the source folder **C:\Program Files\Microsoft Configuration Manager\OSD\Tools\WTG\BitLocker**; then click **OK**, followed by **Next**.

6. On the **Program Type** page, select **Do not create a program** and click **Next**.

7. On the **Summary** page, click **Next**.

8. Next, right-click the **BitLocker for Windows To Go** package and choose **Distribute Content**.

9. On the **General** page, click **Next**.

10. On the **Content Destination** page, click **Add / Distribution Point**, select **CM01.CORP.VIAMONSTRA.COM**, and then click **OK** and **Next**.

11. On the **Summary** page, click **Next**.

12. On the **Completion** page, click **Close**.

Prepare the Task Sequence for Windows To Go

The BitLocker package you created in the preceding section must be run at some point in time, and that would be during OS installation when installing it to the Windows To Go USB memory stick.

1. On **CM01**, using the **ConfigMgr console**, in the **Software Library** workspace, expand **Operating Systems**, and click **Task Sequences**.

2. Right-click the **Task Sequence** named **Windows 8.1 Enterprise Edition (x64)** and choose **Edit**.

3. Scroll down until you find **Setup Windows and ConfigMgr**. Click that line and then click the **Add** button, followed by **General / Run Command Line**. Then enter the following information:

    o   Name: **Enable BitLocker for Windows To Go**

    o   Command line: **x64\osdbitlocker_wtg.exe /Enable /pwd:AD /wait:FALSE**

    o   Package: **BitLocker for Windows To Go**

4. Now click the **Options** tab. You need to make sure that this step in the task sequence is run only when running Windows To Go.

5. Click the **Add Condition** button, click **Task Sequence Variable**, and then enter the following information before clicking **OK**:

    o   Variable: **_SMSTSWTG**

    o   Condition: **Equals**

    o   Value: **True**

6. Click **OK** to close the Task Sequence editor.

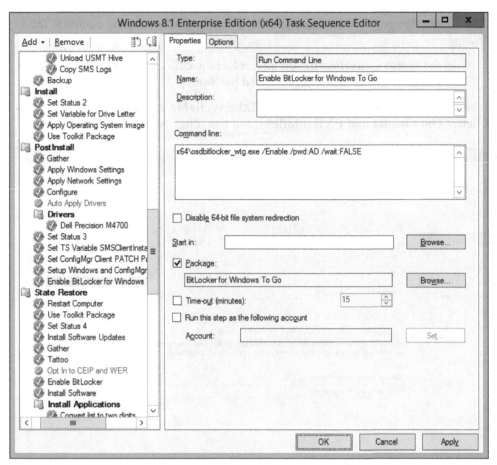

The task sequence should look like this, a custom command to enable BitLocker on the Windows To Workspace during deployment.

Deploy the Task Sequence

As the task sequence is not included in the media you create, it needs to be deployed and thereby made available to the users for when they use their Windows To Go workspaces.

1. On **CM01**, log on as **VIAMONSTRA\Administrator**, and start the **ConfigMgr console** if it is not already started.

2. Click the **Software Library** tab, expand **Operating Systems**, and click **Task Sequences**.

3. Right-click the **Task Sequence** named **Windows 8.1 Enterprise Edition (x64)** and choose **Deploy**.

4. On the **General** page, click the **Browse** button next to **Collection** and complete the following:

> In the **Select Collection** dialog box, select the collection **All Windows 8.1 Systems** and then click **OK**, followed by **Next**.

5. On the **Deployment Settings** page, in the **Make available to the following:** dropdown list, select **Only media and PXE (hidden)**, and then click **Next**.

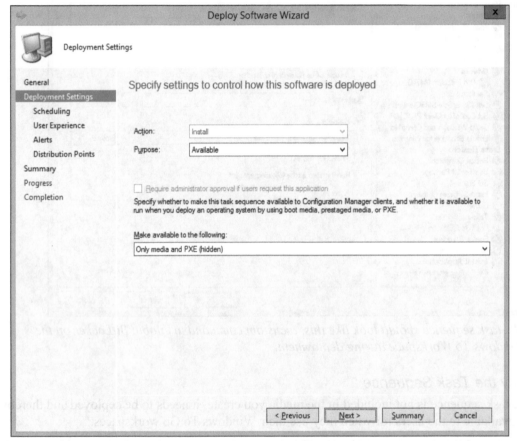

Configuring the deployment settings.

6. On the **Scheduling** page, click **Next**.

7. On the **User Experience** page, click **Next**.

8. On the **Alerts** page, click **Next**.

9. On the **Distribution Points** page, click **Next**.

10. On the **Summary** page, click **Next**.

11. On the **Completion** page, click **Close**.

Create the Prestaged Media

Now you need to create the image WIM file that will be deployed to the USB thumb drive when users create their Windows To Go workspace.

1. On **CM01**, log on as **VIAMONSTRA\Administrator**, and start the **ConfigMgr console** if it is not already started.

2. In the **Software Library** workspace, expand **Operating Systems**.

3. Select the **Task Sequences** node, select the **Windows 8.1 Enterprise Edition (x64)** task sequence and click the **Deployments** tab. Then right-click the column row, and select to display Deployment ID.

4. Make a note of the **Deployment ID** for the **Windows 8.1 Enterprise Edition (x64)** task sequence, in our case it was **P0120001** but it may be different in your environment.

Note: You can also use PowerShell to get the Deployment ID. Simply start PowerShell from within ConfigMgr console and run the following command:

Get-CMDeployment | Where-Object SoftwareName -like *Enterprise* |
Select SoftwareName, DeploymentID

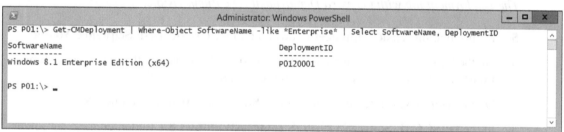

Using PowerShell to find out the Deployment ID.

261

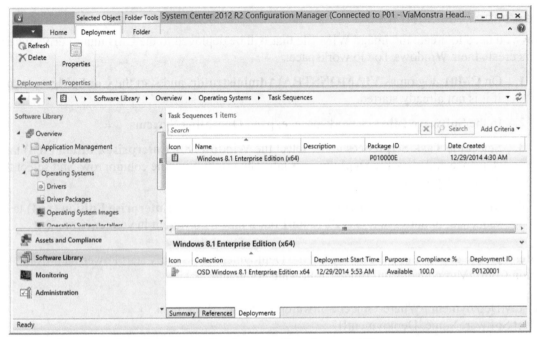

The Deployment tab with the extra Deployment ID column visible.

5. Right-click the **Task Sequences** node and choose **Create Task Sequence Media**.

6. On the **Select Media Type** page, select **Prestaged media** and the check box **Allow unattended operating system deployment**, and then click **Next**.

7. On the **Media Management** page, select **Site-based media**, and click **Next**.

8. In the **D:\SCCM_Source$\OSD\OS Images\Windows 8.1** folder, create a subfolder named **WTGx64**

9. On the **Media Properties** page, in the **Media file** input area, type **D:\SCCM_Source$\OSD\OS Images\Windows 8.1\WTGx64\WindowsToGo.wim** and then click **Next**.

> **Note:** If you get an error message saying you are not allowed to write content to that folder, it's because the folder structure is not in place. This means you must make sure that all the folders in the preceding path actually exist before proceeding.

10. On the **Security** page, clear the **Protect media with a password** check box and click **Next**.

11. On the **Task Sequence** page, click the **Browse** button.

12. In the **Select a Task Sequence** dialog box, choose the **Task Sequence** named **Windows 8.1 Enterprise Edition (x64)** and click **OK**, followed by **Next**.

13. On the **Boot Image** page, click the **Browse** button next to **Distribution point** and complete the following:

> In the **Select Distribution Point** dialog box, select the distribution point **CM01.CORP.VIAMONSTRA.COM** and click **OK**.

14. Still on **Boot Image** page, click the **Browse** button next to **Management point** the and complete the following:

> In the **Add Management Points** dialog box, select the management point **CM01.corp.viamonstra.com** and click **OK**. Then click **Next**.

15. On the **Images** page, click the **Browse** button next to **Distribution point** and complete the following:

> In the **Select Distribution Point** dialog box, select the distribution point **CM01.CORP.VIAMONSTRA.COM** and click **OK**, followed by **Next**.

16. On the **Select Applications** page, click **Next**.

17. On the **Select Package** page, click **Next**.

18. On the **Select Driver Package** page, click **Next**.

Note: In the real world, you would have additional driver packages containing drivers needed for the hardware on which your users will use the Windows To Go workspace, i.e. drivers that are not available inbox. There is more about drivers in Windows To Go later in this chapter.

---

19. On the **Distribution Points** page, select **CM01.corp.viamonstra.com**, click the **Add** button and then **Next**.

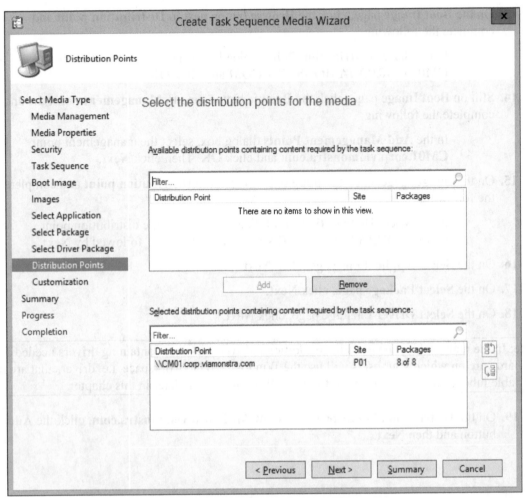

This step verifies that the content required is actually available on the distribution points.

20. On the **Customization** page, click the **yellow star** button and complete the following:

    a. In the **<New> Variable** dialog box, enter the following information then click **Next**:

        ■ Name: **SMSTSPreferredAdvertID**

        ■ Value: **<The deployment ID of the task sequence>**

    b. Enter another variable with the following information:

        ■ Name: **OSDBitLockerPIN**

        ■ Value: **P@ssw0rd**

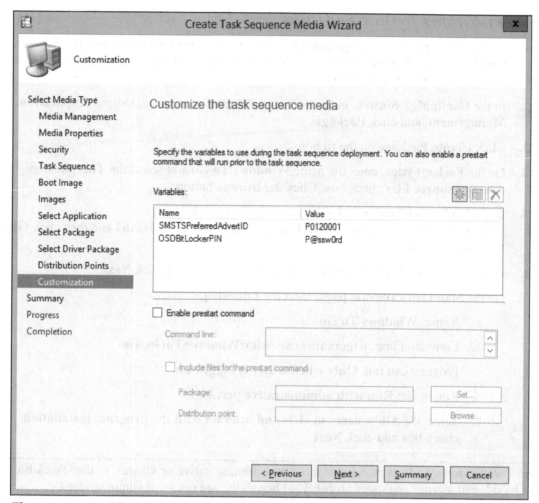

The custom variables are required to point to the correct task sequence and also to set the password for BitLocker.

21. On the **Summary** page, click **Next**. When a UAC message says that Configuration Manager wants to make changes to your computer, click **Yes**. Then wait for the Windows To Go building process to finish. It takes a *really long time* (often more than 45 minutes) to finish, so this is a great time for another coffee break, lunch, or a maybe even a power nap. ☺

22. On the **Completion** page, click **Close**.

Provision Windows To Go to End Users

1. On **CM01**, copy the file **wtgcreator.exe** from **C:\Program Files\Microsoft Configuration Manager\OSD\Tools\WTG\Creator** to **D:\SCCM_Source$\OSD\OS Images\Windows 8.1\WTGx64**.

2. In the **ConfigMgr console**, in the **Software Library** workspace, expand **Application Management**, and click **Packages**.

3. Click **Create Package** on the ribbon.

4. On the **Package** page, enter the name **Windows To Go** and select the **This package contains source files** check box. Click the **Browse** button.

5. In the **Set Source Folder** dialog box, enter the source folder **\\CM01\SCCM_source$\OSD\OS Images\Windows 8.1\WTGx64** and then click **OK**, followed by **Next**.

6. On the **Program Type** page, accept the default settings and click **Next**.

7. On the **Standard Program** page, enter the following:

   a. Name: **Windows To Go**

   b. Command line: **wtgcreator.exe /wim:WindowsToGo.wim**

   c. Program can run: **Only when a user is logged on**.

   d. Run mode: **Run with administrative privileges**.

   e. Select the **Allow users to view and interact with the program installation** check box and click **Next**.

Note: The Windows To Go Creator tool must have administrative privileges, so that check box must be selected as your end users probably, or hopefully, are not local administrators.

---

8. On the **Requirements** page, click **Next**.

9. On the **Summary** page, click **Next**.

10. On the **Completion** page, click **Close**.

Distribute and Deploy Windows To Go to the Users

1. In the **ConfigMgr console**, still in the **Packages** node, right-click the package **Windows To Go** and choose **Deploy**.

2. On the **General** page, click the **Browse** button to the right of **Collection** and complete the following:

   In the **Select Collection** dialog box, choose **Device Collections** and then the collection **All Windows 8.1 Systems**. Click **OK** and then **Next**.

3. On the **Content** page, click the **Add / Distribution Point**, select the distribution point **CM01.CORP.VIAMONSTRA.COM**, click **OK** and then **Next**.

4. On the **Deployment Settings** page, change **Purpose** to **Available** and then click **Next**.

5. On the **Scheduling** page, click **Next**.

6. On the **User Experience** page, click **Next**.

7. On the **Distribution Points** page, click **Next**.

8. On the **Summary** page, click **Next**.

9. On the **Completion** page, click **Close**.

Create the Windows To Go Workspace

Finally, it is time to create the USB stick. That cannot be done using the Windows To Go Creator tool as it will not detect the USB drive in the virtual machine, not even if you add it as a physical drive to the virtual machine. Therefore, you need to create the Windows To Go stick on a physical machine.

Typically, in the enterprise scenario, your end users would start Software Center, select Windows To Go, and click Install. That initiates the download and installation of the Windows To Go Creator tool. Then the user would follow the guide to create the Windows To Go device.

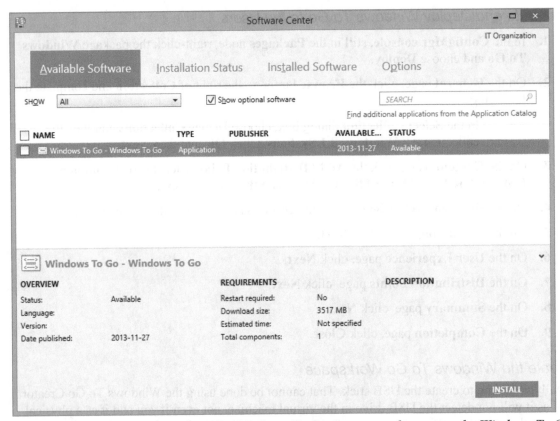

In Software Center, users can have the Windows To Go Creator tool to create the Windows To Go workspace.

Optional – Use the Create a Windows To Go Workspace guide manually

If you haven't installed the ConfigMgr 2012 R2 client an a physical machine, you can follow this guide to use the built-in Create a Windows To Go Workspace tool manually on a physical machine.

1. On a physical machine running **Windows 8.1 Enterprise**, log in and run the **Create a Windows To Go Workspace** guide (available on the Start screen as Windows To Go).

2. Copy the **WindowsToGo.wim** file from **CM01** to a folder on the physical machine and specify that folder during in the **Create a Windows To Go Workspace** guide.

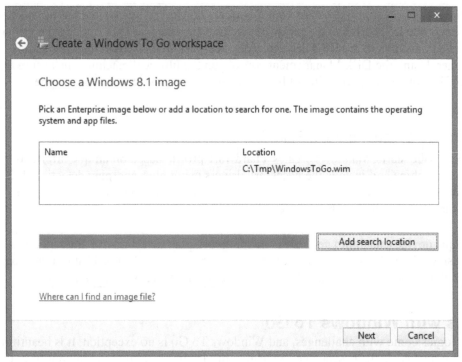

Running the Create a Windows To Go Workspace guide manually.

Use Your Windows To Go Workspace

Now that you've created your Windows To Go workspace, you need to boot it off a physical machine of your choice. Insert the USB memory stick in (or connect a USB hard drive to) a physical machine and boot it up. Make sure that you set the boot order to boot first to USB devices, or set it so that the boot type is selected manually, to ensure that the machine boots to the USB device each time you want to boot to your Windows To Go workspace.

> **Real World Note**: If you would like to test your Windows To Go USB drive in a virtual machine, you need to connect the USB drive to the physical machine on which you are running the virtual machine. Then you have to add the USB drive as a physical disk in the virtual machine settings in Hyper-V Manager. Using the Disk Management console on the physical machine, make sure the USB drive is offline; otherwise, you will not be able to use it as a physical disk on a Hyper-V virtual machine.

Hardware Profiles Unique to Each Model

When Windows To Go starts, Windows creates a hardware profile based on unique information on that particular machine and installs the necessary drivers using plug-and-play detection. It is like a normal Windows 8.1 machine now, and you can do basically everything you can with a traditional installation on a physical hard drive.

> **Note**: Each unique device (machine) generates new plug-and-play detection of hardware on its initial boot, causing a boot delay of a couple of minutes on average hardware. That is a once per unique machine thing, though, so the next boot on that same hardware will be immediate.

Challenges with Windows To Go

All new technologies come with challenges, and Windows To Go is no exception. It is beautiful in many ways, but it has its challenges, such as managing drivers and getting users to boot from the USB device.

Driver Management

It's funny that when we talk about deploying Windows, we always recommend separating the drivers for all the computer models you have in your environments. Windows To Go sort of makes you do the opposite. The drivers that are included in Windows 8 and 8.1 cover most of the hardware released up to Windows 8 RTM and 8.1 RTM, respectively. In the long run, however, new hardware models are released and their drivers will be missing. You must be able to handle that, and the way to do it is to put the necessary drivers in the local driver store.

> **Real World Note**: Network and especially wireless network drivers are essential in your Windows To Go image. Microsoft lists network drivers that are not included in the Windows 8.1 media for easy download at:
>
> http://technet.microsoft.com/en-us/library/jj592685.aspx#wtg_imagedep.

The local driver store solution, however, only covers running Windows To Go on your corporate machines. Windows To Go also will be run on consumer devices, and the drivers for your corporate machines will not help in that scenario. Keeping a generic driver library of NVIDIA, AMD, and Intel graphics drivers, among others, can be a good idea. Also consider letting the Windows To Go workspaces pick up drivers from Windows Update.

USB Boot

For Windows To Go to work, you need to boot from your USB device. On the machines you control in your domain environment, you can set them to boot automatically from Windows To Go if it is present. But what about the rest of the machines out there, such as those in internet cafes and your users' home environments?

Trying to boot a machine from USB can be a real challenge as you have all kinds of hardware to deal with. On some machines, you press F11, and on others F10, Esc, Del, F1, F2, etc., etc., etc. I'm pretty sure you get the point. Getting your users to do this can be easier said than done.

Set USB Boot as the Default

When you are running Windows 8 or 8.1 on your machines and want to be able to use Windows To Go on them, you can activate the group policy to make the computers boot from USB when started.

1. Log in to a domain controller for the domain of which your Windows 8 or Windows 8.1 machine is a member, and start the **Group Policy Management** console.

2. In the OU where the Windows 8 or Windows 8.1 computer account resides, create a new GPO and configure it in the following step.

3. In the **Computer Configuration / Policies / Administrative Templates / Windows Components / Portable Operating System** node, configure the following:

   Enable the **Windows To Go Default Startup Options** policy.

Note: This Group Policy setting is good for your domain environment. You also can instruct your users that if they are running Windows 8 or 8.1, they can search for "Change Windows To Go startup options" and set "Do you want to automatically boot your PC from a Windows To Go workspace" to Yes.

Chapter 10

Service Manager

Although all information about a device is gathered and stored in Configuration Manager, it does not fulfill the requirements for a configuration management database (CMDB) system. Also, because Configuration Manager purges the data in the database, it really serves as a bad CMDB when it comes to tracking resources that haven't reported in for a while. One might be tempted to change the settings so that Configuration Manager doesn't purge the old data but stores it and use Configuration Manager as a CMDB, but doing so will give you less then optimal performance when operating your Configuration Manager environment, and it will not give you all the other features that the CMDB feature within System Center Service Manager gives you, plus its other capabilities.

Even though you'll use Service Manager only for its CMDB in this scenario, the product is outstanding for ticketing systems for the Service Desk and as a Request For Change system, as it is built on top of the ITIL mindset. One feature that is really neat is that if Service Desk operators connect tickets from the end users to the related resource in the CMDB in Service Manager, you can produce reports that helps you see trends. Perhaps a specific computer model gives you more Service Desk tickets due to a malfunctioning driver. Using these reports, you can pinpoint the root cause of a frequent problem and solve it once and for all.

When Microsoft first started developing Service Manager, it did so with the best practices described in Microsoft Operations Framework (MOF) and the Information Technology Infrastructure Library (ITIL) in mind. At the time of this writing, MOF is up to version 4.0.

Note: You can read more about the Microsoft Operations Framework at http://go.microsoft.com/fwlink/p/?LinkID=116391.

Installing Service Manager

With the increasing complexity in all the different System Center products, installation has grown in complexity, although it is still possible to install each and every product by simply stepping through the installation wizard. To achieve the best performance and scalability and get the "most bang for the buck," some special steps need to be taken with Service Manager just as with any other System Center product. A helping hand in this process comes from the Service Manager Sizing Helper tool that is included in the Service Manager job aids documentation set that you can find at http://go.microsoft.com/fwlink/p/?LinkID=232378. A typical implementation for a medium-sized organization containing 2000–5000 users, 3000 computer objects and 15–30 concurrent operators in Service Manager requires at least three Service Manager servers: the Service Manager server, the Data Warehouse server, and the Self-Service Portal server. In this lab setup, one server works fine because we are not going to use the Self-Service Portal which requires at least a second server.

Install .NET Framework 3.5.1

1. Mount the **Windows Server 2012 R2 ISO**, and note which drive letter has been assigned as it is used in the next step. If it is not E:, as in the step 2 example, please replace E: with the drive letter of your choice.

2. Start an **elevated command prompt** (run as administrator), and run the following command:

```
Dism.exe /Online /Enable-Feature /All /FeatureName:NetFX3
/Source:E:\sources\sxs
```

Install SQL Server

1. On **SM01**, start the **SQL Server 2012 with SP1** Setup from the installation media.

2. In the **SQL Server Installation Center**, navigate to **Installation** and click **New SQL Server stand-alone installation or add features to an existing installation** to start the installation process.

3. In the **SQL Server 2012 Setup** wizard, when the **Setup Support Rules** have been processed, click **OK**.

4. Wait until the setup continues, then on the **Product Key** page, click **Next**.

5. On the **License Terms** page, select **I accept the license terms**, and if applicable for you, select the check box to send usage data to Microsoft. **Click Next**.

6. On the **Product Updates** page, if your environment does not have Internet connectivity, you see an exception that SQL Server Setup could not search for updates, which is ok for this setup. Click **Next**.

7. When the installation of setup files has been completed, on the **Install Setup Files** page, click **Install**.

8. Again **Setup Support Rules** are processed, and you will see a warning for **Windows Firewall**. Ignore that warning for now, and click **Next**.

9. On the **Role Setup** page, make sure **SQL Server Feature Installation** is selected and click **Next**.

10. On the **Feature Selection** page, select **Database Engine Services, Full-Text and Semantic Extractions for Search, Analysis Services, Reporting Services – Native**, and **Management Tools – Complete**, and then click **Next**.

11. When the operation is complete, on the **Installation Rules** page, click **Next**.

12. On the **Instance Configuration** page, change the **Instance root directory** to **D:\MSSQL**, but leave the **Instance ID** as it is and click **Next**.

13. On the **Disk Space Requirements** page, click **Next** after examining the calculation.

14. On the **Server Configuration** page, in the **Service Accounts** tab, change the **Account Name** for the **SQL Server Database Engine** to **NT AUTHORITY\SYSTEM** (type SYSTEM in the Browse dialog box).

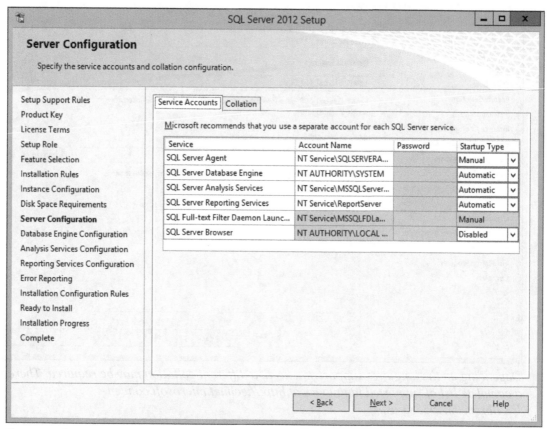

Running the Database Engine service as System works well in this scenario but might not work in all production environments.

15. In the **Collation** tab, change the **Database Engine** and **Analysis Services** to use the **Latin1_General_100_CI_AS** collation, and then click **Next**.

Note: The Latin1_General_100 collation is listed in "Windows collation designator and sort order", and is named Latin1_General_100 in the list. You also need to select the Accent-sensitive option.

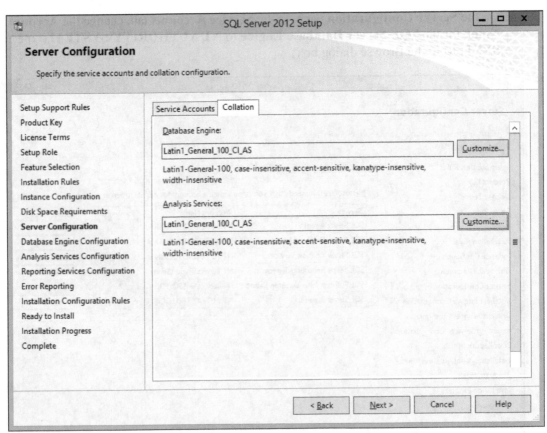

Depending on the language support you need, a different collation may be required. There is a complete list of supported languages at http://technet.microsoft.com/en-US/library/hh495583.aspx.

16. On the **Database Engine Configuration** page, in the **Server Configuration** tab, , **Authentication Mode** should be set to **Windows authentication mode**. Add the current Administrator account as **SQL Server administrators** by clicking **Add Current User**. Also add the **SM01\Administrators** group, by clicking **Add** (will be renamed to BUILTIN\Administrators after being added).

17. Still on the **Database Engine Configuration** page, in the **Data Directories** tab, note the paths for all file types and click **Next**.

18. On the **Analysis Services Configuration** page, click **Add Current User** in the **Server Configuration** tab. Also add the **SM01\Administrators** group, by clicking **Add**, and then click **Next**.

19. On the **Reporting Services Configuration** page, make sure **Install and configure** is selected and click **Next**.

20. On the **Error Reporting** page, if applicable for you, select the check box to send error reports to Microsoft and click **Next**.

21. When the operation is complete, on the **Installation Configuration Rules** page, click **Next**.

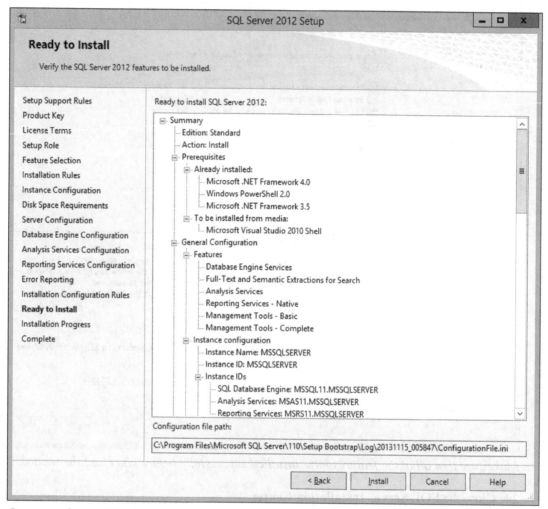

Just as with any SQL Server installation, when the wizard has finished, it actually creates an unattend file. Closing the wizard at this point allows for running the setup unattended using the file produced by the wizard.

22. On the **Ready to Install** page, note that the complete unattended file for this SQL Server installation has been saved in the **Configuration file path**. Click **Install** to start the SQL Server 2012 SP1 installation.

23. When the installation is complete, on the **Complete** page, review the status for each feature, and then click **Close** to complete the installation.

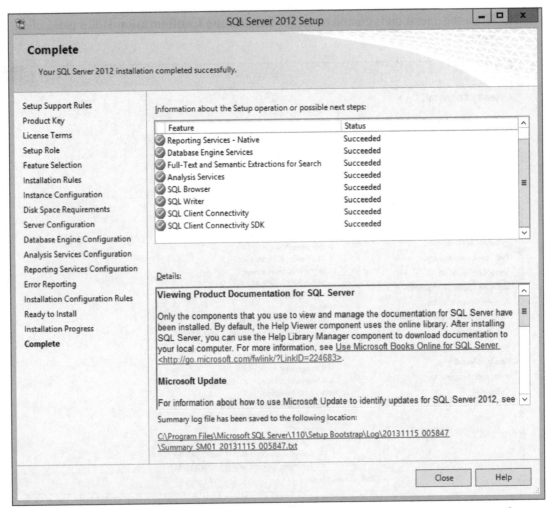

Make sure that all of the features have installed successfully before you close the wizard.

24. Close the **SQL Server Installation Center**.

Install the Microsoft Report Viewer

The Microsoft Report Viewer 2008 SP1 is required to complete the Service Manager installation.

1. On **SM01**, start the **ReportViewer.exe** from **E:\Prerequisites** on the Service Manager 2012 R2 installation media.

2. Click **Next** in the **Microsoft Report Viewer Redistributable 2008** wizard.

3. Select **I have read and accept the license terms** and click **Install**.

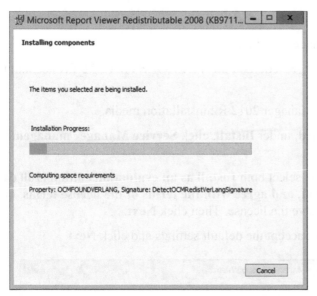

The Report Viewer installation might qualify as the quickest installation in the whole book.

4. When the installation is complete, click **Finish** to close the wizard.

Create the Service Accounts and Administrator Group

Before you can start the Service Manager installation, you need to create a few service accounts and a group .

1. On **DC01**, start **Active Directory Users and Computers** and navigate to the **ViaMonstra / Service Accounts** OU.

2. On **Action** menu, select **New / User**.

3. Enter **SM_SA** in both **Full name** and **User logon name**, and then click **Next**.

4. Enter **P@ssw0rd** as password for the new account and confirm it. Clear the **User must change password at next logon** check box, select both **User cannot change password** and **Password never expires**, click **Next** and then click **Finish**.

5. Repeat step 2 – 4 for the **VIAMONSTRA\SM_WFA** account.

6. In the **Security Groups OU**, create a **Global** security group named **Service Manager Management Group Administrators**.

7. To the **Service Manager Management Group Administrators** group, add the group **Domain Admins**.

Install Service Manager

Now you are ready to install Service Manager 2012 R2.

1. On **SM01**, using **Computer Management**, add the **VIAMONSTRA\SM_SA** account to the local **Administrators** group.

2. Start **Setup.exe** from the Service Manager 2012 R2 installation media.

3. In **Service Manager Setup Wizard**, under **Install**, click **Service Manager management server**.

4. On the **Product registration** page, select both **Install as an evaluation edition (180 day trial)** and **I have read, understood, and agree with the terms of the license terms**, or use your real product key if you have the license. Then click **Next**.

5. On the **Installation location** page, accept the default settings and click **Next**.

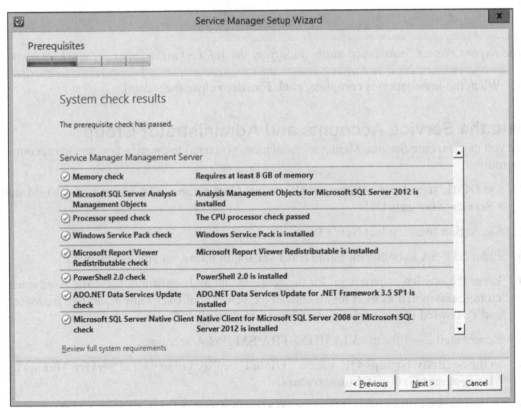

Running Service Manager on less than 8 GB of RAM is possible but not recommended due to performance.

6. When the setup is done checking all requirements, click **Next**.

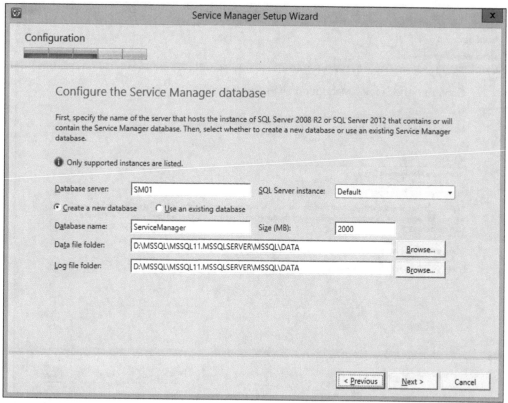

The database can be precreated, and thus is it possible to use an existing database.

7. On the **Configure the Service Manager database** page, make sure that **Create a new database** is selected and click **Next**.

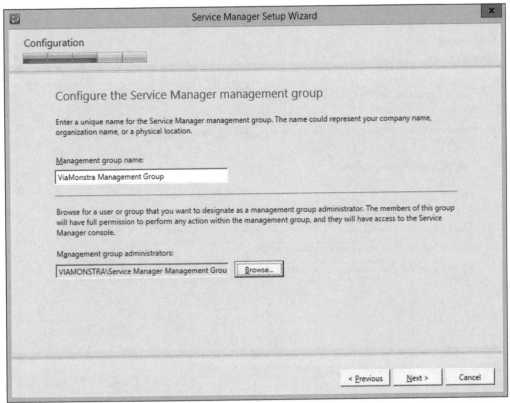

If you use a name for the management group that is too long you'll get an error so keep it short.

8. On the **Configure the Service Manager management group** page, enter **ViaMonstra Management Group** in the **Management group name** field.

9. On the **Configure the Service Manager management group** page, click **Browse** next to **Management group administrators**, and then select the Active Directory group **Service Manager Management Group Administrators**. Continue by clicking **Next**.

10. On the **Configure the account for Service Manager services** page, select **Domain account**, enter user name **VIAMONSTRA\SM_SA** and the account password, and then click **Test Credentials**. When the informative text shows that the credentials were accepted, click **Next**.

11. On the **Configure the Service Manager workflow account** page, select **Domain account**, enter user name **VIAMONSTRA\SM_WFA** and the account password, and then click **Test Credentials**. When the informative text shows that the credentials were accepted, click **Next**.

12. On the **Help improve Microsoft System Center 2012 R2 Service Manager** page, select what's applicable for you and click **Next**.

13. On the **Use Microsoft Update to help keep your computer secure and up-to-date** page, select **Use Microsoft Update when I check for updates (recommended)** and click **Next**.

14. Review the information on the **Installation summary** page, and then click **Install** to start the Service Manager installation.

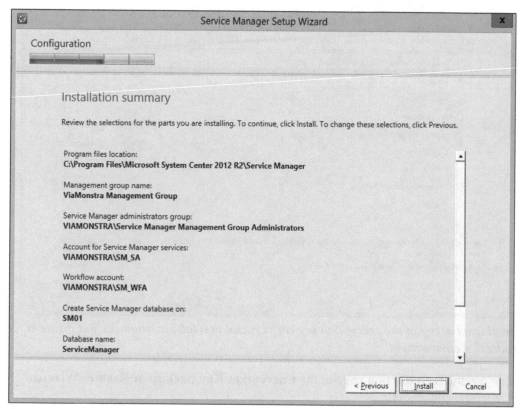

It is a good time to review all accounts, groups, and paths just before the installation starts.

15. When the installation is complete, click **Close**, leaving the default check box selections. This automatically starts the **Encryption Key Backup or Restore Wizard**.

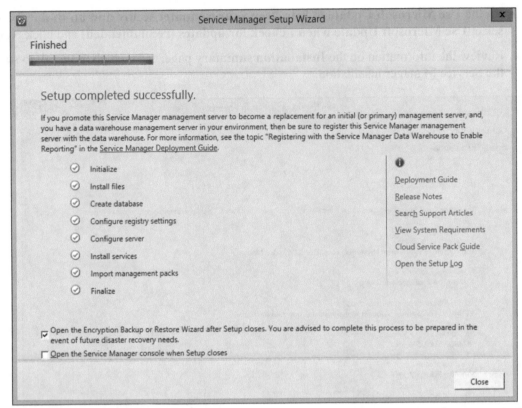

Creating a backup of the encryption key isn't crucial in a lab environment, but it sure is for a production environment.

16. When the **Introduction** page of the **Encryption Key Backup or Restore Wizard** appears, click **Next**.

17. On the **Backup or Restore?** page, leave **Backup the Encryption Key** selected and click **Next**.

18. On the **Provide a Location** page, enter **\\DC01\C$\Setup\SM01_BackupKey.bin** in the **Path** field and click **Next**.

19. On the **Provide a Password** page, enter **P@ssw0rd** twice and click **Next**.

20. When the backup is done and the **Secure Storage Backup Complete** notice appears, click **Finish** to complete the wizard.

Integrate Active Directory with Service Manager

Since you probably have a place where all your users are stored in a nice, commonly known, format, it is a good idea to use that as a source when you populate Service Manager with all your users. That is achieved by creating a *connector* from Service Manager to Active Directory. The connector can then run on a schedule and find all new or modified user accounts and populate them into the Service Manager database.

Create the Run As Account

The Run As account must have read access to the OU where your users reside. Typically, all users have this permission out of the box with Active Directory, so there is no need to grant extra permissions to the account.

1. On **DC01**, start the **Active Directory Users and Computers** snap-in.

2. Create a new **User** account in the **ViaMonstra / Service Accounts** OU.

3. On the **New Object – User** page, enter **SM_RAA_AD** in both the **Full name** and the **User logon name** fields, and then click **Next**.

Real World Note: There is always a big demand for service accounts in any environment. Creating a service that allows service account generation in order to keep the naming convention correct is a good idea. The same goes for using a service to store the passwords for service accounts. You never know when you'll need it next.

Only Full name, User logon name and the pre-Windows 2000 User logon name need to be completed in order to create an account.

4. Enter **P@ssw0rd** in the **Password** and **Confirm password** fields; make sure that only **User cannot change password** and **Password never expires** are selected; and click **Next**, and the then click **Finish**. This account will be used later on in the "Set Up the Active Directory Connector" section.

You also can use the following PowerShell script to create this user account in Active Directory. If you do, you also can use it to create the user account in the "Integrate Configuration Manager with Service Manager" section later in this chapter.

```
New-ADUser -Name:"SM_RAA_AD" -Path:"OU=Service
Accounts,OU=ViaMonstra,DC=corp,DC=viamonstra,DC=com"
-SamAccountName:"SM_RAA_AD"
-Type:"user" -UserPrincipalName:"SM_RAA_AD@corp.viamonstra.com"
-Verbose

Set-ADAccountPassword -Identity:"CN=SM_RAA_AD,
OU=Service Accounts,OU=ViaMonstra,DC=corp,DC=viamonstra,DC=com"
-NewPassword:(ConvertTo-SecureString -String "P@ssw0rd"
-AsPlainText -Force) -Reset:$true
-Verbose

Enable-ADAccount -Identity:"CN=SM_RAA_AD,OU=Service
Accounts,OU=ViaMonstra,DC=corp,DC=viamonstra,DC=com" -Verbose

Set-ADAccountControl -AccountNotDelegated:$false
-AllowReversiblePasswordEncryption:$false
-CannotChangePassword:$true -DoesNotRequirePreAuth:$false
-Identity:"CN=SM_RAA_AD,OU=Service
Accounts,OU=ViaMonstra,DC=corp,DC=viamonstra,DC=com"
-PasswordNeverExpires:$true -UseDESKeyOnly:$false -Verbose

Set-ADUser -ChangePasswordAtLogon:$false
-Identity:"CN=SM_RAA_AD,OU=Service
Accounts,OU=ViaMonstra,DC=corp,DC=viamonstra,DC=com"
-SmartcardLogonRequired:$false -Verbose
```

Running this script requires that the PowerShell prompt or ISE is running with elevated privileges.

Set Up the Active Directory Connector

Before you complete the following step-by-step instructions, we recommended that you have at least one user account in the ViaMonstra / Users OU in Active Directory. In our lab, the user Don.

1. On **SM01**, start the **Service Manager Console**, and in the **Connect to Service Manager Server** dialog box, click **Connect**.

2. In the **Administration** workspace, right-click the **Connectors** node and select **Create connector / Active Directory connector**.

3. On the **Before You Begin** page, click **Next**.

4. On the **General** page, enter **ViaMonstra Inc. Active Directory Users** in the **Name** field and click **Next**.

5.   On the **Domain/OU** page, use the following settings and click **Next**:

   o   Server Information: Select **Let me choose the domain or OU**, and then click **Browse** and select the **ViaMonstra / Users** OU.

   o   Credentials: Create a new **Run As account** by clicking the **New** button and entering **Active Directory Connector Account** as the **Display Name** and using the username and password from the preceding "Create the Run As Account" section (VIAMONSTRA\SM_RAA_AD).

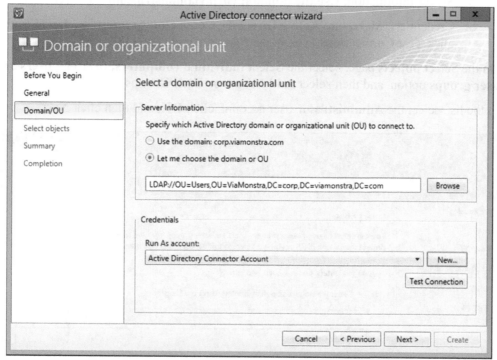

Depending on your OU structure in Active Directory, you might need to create multiple connectors to Active Directory.

6.   On the **Select objects** page, leave the **All computers, printers, users and user groups** button selected and click **Next**.

7.   Review the settings on the **Summary page** and click **Create**.

8.   When the connector creation is complete and the **Completion** page appears, click **Close** to exit the wizard.

9.   Repeat steps 2–7, but this time name the connector **ViaMonstra Inc. Active Directory Servers** and use the following LDAP path:

   LDAP://OU=Servers,OU=ViaMonstra,DC=corp,DC=viamonstra,DC=com.

10. In the **Administration** workspace, right-click the **Connectors** node once again, and select **Create connector / Active Directory connector**.

11. On the **Before You Begin** page, click **Next**.

12. On the **General** page, enter **ViaMonstra Inc. Active Directory Admins** in the **Name** field and click **Next**.

13. On the **Domain/OU** page, use the following settings and click **Next**:

    o Server Information: **Use the domain: corp.viamonstra.com**

    o Credentials: Make sure **Active Directory Connector Account** is selected, and click **Test Connection**. Type in the password and click **OK**.

14. On the **Select objects** page, select the **Select individual computers, printers, users or user groups** option, and then select **Add / Users or User Groups**.

15. In the list, select the **Administrator** user account, click **OK**, and then click **Next**.

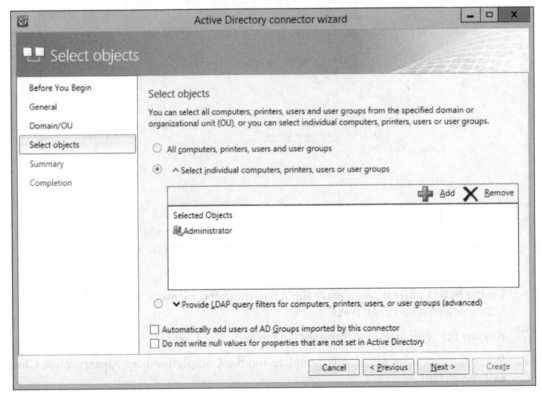

Selecting a specific user.

16. Review the settings on the **Summary page** and click **Create**.

17. When the connector creation is complete and the **Completion** page appears, click **Close** to exit the wizard.

The time required to run the initial synchronization depends on how many objects you have in your environment, as well as the performance on the server. In the lab environment, the initial synchronization shouldn't take longer than five minutes to complete.

> **Note**: For a complete, comprehensive mapping list between Active Directory attributes and object properties in Service Manager, see http://technet.microsoft.com/library/hh524307.aspx.

Integrate Configuration Manager with Service Manager

When you integrate Configuration Manager with Service Manager, you get the benefits of the discovery features in Configuration Manager together with the data warehouse and CMDB capabilities in Service Manager. This enables you to track information about computers and servers that you had in Configuration Manager further back in history, as well as link incidents that a user reports directly to a computer object that the user has the issue with. Collecting all this data gives you a better understanding of your environment so that you can make better decisions. For example, if your end users frequently have issues with a specific computer model, you can decide to go with a different vendor the next time you purchase computers, or perhaps simply replace one user's computer of that model and dive deeper into what the root cause of the issue is and fix it once and for all.

> **Real World Note**: After the connection between different System Center products has been made, it is always very important to make sure that upgrades to the different components are made in the right sequence. During the upgrade from 2012 SP1 to 2012 R2, Service Manager had to be upgraded before Configuration Manager was upgraded. The upgrade sequence from 2012 R2 to vNext might be different.
>
> The upgrade sequence to 2012 R2 can be found here: http://technet.microsoft.com/en-us/library/dn521010.aspx.

Create the Run As Account

> **Note:** You can reuse the script from "Create the Run As Account" in the preceding "Integrate Active Directory with Service Manager" section with some small modifications so that the account names match.

1. On **DC01**, start the **Active Directory Users and Computers** snap-in.

2. Create a new **User** account in the **ViaMonstra / Service Accounts** OU.

3. On the **New Object – User** page, enter **SM_RAA_CM** in both the **Full name** and the **User logon name** fields, and then click **Next**.

4. Enter **P@ssw0rd** in the **Password** and **Confirm password** fields; make sure that only **User cannot change password** and **Password never expires** are selected; and click **Next**. This account will be used later in the "Set Up the Configuration Manager Connector" section.

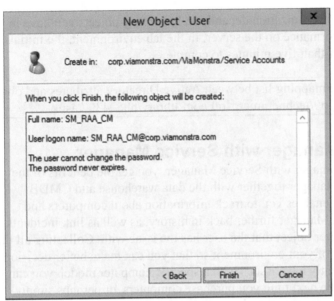

A service account typically has "The password never expires" option selected. Doing so implies that the password should be really long and complex so the need to change it is less frequent.

5. Click **Finish** to close the wizard and create the account.

6. On **CM01** (the ConfigMgr 2012 R2 Site Server), start **SQL Server Management Studio**.

7. In the **Connect to Server** dialog box, make sure that **CM01** is used in the **Server name** field and that **Windows Authentication** is selected in the **Authentication** list; then click **Connect**.

8. Expand the top **Security** node on the **Object Explorer** pane to the left, and expand the **Logins** node beneath it.

9. Right-click the **Logins** node and select **New Login**.

10. In the **Login – New** dialog box, click **Search**, and then type **VIAMONSTRA\SM_RAA_CM** in the **Select User or Group** dialog box and click **OK**.

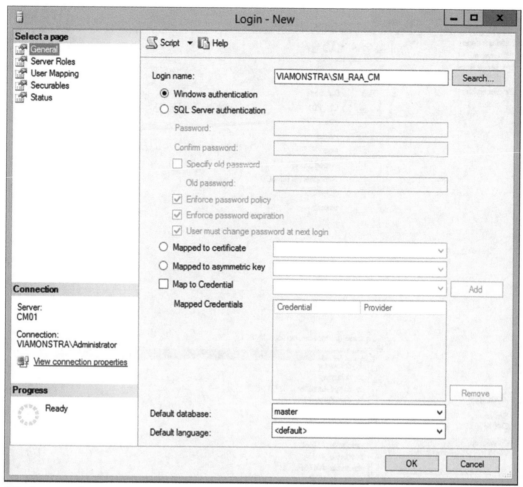

Windows authentication in SQL Servers both local as well as domain accounts.

11. On the left hand side of the **Login – New** dialog box, select the **User Mapping** page.

Selecting database roles to a login in SQL is equivalent to adding a user account into groups in Active Directory in order to give an account permissions on a file share or in this case a database.

12. On the **User Mapping** page, select the **Map** check box next to **CM_P01**; then in the **Database role membership for: CM_P01** list, select both **db_datareader** and **smsdbrole_extract;** and click **OK**.

You can achieve the same permission delegation in SQL by executing the following script:

```
USE [master]

CREATE LOGIN [VIAMONSTRA\SM_RAA_CM] FROM WINDOWS WITH
DEFAULT_DATABASE=[master]

GO

USE [CM_P01]

GO

CREATE USER [VIAMONSTRA\SM_RAA_CM] FOR LOGIN
[VIAMONSTRA\SM_RAA_CM]

ALTER ROLE [db_datareader] ADD MEMBER [VIAMONSTRA\SM_RAA_CM]

ALTER ROLE [smsdbrole_extract] ADD MEMBER [VIAMONSTRA\SM_RAA_CM]

GO
```

Set Up the Configuration Manager Connector

1. On **SM01**, start the **Service Manager Console**, navigate to the **Administration** workspace and click **Connectors**.

2. On the right side, in the **Tasks** menu, select **Create connector / Configuration Manager connector**.

3. On the **Before You Begin** page of the **System Center Configuration Manager connector wizard**, click **Next**.

4. On the **General** page, enter **ViaMonstra ConfigMgr Primary Site** in the **Name** field and click **Next**.

5. On the next page, select **System Center Configuration Manager 2012 Connector Configuration** in the **Management pack** list and then click **Next**.

Note: Make sure to select the ConfigMgr 2012 version of the management pack or you get a warning about the connector configuration not being appropriate for the 5.00.7958.1000 of Configuration Manager.

6. On the **Database** page, enter **CM01** as the **Database server name** and **CM_P01** as the **Database name**; then in the **Credentials** area, click **New** next to **Run As account**.

7. In the **Run As Account** dialog box, enter **Configuration Manager Connector Account** in the **Display name** field and **SM_RAA_CM** in the **User name** field. Also, enter the **password** assigned to the account in the preceding "Create the Run As Account" section, and then click **OK**.

Creating different accounts for different things is a good security practice to follow because you will not end up having one account that has a lot of permissions on different systems.

8. Back in the **System Center Configuration Manager connector wizard**, note that the newly created Run As account has been selected, and then click **Test Connection**.

9. When the **Test Connection** message box appears telling you that the connection was successful, click **OK** to close the window, and then click **Next** back in the **System Center Configuration Manager connector wizard**.

10. On the **Collections** page, select at least **All Windows 8.1 Systems** in the list of collections and click **Next**.

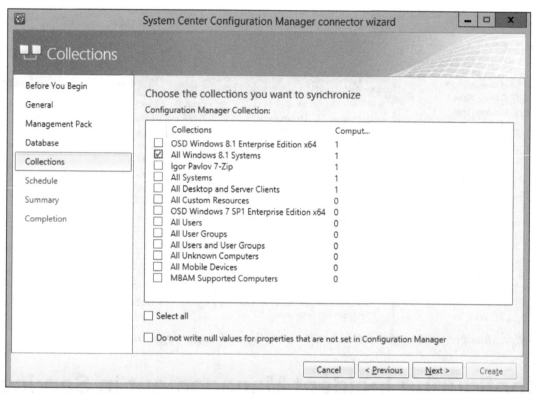

You must select at least one collection to synchronize. While All Systems might be tempting, it is not always the best collection to use because you cannot filter it.

11. On the **Schedule** page, leave the schedule as it is and click **Next**.

12. Review the settings on the **Summary** page and then click **Create**. When the **Completion** page appears, click **Close** to finish and close the wizard.

Running the synchronization does take some time, and while you wait for your coffee to be at a more drinkable temperature, you can follow the process both in the console and the Event Viewer.

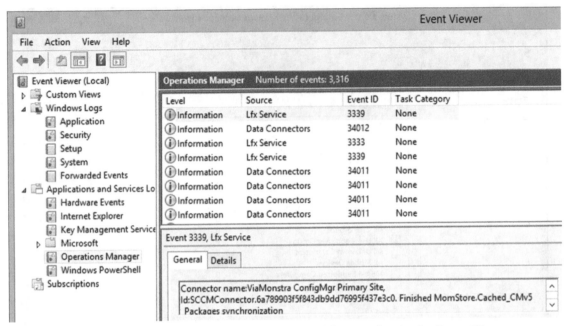

Service Manager writes information to the Operations Manager log in the Event Viewer.

Configuring Incident Management in Service Manager

Incident management might be one of the most common things in any IT organization. Regardless of how it is done, one way or another we keep track of what's not working in our environments—whether it be small yellow pieces of paper or a guy standing in the middle of the room shouting out everything he remembers that has stopped working. A better way than those two, of course, is to use a digital system in which incidents can be delegated to a technician who can fix them. By using a digital system, you also can search all old and ongoing incidents and see what is repeating itself. Based on that information, you can then create a *problem* that needs investigation so that you can stop putting out fires and instead free that time and be more productive.

Configure Incident Priority Calculation

For you and your coworkers to know what incident to start working with first, priority can be a great help. With Service Manager, the priority value of an incident is automatically calculated based on the impact and the urgency. One way to think about the *impact* is to take into consideration how many users the incident affects. If it is only one, two, or at least very few users, the impact is low; for a department or multiple users, the impact is medium-size; and when most if not all users in the organization are affected by the incident, then the impact is set to high.

Urgency is then measured by the nature on how quickly something needs to be done. In the case of a user who cannot log on, the urgency is probably high or at least medium. Now, the incident doesn't make high urgency just because all the domain controllers are offline and no one can log on. That is what the impact is for as we just discussed. The question is how urgent it is to fix the problem of users, regardless of how many, not being able to log on. Perhaps your organization has impeccable offline routines, so logon issues aren't that big of a deal. Urgency then should be set to low or medium.

Before starting with *priority calculation*, it is important that everyone has the same idea of what the different scales of impact and urgency are.

1. In the **Service Manager Console**, in the **Administration** workspace, select the **Settings** node.

2. Double-click the **Incident Settings** item.

3. In the **Incident Settings** dialog box, click **Priority Calculation** on the left side.

4. Fill in the nine fields with 9 through 1 starting on the top left and ending on the bottom right, as shown in the figure.

Tip: Use Tab and the number keys to move between the fields and set the correct values.

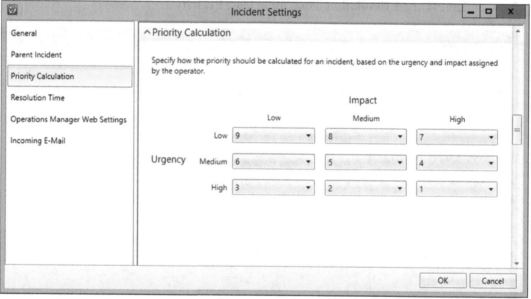

Using this setup, an incident with High Impact for one or few users never gets higher priority than a Low Impact incident for a department or many users. Although this helps to calculate priority, in the end it's up to the person who creates the incident to weigh the input and information.

5. Click **OK** to save the values and close the **Incident Settings** dialog box, or leave it open and continue with the next section, "Configure Target Resolution Time."

Configure the Target Resolution Time

The target resolution time is used to measure whether an incident is solved within the service level agreement (SLA). Based on the priority on an incident, which is calculated based on urgency and impact, as we discussed in the preceding section, a target resolution time can be set automatically. This helps you track the performance on the service desk as a whole and can be used as one of many pointers to determine whether you are properly staffed.

> **Real World Note**: It is never as easy as looking at one parameter to know whether a department is properly staffed, but without a negotiated SLA, everything tends to have the highest priority and no one knows when something must be done. That often results in one of two things, everything needs to be done *now* or *never*.

In the following example, you assign a target resolution time of four hours to a Priority 3 incident. That means that an incident with that priority must be set to the Resolved status within four hours after it is created or the SLA will be broken.

1. Double-click the **Incident Settings** item and select **Resolution Time** on the left side.

2. Configure **Target Resolution Time** for at least **Priority 1**.

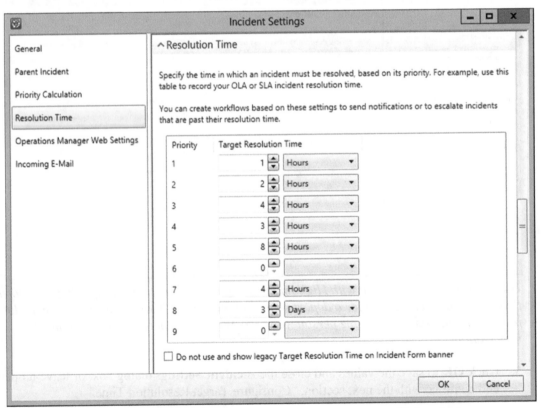

Depending on the size of your organization and the IT department's SLA with the organization, different target resolution times apply.

3. Click **OK** to save the settings and close the **Incident Settings** dialog box, or leave it open and continue to the next section.

Configure File Attachment Limits

A picture can say more than a thousand words, they say. Therefore, sometimes it is better to attach a picture of an error than try explaining it. Log files also are often quite good at explaining an error. Both pictures and log files have a tendency to be larger than the standard attachment limit of 2 MB, so it is a good idea to change the setting to 5 MB.

1. Double-click the **Incident Settings** item and select **General** on the left side.

2. Change the **Maximum size (KB)** value to **5120** which translates into 5 MB.

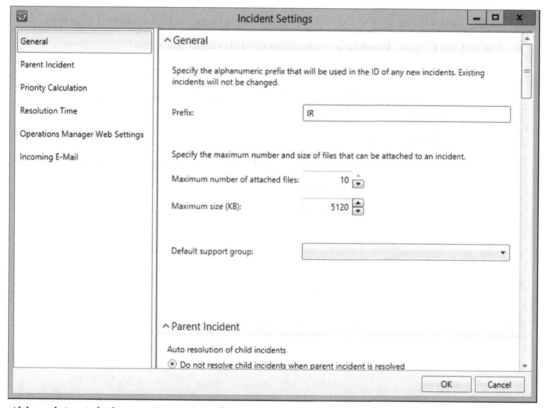

Although it might be tempting to set the maximum size to a larger number, remember that 10 files each can be stored with that size, allowing for each incident to be as large as 50 MB. The numbers quickly add up to one very large database.

3. Click **OK** to save the settings and close the **Incident Settings** dialog box.

Create an Incident Template

A template allows an operator to create an incident more easily and faster for typical issues that arise within your organization. It is always best if you can empower your end users so that they can solve things by themselves instead of contacting the IT department, but that is not always feasible. Also, regardless of how much you empower your users, some will always contact the IT department as the first action when an issue arises. In such cases, it's good to be able to complete those incidents as quickly as possible.

An incident template holds typical information for a specific type of incident. Such information can include to whom the case should be escalated or preferred impact and urgency levels.

1. Using the **Service Manager Console** on **SM01**, in the **Library** workspace, navigate to the **Templates** node.

2. In the **Tasks** menu on the right side, under **Templates**, select **Create Template**.

3. Fill out the **Create Template** form using the following attributes:

   o Name: **User Forgot Password**

   o Description: **Use this template when a single user has forgotten his or her password.**

   o Class: **Incident**

   o Management Pack: **Service Manager Incident Management Configuration Library**

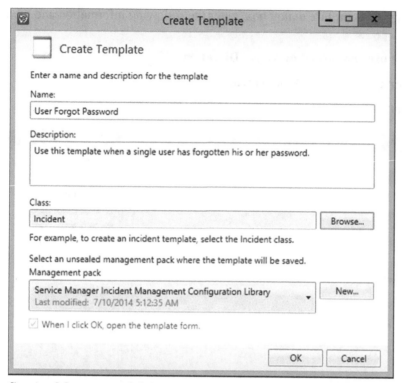

Service Manager and Operations Manager share the schema on extensions using management packs to store changes such as a new template.

4. Click **OK** to close the initial dialog box and start customizing the template.

5. In the newly opened **Incident Template – User Forgot Password** dialog box, populate the following fields on the **General** tab with their respective values:

- o   Title: **User forgot password**

- o   Classification category: **Software Problems**

- o   Impact: **Low**

- o   Urgency: **High**

- o   Support group: **Tier 1**

6. While still in the **Incident Template – User Forgot Password** dialog box, select the **Activities** tab and click the **Add** button.

7. In the **Select a Class** dialog box, select **Manual Activity** and click **OK**.

8. In the **Select Template** dialog box, click **OK**.

9. In the **Manual Activity Template** dialog box, enter the following information and then click **OK**:

    o   Title: **Reset user password in Active Directory**

    o   Area: **Security \ Account Management**

    o   Priority: **Immediate**

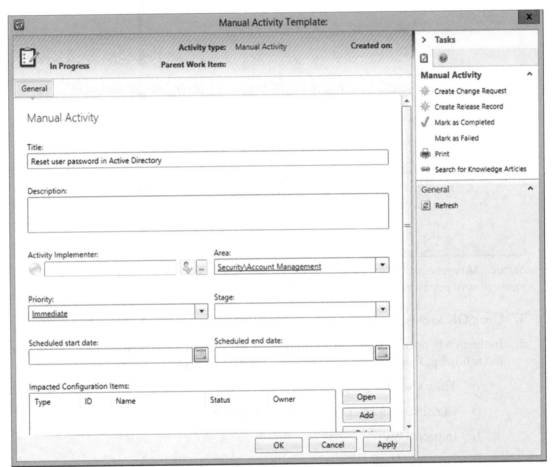

Activities are great for creating lists of things to do in order to solve a specific incident. Activities can be manual steps as well as automated steps using runbooks in System Center Orchestrator.

10. Back in the **Incident Template – User Forgot Password** dialog box, click **OK** to save the template.

Manage Your First Incident

Assume that you have a user who have lost his or her password and calls the service desk to reset the password. The following step-by-step guide walks you through the steps needed now that you have created an incident template for that type of incident.

> **Note**: Throughout the guides with Service Manager, you will see references to numbers at incidents (IR), problems (PR), and so forth, and those numbers are automatically generated so they likely will not be the same in your environment.

1. On **SM01**, in the **Service Manager Console**, in the **Work Items** workspace, navigate to the **Incident Management** node.

2. Click **Create Incident** in the **Tasks** menu on the right side.

3. After the form loads, in the **Incident IR<number> - - New** dialog box, click **Apply Template** in the **Tasks** menu.

> **Note**: This also can be achieved by selecting the "Create Incident from Template" option from the Tasks menu in step 2.

4. Scroll down until you find **User Forgot Password** in the **Apply Template** dialog box, or use the Filter text box. Then select the template and click **OK**.

5. Back in the **Incident** dialog box, notice that some fields have been populated and the dialog box title is updated, as well. In the user name field, in the **Affected user** area, type in **Don**, and then select **VIAMONSTRA\Don**.

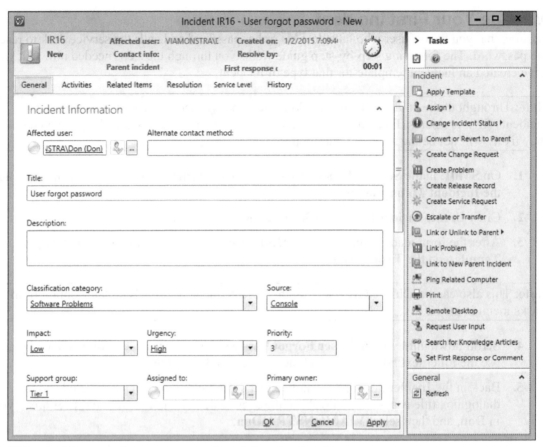

Using incident templates can save a lot of time for first-line operators.

6. Navigate to the **Activities** tab and notice that an activity has already been added to the list. Click **Open**.

7. In the **MA<number>: Reset user password in Active Directory** dialog box, click **Mark as Completed** in the **Tasks** menu and enter **Completed** as a comment in the dialog box before you click **OK** twice.

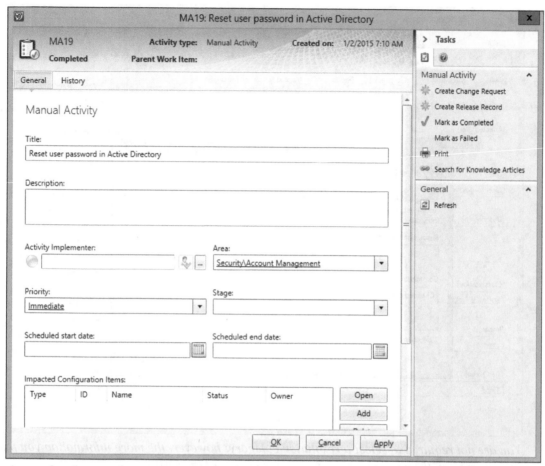

A completed manual activity.

8. Back in the **Incident** dialog box, in the **Tasks** menu, under **Change Incident Status**, click **Resolve**.

9. Enter **Changed the password in Active Directory** as a comment in the **Resolve** dialog box and click **OK**.

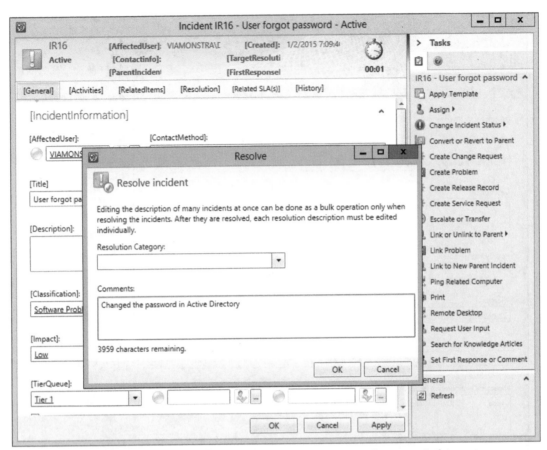

You are not required to select a resolution category; however, the more information you put into the system, the more information you can get out of the system.

10. Click **OK** in the **Incident** dialog box to close it.

> **Note:** If you see a dialog box saying that "Time worked can be added only for imported or created users in Service Manager" it's normally because the user running the console have not been added as a user in Service Manager. You can see synchronized users in the Configuration Items workspace, in the Users node.

After the incident have been resolved, you can find it in the All Incidents view. Incidents that have been created but yet not resolved can be found in the All Open Incidents view found under the Incident Management node.

Of course, in a real-world production environment, an incident might not be this easy to solve. Service Manager, therefore, has support for different tiers of support so that the first tier that perhaps receives a phone call or contact from a user in any form can escalate the issue to the second tier or the third tier where operators with deeper knowledge of the different products work. There also is support for assigning an incident to an operator so that each operator can work with a dedicated queue and a manager can see who has the biggest queue and assign incidents to other operators.

Working with Configuration Items and Incidents

In addition to how you worked with and completed an incident in the preceding section, an incident can be connected to one or many configuration items (CIs). This can be very helpful when a recurring error occurs within your organization.

Let's say that your service desk gets an increase in calls regarding laptops that need to be charged more frequently. The first thing to do might be to troubleshoot a battery on one laptop. If no fault is found on that battery, there is a less clear path ahead.

By collecting as much data as possible, you might be able to find that the issue is related to a specific laptop manufacturer or model. That information together with what Configuration Manager collects for you can give you a comprehensive image on the problem. Perhaps these laptops were purchased at the same time, perhaps they have a legacy UEFI or BIOS version. All this starts by relating configuration items together with incidents.

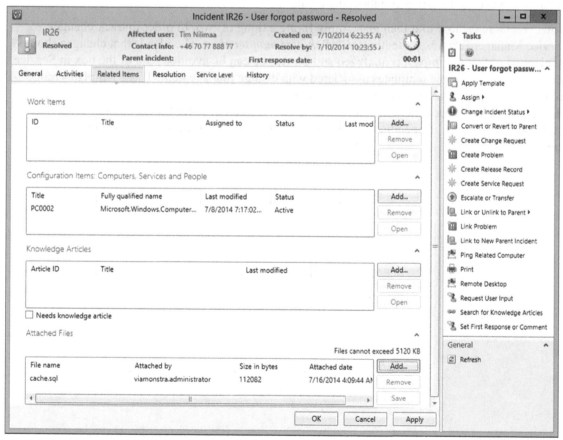

Working with related CIs is done on the Related Items tab on an incident.

Working with Problem and Change Management in Service Manager

Problems, according to ITL, are considered to be both reactive and proactive, meaning that a problem can be used to prevent something from happening. In Service Manager, this takes the form of creating problems based on one or many incidents that coordinate solutions for them or that prevent one or many incidents.

An organization going from only taking care of incidents to managing problems will see an increase in the time spent on administrative efforts, of course, but should see a larger benefit from fewer fires to put out and a more stable infrastructure. By spending less time on recurring incidents, operators can instead spend time on improving the infrastructure so that it is more reliable and up to date with the latest technology.

Problem management includes a crucial part that incidents do not necessarily include, and that is research and documentation. Whereas an operator solving an incident simply closes the ticket, an operator who works with a problem finds a solution not only to close a ticket but also, in the best of worlds, prevents it from ever happening again.

However, there is more to it than just simply fixing a thing or two. In order to track changes, Service Manager features something called *change management*. The idea is that changes should be planned so that the impact is analyzed and downtime can be avoided. Out of the box in Service Manager, there are some templates associated with change management. These templates range from minor to major and include templates for both security and emergency changes, as well. Each template holds some activities that need to be executed in order for the change to be implemented correctly. Depending on the template in question,/ the number and types of steps vary.

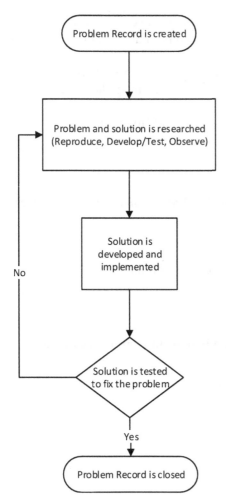

Solving a problem once and for all frees up time for other tasks.

Solving Incidents Using Problem Management

To complete the following guide, it is recommended but not necessary that you have completed the steps in Chapter 4's "Application Model" section.

The Scenario

Tim and Andreas have both traveled to the ViaMonstra branch office in the UK. While there they realize, independent from each other, that they are unable to install TweetDeck using Configuration Manager. They contact the service desk in their own preferred ways and get their incidents created.

> **Note**: To actually experience the problem in this scenario, you would have to add a secondary site using a router to your lab environment. Check http://viamonstra.com for an IP plan. For a router, the guide written by Johan Arwidmark at http://www.deploymentresearch.com/Research/tabid/62/EntryId/81/Using-a-virtual-router-for-your-lab-and-test-environment.aspx gives a good overview how to implement the router in the lab.
>
> To complete the steps in this guide, however, it is not necessary to add any of this to your environment.

Create Two Incidents

1. On **SM01**, using the **Service Manager Console**, in the **Work Items** workspace, select the **Incident Management** node.

2. Click **Create Incident** from the **Tasks** menu on the right.

3. In the **New Incident Form** dialog box, enter the following information:

   o   Affected user: **VIAMONSTRA\Don**

   o   Title: **Unable to install TweetDeck**

   o   Description: **While in UK, the user is unable to install TweetDeck using SCCM.**

   o   Classification category: **Software Problems**

   o   Impact: **Low**

   o   Urgency: **High**

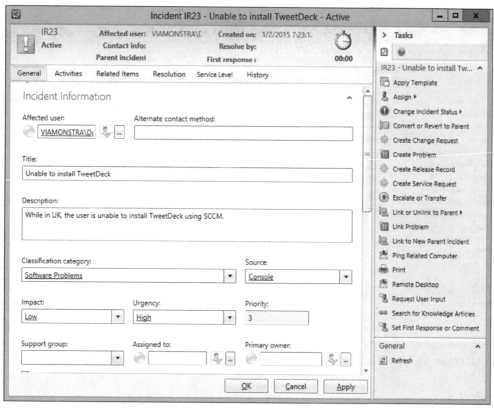

A typical incident, with little information except the experienced problem by the end user.

4. Close and create the new incident by clicking **OK**.

5. Repeat steps 2–4 once more. The exact phrasing on the title and description isn't required. Actually, by differentiating them a bit, you can see more clearly that two incidents have been created.

After you have created at least two incidents, you can review these using the All Open Incidents node under Incident Management in the Work Items workspace.

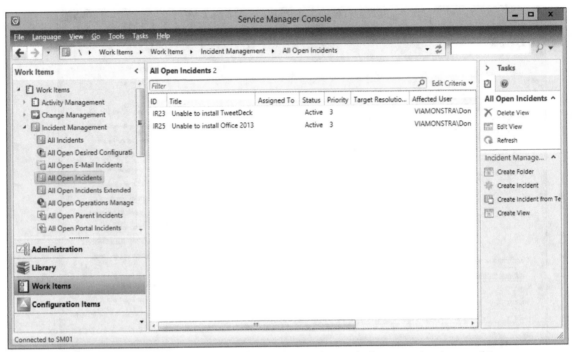

Using the All Open Incidents node shows all open incidents in the organization at this moment.

Related Items

Although Service Manager is a powerful software in many aspects, when it comes to incident management, one of the features that makes it so powerful is the ability to see other items related to what you are working on. The more information you and your colleges put into the system, the more information and understanding can you get out of it, and, in the long run, you have a better understanding of the big, often complex, picture of why a problem occurs.

We have all stumbled upon errors that seem to occur randomly, but computers are quite bad at making things at random. Most often, if not always, we just don't have all information or the complete picture. Using the feature to relate items to an incident or a problem helps us to gather the complete picture of why something happened.

1. In the **Work Items** workspace, open an open incident from the **Incident Management / All Open Incidents** node.

2. Select the **Related Items** tab.

3. In the **Configuration Items: Computers, Services and People** area, click **Add**.

4. In the **Select objects** dialog box, select **Package** from the drop-down list and find **TweetDeck** (or the package that your incident refers to) from the list of available objects. Click **Add** and then **OK**.

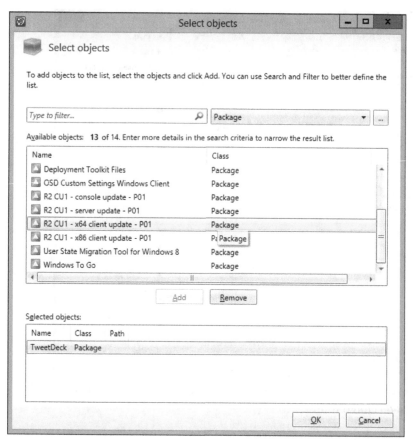

Multiple items of the same or different types can be added at the same time using the Select objects wizard. In this example you see TweetDeck being added.

5. In the **Incident** dialog box, click **Apply** to save the changes and leave the incident form open.

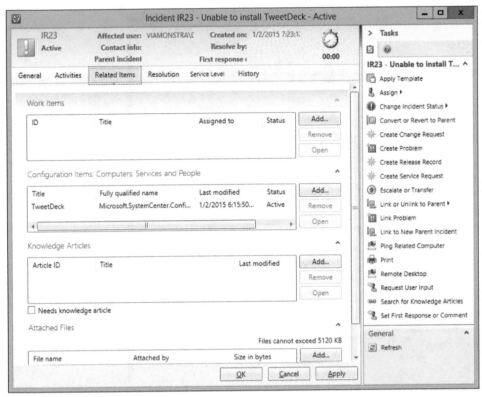

An incident with an item related to it.

Connect the Dots

Although you could create a problem using the problem management view just like you created incidents, this time we'll walk you through creating a problem from the incident form view.

1. If you left the incident form open from the last guide, go ahead to the next step; otherwise, open an open incident from the **All Open Incidents** node in the **Work Items** workspace.

Note: The problem will inherit the title of the selected incident, but it is changeable.

2. On the right side, click **Create Problem** in the **Tasks** menu.

3. In the **New Problem Form** dialog box, enter the following information:

   o   Title: **Unable to install applications in UK**

   o   Description: **Users from Sweden are unable to install applications while at the UK Branch Office.**

   o   Category: **Application**

   o   Impact: **Medium**

   o   Urgency: **Medium**

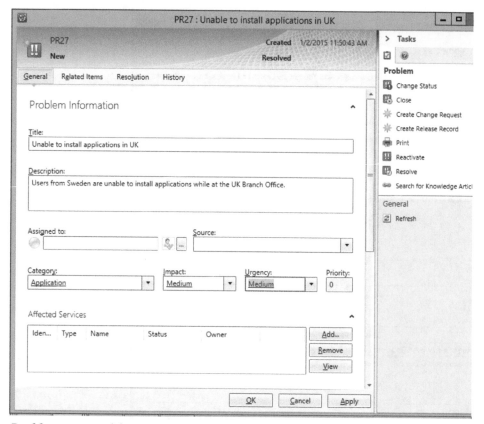

Problem spawned from a preexisting incident in Service Manager.

4. Click **Apply** to create and save the problem.

5. In the problem dialog box, navigate to the **Related Items** tab.

6. In the **Work Items** area, click **Add** to add the other incident that is related to application installation in the UK branch office.

7. In the **Select objects** dialog box, select the incident and click **Add**, followed by **OK**.

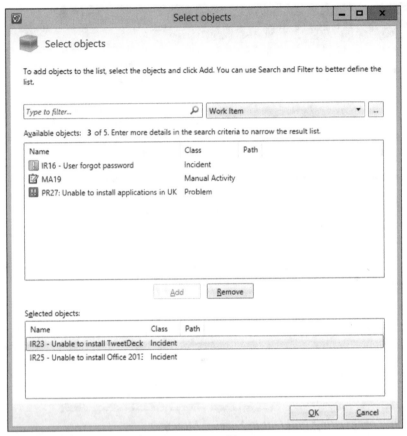

Linking additional work items to a problem.

8. Back in the problem dialog box, click **OK** twice save the information and close the open incident.

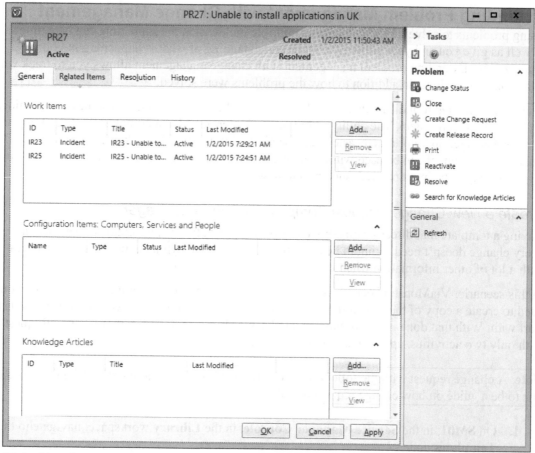

Linked incidents to a problem in Service Manager allow for an operator to quickly gather all information available on a problem to find a solution.

As an operator, you can now go through the problem to the two incidents and note that the problem only occurs when a user travels to the UK site. In a large organization, this problem could now be handed off to the team managing Configuration Manager.

Based on the information in this problem, a skilled Configuration Manager operator can understand that there is something wrong with the setup for at least one application or the distribution point in the UK. Because in this scenario we don't have a distribution point in the UK, it's far more likely something is wrong with the application.

Extending Problem Management with Change Management

Using problems to solve larger incidents or multiple incidents at the same time can be a time saver as well as give you and your colleges a better understanding of what is happening in your organization. Extending problem management with change management allows you to track why things have been done, in addition to how the problems were solved.

A change is created to indicate that something needs to be altered in order to achieve something, such as solving a problem. The ability to link items in Service Manager makes the life of an Service Manager operator much easier because all the information is trackable for all items. Change management can be used without a problem, as well. One such scenario is when you plan for something to be implemented, such as a new server.

Create a New Change Request Template in Service Manager

Having a template that directly corresponds to your organization is important so that each and every change doesn't need fixing to be compliant. This is done by managing templates, just as with a lot of other information when it comes to Service Manager.

In this scenario, ViaMonstra keeps a tight and clean change process for minor changes, and you need to create a copy of the standard Minor Change Request and make it even shorter than it is to start with. With that done, you will have created a ViaMonstra-specific Minor Change Request with only two activities: approval and implementation.

> **Note**: A change request with the following two activities is basically a Standard Change. Consider this to be a guide on how change request templates can be altered.

1. On **SM01**, in the **Service Manager Console**, in the **Library** workspace, navigate to the **Templates** node.

2. Locate and select the **Minor Change Request** in the list of templates, and then click **Duplicate** in the **Tasks** menu on the right side.

3. Leave the **Service Manager Change Management Configuration Library** selected in the **Select management pack** dialog box and click **OK**.

4. Again in the list of templates, locate the **Minor Change Request – Copy** and open its properties dialog box by double-clicking it.

5. In the **Minor Change Request – Copy** dialog box, change the **Name** field to **ViaMonstra Minor Change Request** and click **OK** after making sure that the **When I click OK, open the template form** check box is selected.

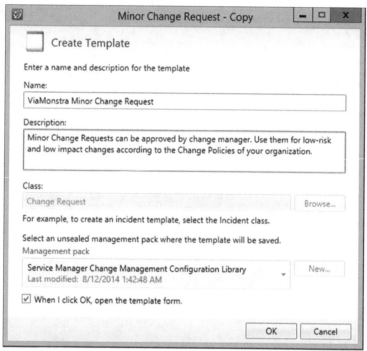

Having a naming standard, including the company name, can be good in a lab environment; otherwise, it is often better to delete the out-of-the-box ones and keep standard names.

6. Once the **Change Request – ViaMonstra Minor Change Request** template dialog box opens, set the following values on the **General** tab:

    o   Impact: **Minor**

    o   Risk: **Low**

7. Navigate to the **Activities** tab and remove the two activities in the middle that contain the words **develop** and **testing,** respectively.

Note: You can delete activities by right-clicking them and selecting Delete Activity.

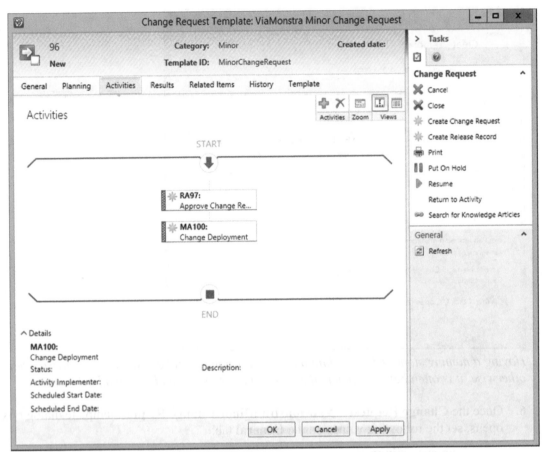

The list of activities can be as long or as short as your organization needs.

8. Click **OK** to save the changes and close the template dialog box.

Create a Change Request in Service Manager

The change request is built from the template that defines what steps, or activities, are normally executed for the type of change. After the change request is created, activities can be added, removed, or altered to match exactly what is needed by the change.

1. On **SM01**, in the **Service Manager Console**, in the **Work Items** workspace, navigate to the **Problem Management / Active Problems** node.

2. Double-click the **Unable to install applications in UK** problem, and in the **Tasks** menu on the right side, click **Create Change Request**.

3. In the **Select Template** dialog box, select the **ViaMonstra Minor Change Request** template and click **OK**.

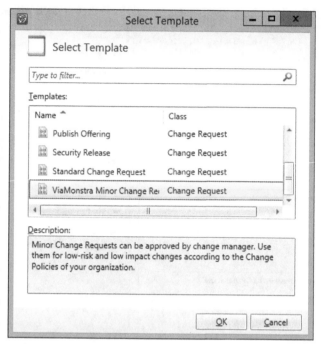

Selecting the ViaMonstra Minor Change Request template.

4. In the **Minor Change Request** dialog box, populate the following values in the **General** tab:

    o   Title: **Change fallback setting on distribution point**

    o   Description: **Distribution point CM01 must be configured to allow to serve fallback clients.**

    o   Reason: **Clients in the UK office are unable to download packages since there isn't a DP in that site.**

    o   Priority: **Immediate**

    o   Config Items To Change: In the **Select objects** wizard, add **CM01** using the **Add** button.

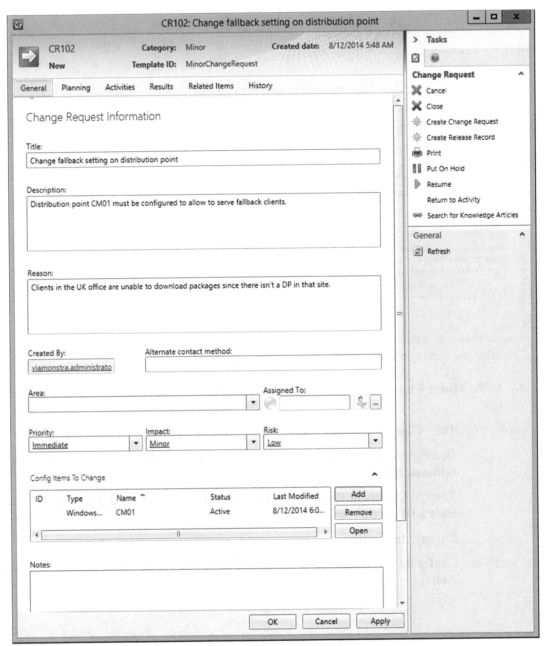

A filled out change request form to change a setting on CM01.

5. Notice that both **Impact** and **Risk** are already populated but that you could change both of them if you wanted to.

6. Click **OK** to save and close the change request, but leave the **Unable to install applications in UK** problem dialog open.

Approve the Change Request in Service Manager

Before the actual fix can be implemented, the change request should be approved. This is so that others know the status of a change. For minor changes it might not seem that important, but you never know when you'll be interrupted from the task at hand, so it is important to document the status of the work. This helps you to do just that.

In a larger organization, it is common that the person approving the change is not the same person who is requesting that a change be made.

1. On **SM01**, using the same problem from the preceding section, select the **Related Items** tab.

2. In the right pane, click **Refresh** see the related change request in the **Work Items** list.

3. In the **Work Items** list, select the change request and click **View**.

4. In the change request dialog box, select the **Activities** tab and double-click the first activity, **Approve Change Request**, to open it.

5. In the **Approve Change Request** dialog box, add the **VIAMONSTRA\Administrator** account as a reviewer, and then select that entry under **Reviewers** and click **Approve**

6. In the **Comments** dialog box, enter **Approved** in the comments field and click **OK**.

7. Back in the **Approve Change Request** dialog box, click **OK** to save the changes and close the dialog box.

8. Back in the **Change fallback setting on distribution** point dialog box, wait until activity is marked as completed and that the next activity is active. Then click **OK**.

Note: Service Manager triggers workflows on a schedule; therefore, it may take a minute before you see that the approve activity is marked as completed and that the next activity is active.

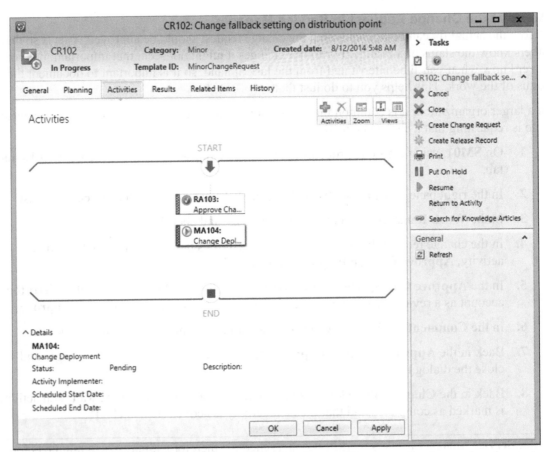

The Activities tab shows the current progress of a change. Views can be changed and zooming done from the upper right corner of the Activities area.

Implement the Change in Configuration Manager

Making sure that a client can access content is crucial when working with Configuration Manager. When an organization expands, it's not always the case that the initial setup of the Configuration Manager infrastructure remains valid. It is therefore a good practice to review the configuration from time to time.

In this scenario, the infrastructure is serving only clients in the Swedish office (ViaMonstra HQ) and not the ones outside it, even if the client originates from the Swedish office. To solve this issue, an operator has to make two changes, one to the infrastructure and one per application deployment type. This allows for smart content management so that a client, for instance, can install small and/or important software, such as antivirus definitions or hotfixes, but perhaps not larger software like the Adobe Creative Suite, which is several gigabyte in size.

Real World Note: When deciding on which distribution points to allow for fallback and where to install a new distribution point, it is a good idea to talk to the networking team early in the process. Bring a bottle of good whiskey and chances are higher that you'll get good help.

1. On **CM01**, start the **ConfigMgr console** if it is not already started and navigate to the **Applications** node in the **Software Library** workspace.

2. Select the **TweetDeck** application and open the **Properties** dialog box by clicking the **Properties** button on the ribbon.

3. In the **Deployment Types** tab, select the **TweetDeck - Windows Installer (*.msi file)** deployment type and click **Edit**.

4. In the **Content** tab, make sure that **Allow clients to use a fallback source location for content** is selected and **Deployment options** is set to **Download content from distribution point and run locally**.

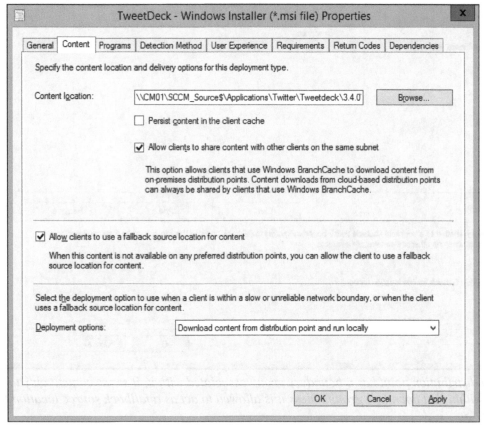

A deployment type that is enabled to allow clients to download the content even if the client isn't located near a distribution point that has the bits and bytes.

5. Click **OK** twice to save the changes and close the dialog boxes.

6. In the **Administration** workspace, select the **Servers and Site System Roles** node under **Site Configuration**.

7. Select the **CM01** server from the upper list, and then open the properties for the **Distribution point** site system role by double-clicking it.

8. In the **Boundary Groups** tab, make sure that **Allow fallback source location for content** is selected.

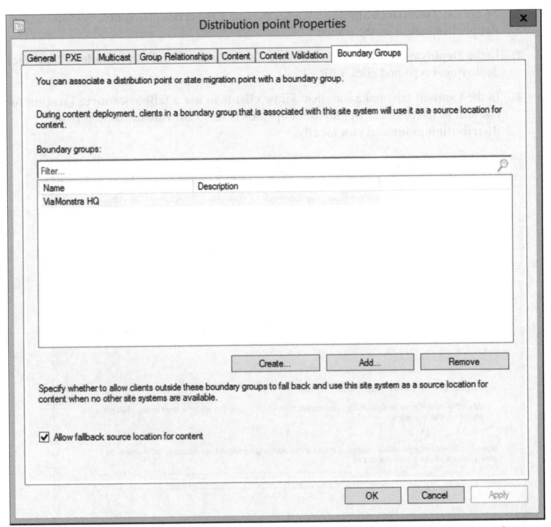

When a distribution point has a boundary group associated with it, it sends content only to clients within that boundary group unless it is allowed to act as a fallback source location for content.

9. Click **OK** to close the dialog box and save the setting.

Update and Close the Change Request

After the changes have been applied to the system as intended and the new functionality has been verified to work as expected, the change request should be marked as completed. This allows for change request tracking, as well as, so that you and your colleges know the status of the change.

1. If you left the change request open from the "Approve the Change Request in Service Manager" section, skip to step 4.

2. On **SM01**, open the **Service Manager Console** if it is not already open, in the **Work Items** workspace, select the **Change Management** node.

3. Select the **All Change Request** node, and open the **Change fallback setting on distribution point** change request by double-clicking it.

4. In the **Activity** tab, open the **Change Deployment** activity by double-clicking it.

5. Optionally, enter information on what you did in Configuration Manager to the activity.

6. Click **Mark as Completed** in the **Tasks** menu.

7. In the **Comments** dialog box, enter **Completed successfully** as a comment, and then click **OK**.

8. In the **Change Deployment** dialog box, click **OK** to save the changes and close the dialog box.

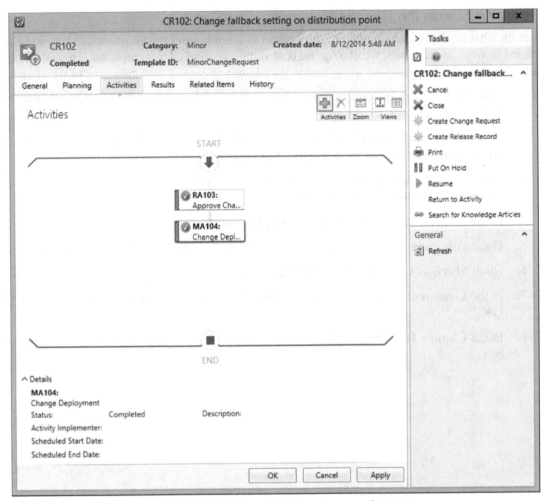

Workflows can be long or short and consist of different types of activities.

9. Click **OK** to close the change request. After all the workflows in Service Manager have been executed, the change request's status will change to Completed.

Update and Resolve the Problem Record

After all the changes have been applied to the system, a problem needs to be closed so that you can start working on something new. And perhaps more important, the clock measuring how long the problem was open will stop, hopefully within the allowed SLA (Service Level Agreement) resolution time.

Problems can be of different nature, and some allow for the operator to close all linked incidents, whereas others require that each and every incident be verified with the affected user. For the sake of this lab, you simply close all the linked incidents.

1. On **SM01**, in the **Service Manager Console**, in the **Work Items** workspace, navigate to the **Active Problems** node under **Problem Management**.

2. Open the **Unable to install applications in UK** problem by double-clicking it.

3. In the **Tasks** menu in the right pane, click **Resolve** and navigate to the **Resolution** tab.

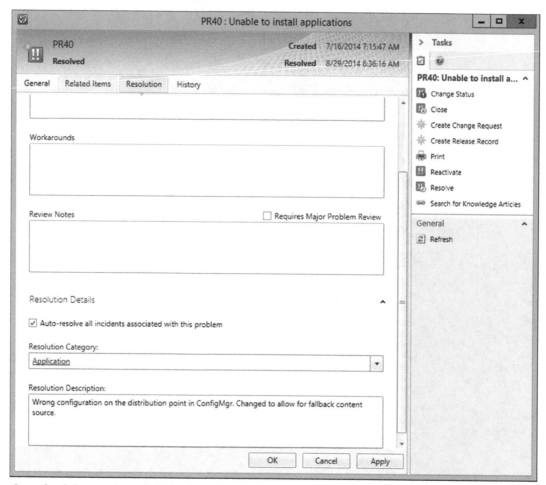

One check box makes all linked incidents resolved at the same time that the problem is resolved. Time efficient!

4. Select the **Auto-resolve all incidents associated with this problem** check box, enter a short but informative description in the **Resolution Description** field (at the bottom of the page), and then click **OK** to save and close the problem record.

Chapter 11

PowerShell

In just a couple of years, PowerShell will actually "turn binary," 10 that is. PowerShell is, in other words, anything but new. Back in 2006, PowerShell 1.0 was released together with Windows Server 2008 and Windows Vista. Since then, a new major release has been shipped together with each new major release of Windows. Together with Windows Server 2012 R2 and Windows 8.1, we now have PowerShell 4.0.

PowerShell is an object- and task-oriented scripting language built on top of the .NET Framework. You might think of it as a "C# light" scripting language if you come from the developer perspective, or CMD-files on futuristic steroids if you come from the IT professional perspective.

The foundation of PowerShell is readable and reusable code. Code PowerShell like every single script should be reusable without alternation, and you will do a lot of good scripting.

Introduction to PowerShell

Object Oriented

PowerShell is an object-oriented scripting language in the sense that all things we have within PowerShell are objects, in comparison to all things we can do in PowerShell which are tasks. When we assign a variable the text "PowerShell is awesome", we actually create an object of the type String that has the value "PowerShell is awesome". How does this differentiate from just a variable that has the value then? The object has properties that it knows about.

For instance, if we have the object Building, we can create multiple buildings, but all of them don't have to be houses. Some of the buildings can be shops or garages, as well. All of them, however, will have and know its properties that we call "NumberOfWalls," "Height," or perhaps "Color."

Querying a variable object of a property is done using a dot followed by the property name, such as we do with the property *Length* on the *MyVariable* variable in the following example. An object's *methods* are invoked in the very same way although some of them require parameters in order to function.

```
Windows PowerShell

Windows PowerShell
Copyright (C) 2013 Microsoft Corporation. All rights reserved.

PS C:\Users\Administrator> $MyVariable = "PowerShell is awesome."
PS C:\Users\Administrator> $MyVariable.Length
22
PS C:\Users\Administrator> $MyVariable | Get-Member


   TypeName: System.String

Name                 MemberType             Definition
----                 ----------             ----------
Clone                Method                 System.Object Clone(), System.Object ICloneable.Clone()
CompareTo            Method                 int CompareTo(System.Object value), int CompareTo(string str8), int IComparab...
Contains             Method                 bool Contains(string value)
CopyTo               Method                 void CopyTo(int sourceIndex, char[] destination, int destinationIndex, int co...
EndsWith             Method                 bool EndsWith(string value), bool EndsWith(string value, System.StringCompari...
Equals               Method                 bool Equals(System.Object obj), bool Equals(string value), bool Equals(string...
GetEnumerator        Method                 System.CharEnumerator GetEnumerator(), System.Collections.Generic.IEnumerator...
GetHashCode          Method                 int GetHashCode()
GetType              Method                 type GetType()
GetTypeCode          Method                 System.TypeCode GetTypeCode(), System.TypeCode IConvertible.GetTypeCode()
IndexOf              Method                 int IndexOf(char value), int IndexOf(char value, int startIndex), int IndexOf...
IndexOfAny           Method                 int IndexOfAny(char[] anyOf), int IndexOfAny(char[] anyOf, int startIndex), i...
Insert               Method                 string Insert(int startIndex, string value)
IsNormalized         Method                 bool IsNormalized(), bool IsNormalized(System.Text.NormalizationForm normaliz...
LastIndexOf          Method                 int LastIndexOf(char value), int LastIndexOf(char value, int startIndex), int...
LastIndexOfAny       Method                 int LastIndexOfAny(char[] anyOf), int LastIndexOfAny(char[] anyOf, int startI...
Normalize            Method                 string Normalize(), string Normalize(System.Text.NormalizationForm normalizat...
PadLeft              Method                 string PadLeft(int totalWidth), string PadLeft(int totalWidth, char paddingChar)
PadRight             Method                 string PadRight(int totalWidth), string PadRight(int totalWidth, char padding...
Remove               Method                 string Remove(int startIndex, int count), string Remove(int startIndex)
Replace              Method                 string Replace(char oldChar, char newChar), string Replace(string oldValue, s...
Split                Method                 string[] Split(Params char[] separator), string[] Split(char[] separator, int...
StartsWith           Method                 bool StartsWith(string value), bool StartsWith(string value, System.StringCom...
Substring            Method                 string Substring(int startIndex), string Substring(int startIndex, int length)
ToBoolean            Method                 bool IConvertible.ToBoolean(System.IFormatProvider provider)
ToByte               Method                 byte IConvertible.ToByte(System.IFormatProvider provider)
ToChar               Method                 char IConvertible.ToChar(System.IFormatProvider provider)
ToCharArray          Method                 char[] ToCharArray(), char[] ToCharArray(int startIndex, int length)
ToDateTime           Method                 datetime IConvertible.ToDateTime(System.IFormatProvider provider)
ToDecimal            Method                 decimal IConvertible.ToDecimal(System.IFormatProvider provider)
ToDouble             Method                 double IConvertible.ToDouble(System.IFormatProvider provider)
ToInt16              Method                 int16 IConvertible.ToInt16(System.IFormatProvider provider)
ToInt32              Method                 int IConvertible.ToInt32(System.IFormatProvider provider)
ToInt64              Method                 long IConvertible.ToInt64(System.IFormatProvider provider)
ToLower              Method                 string ToLower(), string ToLower(cultureinfo culture)
ToLowerInvariant     Method                 string ToLowerInvariant()
ToSByte              Method                 sbyte IConvertible.ToSByte(System.IFormatProvider provider)
ToSingle             Method                 float IConvertible.ToSingle(System.IFormatProvider provider)
ToString             Method                 string ToString(), string ToString(System.IFormatProvider provider), string I...
ToType               Method                 System.Object IConvertible.ToType(type conversionType, System.IFormatProvider...
ToUInt16             Method                 uint16 IConvertible.ToUInt16(System.IFormatProvider provider)
ToUInt32             Method                 uint32 IConvertible.ToUInt32(System.IFormatProvider provider)
ToUInt64             Method                 uint64 IConvertible.ToUInt64(System.IFormatProvider provider)
ToUpper              Method                 string ToUpper(), string ToUpper(cultureinfo culture)
ToUpperInvariant     Method                 string ToUpperInvariant()
Trim                 Method                 string Trim(Params char[] trimChars), string Trim()
TrimEnd              Method                 string TrimEnd(Params char[] trimChars)
TrimStart            Method                 string TrimStart(Params char[] trimChars)
Chars                ParameterizedProperty  char Chars(int index) {get;}
Length               Property               int Length {get;}

PS C:\Users\Administrator> _
```

Using the Cmdlet Get-Member, you get all the members of your variable and its object type.

Task Oriented

When running code in PowerShell, we work with the different objects. We interact with the objects using cmdlets (pronounced *command-lets*). Each cmdlet is in the form of a verb combined with a noun, for instance the verb Get can be combined with the noun Credentials creating the task to Get (your) Credentials. The task is then combined with a dash and forms Get-Credentials.

Cmdlets, Scripts, and Modules

PowerShell is a language that is easy to read and understand. It is therefore very suitable for sharing. In PowerShell 1.0, however, it was somewhat troublesome to share larger portions of code because it only had support for what was called snap-ins. Since PowerShell 2.0, that has been made easier by the use of modules. Each function in PowerShell is referred to as a cmdlet, and each script uses one or more of these functions or cmdlets.

Although scripts can be perfect for storing for personal usage or sharing, they are often made for a more or less specific task. One task could be to get an input of a text file and create users in Active Directory based on that. After that, a synchronization with Office365 could be made, and then each user in Office365 could be email enabled. This script can be made very reusable by simply allowing for some input parameters. However, it would be somewhat troublesome to manage and update the script if all the logic had to be placed in that script file. All authentication, error, and whatnot handling that needs to be done while talking to services such as Active Directory and Office365. Reading a text file is a bit easier, even if that also needs error handling – what if the file doesn't exist in the path specified?

In order to make the script more readable and thus useable, a lot of the required cmdlets are put in different modules, depending on what they belong to. For instance, Office365 cmdlets to mail enable a user are put together with other cmdlets for Office365 and shipped by the team behind Office365 at Microsoft. The same goes for the cmdlets for Active Directory.

Getting Started with PowerShell

Installing PowerShell

As of Windows Vista, PowerShell comes preinstalled on both client and server versions of Windows. However, there are new versions of PowerShell released with each new version of Windows. When Windows 6.3 (more commonly known as Windows 8.1 and Windows Server 2012 R2) was released, so was PowerShell 4.0. For earlier versions of Windows, such as Windows 7, PowerShell 4.0 was released in what is called Windows Management Framework 4.0.

Operating System	Shipped PowerShell version
Windows 6.0, Windows Vista / Server 2008	PowerShell 1.0
Windows 6.1, Windows 7 / Server 2008 R2	PowerShell 2.0
Windows 6.2, Windows 8 / Server 2012	PowerShell 3.0
Windows 6.3, Windows 8.1 / Server 2012 R2	PowerShell 4.0

Windows Management Framework 4.0 is delivered for Windows 6.1 as an update file (MSU) and can be downloaded from http://www.microsoft.com/en-us/download/details.aspx?id=40855. The update exists in both x86 and x64 versions for Windows 6.1 and additionally for the ARM platform for Windows 6.2 RT. By installing the update for Windows Management Framework 4.0, PowerShell is upgraded from 2.0 to 4.0.

This means that other than installing upgrades, there is no real need to install anything to be able to run PowerShell code on any operating system from Microsoft since Windows Vista, including Windows RT and Windows Server Core. Later, support for .NET Framework has been added to Windows Preinstallation Environment, enabling support for PowerShell even there.

With PowerShell having such a tight integration with the .NET Framework, it is even possible to write graphical "applications" using PowerShell. Of course, they require the .NET Framework and PowerShell to execute on a PC because it is still just a script that loads modules from .NET Framework and draws a form on the screen, but it is possible. Working closely with customers, we've seen IT professionals implementing small and big tools and helping their colleagues perhaps not to automate everything, but to help them with their daily tasks. One example of a tool written in PowerShell draws a GUI that allows a technician to deploy a VM in VMware (!) with a preset of VM sizes referred to as Small, Medium and Large. Each size has a preset of vCPUs, RAM, and so forth making the VMs in the datacenter more standardized than if each technician were allowed to create a VM of their own. All done with PowerShell.

Running the First Command

Throughout this book, we have suggested, from time to time, that you run PowerShell scripts to automate steps. If you took the GUI (graphical user interface) approach then and still haven't gotten started with PowerShell, now is about time.

A PowerShell command is, as we mentioned, built from a verb and a noun, but there often is more to a command than just the command. Each command often has a set of parameters that come along with it. As an example, the Write-Host cmdlet wouldn't do much good without the -Object parameter telling the command which object it should write to the host (most often the console on the local machine). Remember, even if we pass the string "PowerShell is awesome" to the -Object parameter, it's not just a string that we have defined; it's an object of the type String with the value "PowerShell is awesome".

Create an User in Active Directory

While we could go for the traditional "Hello World" concept for teaching a new scripting or programming language, we'll go with something a bit more useful. After completing these steps, you will have created a normal user account within Active Directory.

1. On **DC01**, log on as **VIAMONSTRA\Administrator**, start an elevated **PowerShell** prompt or the ISE.

2. Run the following command to create a user account. Feel free to change the values from Firstname and Lastname to your own name.

```
New-ADUser -GivenName "Firstname" -Surname "Lastname"
-DisplayName "Firstname Lastname" -Name "Firstname Lastname"
-SamAccountName "Firstname.Lastname " -UserPrincipalName
"Firstname.Lastname@corp.viamonstra.com" -Path
"OU=Users,OU=ViaMonstra,DC=corp,DC=viamonstra,DC=com"
-Verbose
```

> **Note:** If you were to look up the user account in Active Directory Users and Computers, you would notice that the account is disabled. That is because the account doesn't have a password assigned yet. Although we could do all of this in one line of code, for clarity we go about it step by step.

3. Run the following command to assign a password to the account:

```
Set-ADAccountPassword
-Identity:"CN=Firstname.Lastname,OU=Users,OU=ViaMonstra,
DC=corp,DC=viamonstra,DC=com"
-NewPassword:(ConvertTo-SecureString -String "P@ssw0rd"
-AsPlainText -Force)
-Reset:$true -Verbose
```

> **Note**: The password parameter actually accepts only the password in the form of a SecureString object; therefore, we need to convert the plain text string that we can type on a command line to that kind of object. This is achieved by enclosing the command in a parentheses.

4. Now that the user account has a password that is compliant with the password policy in the domain, you can go ahead and activate the account using the following command line:

```
Enable-ADAccount
-Identity:"CN=Firstname Lastname,OU=Users,OU=ViaMonstra,
DC=corp,DC=viamonstra,DC=com" -Verbose
```

5. As this is a user account, we want to make sure that the end user changes the password at the first logon. Set this using the following command line:

```
Set-ADUser -ChangePasswordAtLogon:$true
-Identity:"CN=Firstname Lastname,OU=Users,OU=ViaMonstra,
DC=corp,DC=viamonstra,DC=com" -Verbose
```

```
Windows PowerShell
Copyright (C) 2013 Microsoft Corporation. All rights reserved.

PS C:\windows\system32> New-ADUser -GivenName "Firstname" -Surname "Lastname" -DisplayName "Firstnam
e Lastname" -Name "FirstName Lastname" -SamAccountName "Fistname.Lastname" -UserPrincipalName "First
name.Lastname@corp.viamonstra.com" -Path "OU=Users,OU=ViaMonstra,DC=corp,DC=viamonstra,DC=com" -Verb
ose
VERBOSE: Performing the operation "New" on target "CN=FirstName
Lastname,OU=Users,OU=ViaMonstra,DC=corp,DC=viamonstra,DC=com".
PS C:\windows\system32>
PS C:\windows\system32> Set-ADAccountPassword -Identity:"CN=Firstname Lastname,OU=Users,OU=ViaMonstr
a,DC=corp,DC=viamonstra,DC=com" -NewPassword:(ConvertTo-SecureString -String "P@ssw0rd" -AsPlainText
 -Force) -Reset:$true -Verbose
PS C:\windows\system32>
PS C:\windows\system32> Enable-ADAccount -Identity:"CN=Firstname Lastname,OU=Users,OU=ViaMonstra,DC=
corp,DC=viamonstra,DC=com" -Verbose
VERBOSE: Performing the operation "Set" on target "CN=FirstName
Lastname,OU=Users,OU=ViaMonstra,DC=corp,DC=viamonstra,DC=com".
PS C:\windows\system32>
PS C:\windows\system32> Set-ADUser -ChangePasswordAtLogon:$true -Identity:"CN=Firstname Lastname,OU=
Users,OU=ViaMonstra,DC=corp,DC=viamonstra,DC=com" -Verbose
VERBOSE: Performing the operation "Set" on target "CN=FirstName
Lastname,OU=Users,OU=ViaMonstra,DC=corp,DC=viamonstra,DC=com".
PS C:\windows\system32>
PS C:\windows\system32> _
```

All three lines of PowerShell code required to create a user in Active Directory.

The user account is now created, and you should be able to log on with the account on PC0001 or PC0002.

Running the First Script

As you might have noticed while creating the user account in the preceding section, there was a lot of typing the same thing over and over. So in the event that you had to do the same thing over and over, a great way of doing it would be to save the rows into a script file that you could execute with PowerShell every time you needed it. You might have gotten this far already, but the need to recreate the same user account over and over might not be that necessary so in an upcoming section, we cover how to take input into the script. But one thing at a time, and Rome will be built over and over every day with as little as a keystroke from you.

1. On **DC01**, start the **PowerShell** ISE in elevated mode.

2. Enter the following text into the upper section of the ISE:

```
$UserOU =
"OU=Users,OU=ViaMonstra,DC=corp,DC=viamonstra,DC=com"

$Givenname = "Firstname"

$Surname = "Lastname"

$Displayname = "$($Givenname) $($Surname)"

$SamAccountName = "$($Givenname).$($Surname)"

New-ADUser -GivenName $Givenname -Surname $Surname
-DisplayName $Displayname -Name $Displayname -SamAccountName
$SamAccountName

-UserPrincipalName "$($SamAccountName)@corp.viamonstra.com"
-Path $UserOU -Verbose

Set-ADAccountPassword -
Identity:"CN=$($Displayname),$($UserOU)"

-NewPassword:(ConvertTo-SecureString -String "P@ssw0rd"
-AsPlainText -Force) -Reset:$true -Verbose

Enable-ADAccount -Identity:"CN=$($Displayname),$($UserOU)"
-Verbose

Set-ADUser -ChangePasswordAtLogon:$true
-Identity:"CN=$($Displayname),$($UserOU)" -Verbose
```

> **Note:** Make sure to give the user a new Givenname and Surname, or delete the previously created account, or the script will fail.

3. Save the script as **CreateADUser.ps1** to **C:\Setup** using the **Save As** option on the **File** menu.

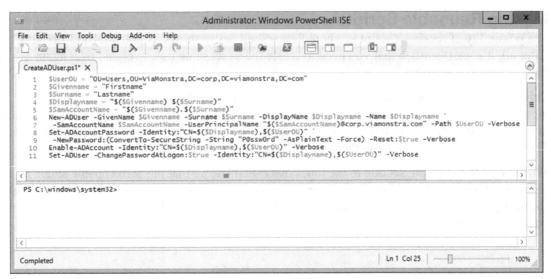

The use of variables makes the script far easier to change for new users because it requires changes in fewer places.

Note: In the figure, we have added the ` character to row 6 and 8 to be able to split them into two rows each so that row 7 and 9 are just the ends of 6 and 8, respectively. When creating the script, you can omit those characters and write the script on a total of nine rows.

---

4. Start an elevated **PowerShell** prompt.

5. Navigate to the folder where you saved the script using the following command:

   ```
   cd C:\Setup
   ```

6. Execute the script using the following command:

   ```
   .\CreateADUser.ps1
   ```

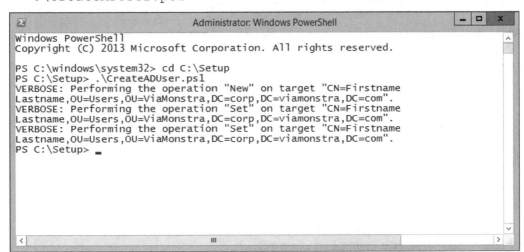

Running a script does not return the executed lines of code as running the commands in the prompt, but thanks to the –Verbose parameter we get some output from the script.

Making Reusable Scripts

The possibility of reusing a script is where PowerShell really shows its potential and strength. After all, it's not that often that you need to create the exact same user over and over again as you did in a previous section.

This time you add some logic to the script so that you can run the script and it prompts for the input required to complete the script. When you start to mass create end-user accounts, you want to make sure that they don't have the same password, even if it's just the initial password. Therefore, you add some logic to the script to generate a password, as well.

When you add the param section to the top, PowerShell knows that the $Givenname and $Surname variables should be populated using parameters to the execution of the script. By also specifying the parameter property Mandatory=$true, PowerShell will throw an exception, or an error, if one or both of them are missing.

```
param(

    [Parameter(Mandatory=$true)]

    $Givenname,

    [Parameter(Mandatory=$true)]

    $Surname
)

$UserOU = "OU=Users,OU=ViaMonstra,DC=corp,DC=viamonstra,DC=com"

$Displayname = "$($Givenname) $($Surname)"

$SamAccountName = "$($Givenname).$($Surname)"

$PasswordCharacters =
"ABCDEFGHJKLMNPQRSTUVWXYabcdefghijkmnpqrstuvwxy0123456789!@#$%&*(
)_-="

$Password = ""

while ($Password.Length -le 12)

{

    $Password += $PasswordCharacters[(Get-Random -Minimum 0
-Maximum $PasswordCharacters.Length)]

}
```

```
try

{

    New-ADUser -GivenName $Givenname -Surname $Surname
-DisplayName $Displayname -Name $Displayname `

     -SamAccountName $SamAccountName -UserPrincipalName
"$($SamAccountName)@corp.viamonstra.com" -Path $UserOU -Verbose

    Set-ADAccountPassword -
Identity:"CN=$($Displayname),$($UserOU)" `

     -NewPassword:(ConvertTo-SecureString -String "P@ssw0rd"
-AsPlainText -Force) -Reset:$true -Verbose

    Enable-ADAccount -Identity:"CN=$($Displayname),$($UserOU)"
-Verbose

    Set-ADUser -ChangePasswordAtLogon:$true
-Identity:"CN=$($Displayname),$($UserOU)" -Verbose

    Write-Output "Created the user account $($SamAccountName)
with password '$($Password)' ."

}

catch

{

    Write-Error "Unable to create the user account
$($SamAccountName)."

}
```

In the preceding script, we use a try/catch scenario in which PowerShell should try to execute a series of commands, and in the event of an error, it should catch that error and execute a different command, Write-Error, telling the console that an error occurred. This is a better way to write code because you can have different catches and catch different errors and thus return different error messages depending on what error has occurred.

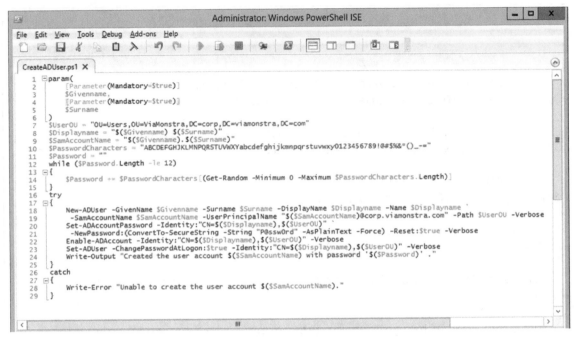

A complete script to generate user accounts.

The part that generates the password is the while loop. It will add a random character to the $Password variable from the $PasswordCharacters string until the $Password string variable length is "less than or equal" to 12 characters long.

Execute the Script

1. On **DC01**, update the **CreateADUser** script with the code in preceding section.

2. Again, execute the script in an elevated **PowerShell** prompt:

   a. Navigate to **C:\Setup** in the prompt using:

   ```
   cd C:\Setup
   ```

   b. Execute the script using:

   ```
   .\CreateADUser.ps1 -Givenname "Firstname" -SurName "Lastname"
   ```

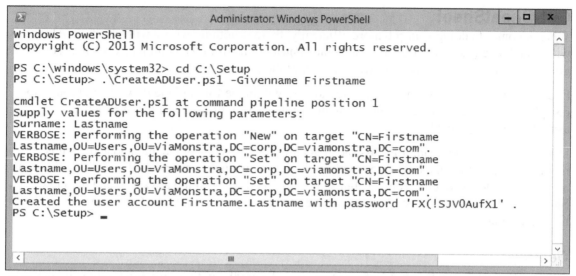

Failure to provide a mandatory parameter will cause PowerShell to prompt for the parameter.

Providers

A part of PowerShell that makes it so useful is its *providers*. A provider is simply a program that helps PowerShell access different kinds of data. In VBScript, you had to take care of this yourself.

A provider provides, or exposes, the data it provides using a drive letter. Therefore, to access the registry, you simply change drive letter like in a command prompt. For High Key Local Machine, that is HKLM:\ just as the local system drive is C:\.

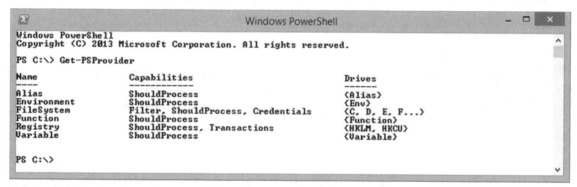

A list of all different providers and their drives.

When using PowerShell together with Configuration Manager, the PowerShell Module for Configuration Manager adds a dedicated provider for Configuration Manager. That provider has the "drive letter" of the site code. So if you have a Configuration Manager site with site code P01, you would access that site using the drive letter P01:\ in PowerShell.

341

Get-CheatSheet

When it comes to doing your job more efficiently, there is nothing wrong with cheating. Along with search engines on the web and awesome contributions from the community, there is some great stuff hidden in the core of PowerShell out of the box.

First is the IntelliSense that allows you to tab both within the ISE and the PowerShell prompt to complete a variable, command, and so on, or simply to walk through the list of parameters available for a command.

Using the Show-Command, it is possible to get a visual overview of a command and what is required in order to make it work. Sometimes it gives you a better overview than cycling through all the parameters using the Tab key, but some commands are just too advanced and the view from Show-Command is just messy. In that case the –Example parameter to the Get-Help command can be of great help.

Get-Help

The Get-Help command extracts information from the cmdlet with information written by the cmdlet author. The built-in modules and most of the modules from Microsoft contain this kind of information.

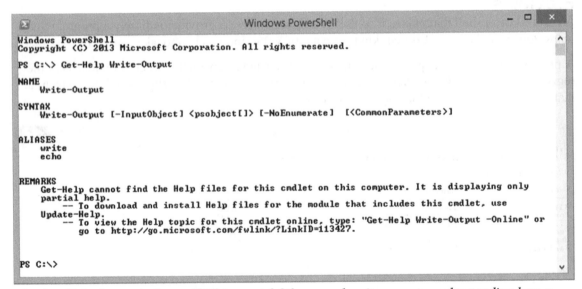

The Get-Help feature in PowerShell is a quick lifesaver when it comes to understanding how a cmdlet works. It will save you both once and twice from reaching for Internet Explorer.

Before you can use Get-Help, the information must be downloaded from the Internet using the command Update-Help, which requires your lab environment to have access to the Internet. This allow you to keep your offline help information up to date, and not only contain the information as it were when the product was shipped by Microsoft. Save-Help, a cleaver feature for those machines lacking internet connection, was released in PowerShell 4.0. You can read more about how to use that Cmdlet in the "What's New in PowerShell" section later in this Chapter.

Show-Command

Another very cool feature in PowerShell that sometimes can be handy and other times, let's say, not that handy is the Show-Command command. In a way, it is like Get-Help in that it shows you what parameters a command takes in order to work, but on the other hand, it is not like Get-Help because it does not show you any examples.

The command Show-Command gives you, in spite PowerShell being a script language, a GUI overview of a command.

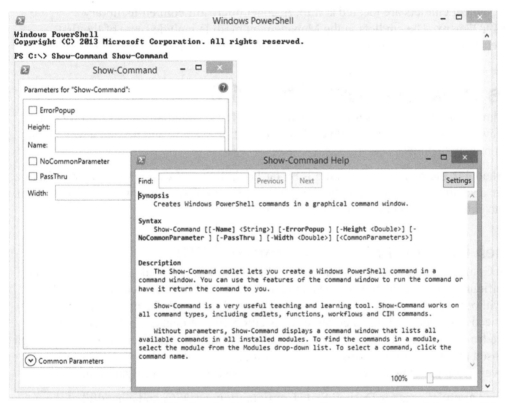

Here we see the help available for the Show-Command command opened from the Show-Command GUI window.

Online Reference

This information should get you going on your very first script with PowerShell. Basically there is just one way to learn PowerShell, and that is by starting to use it. Start simple like creating some users just as we showed you in the previous sections. Perhaps, like many others, you've found a great way to create service accounts in your Active Directory domain.

On TechNet, there is a great amount of documentation on the different modules and their cmdlets in PowerShell. For the core part, that can be a good reference when starting writing scripts, and for as long as you write scripts, there are some key sites on the web to look at:

- Utility cmdlets are located at http://technet.microsoft.com/en-us/library/hh849958.aspx. Here you will find important information for very useful cmdlets like ConvertFrom-Csv, Get-Random, and the popular Write-Progress.

- Security cmdlets are located at http://technet.microsoft.com/en-us/library/hh849807.aspx. Here you will find both ConvertTo and ConvertFrom-SecureString that are very important when handling passwords, but also the Get-Credential command that helps you authenticate to different services.

- Management cmdlets are located at http://technet.microsoft.com/en-us/library /hh849827.aspx. The cmdlets in the Management module include some of the first cmdlets that you probably will use, such as Get-Content, Join-Path and New-Item.

What's New in PowerShell 4.0

Automation through PowerShell is something that Microsoft has been hard at work on for quite some time. New versions are released with each new operating system, and in each new version, there are a lot of new features.

With PowerShell 4.0, the biggest new feature is by far Desired State Configuration, as we discuss later on. There also are features added to the Integrated Scripting Environment (ISE), one of them is the ability to debug code running in a remote session.

PowerShell Desired State Configuration (DSC)

Desired State Configuration is an extension to PowerShell and is a way to deploy, measure, and remediate configurations on a PC or server using scripts. One can think of them as Group Policy objects, but without the limitations in GPOs, such as the need for an administrative template, the fact that you need a domain, and that a policy often is enforced in a manner that an end user cannot deviate from the baseline. Now you might think of Group Policy preferences, and although those can be used to set a preferred setting, the other things still apply making a GPO preference settings not even close to being as flexible as PowerShell Desired State Configuration.

There is a wide variety of uses for Desired State Configuration, or DSC, and a handful of them are:

- Manage registry settings

- Manage files and directories

- Stop, start, and manage both Windows services as well as processes

- Install or remove Windows roles and features

- Manage local users and groups

- Run PowerShell scripts

The last point in that bullet list is really a wild card because a PowerShell script pretty much can be anything at all.

To use DSC, you need a configuration that lists the different components and their desired states. In the following example, you see how to create a local group on a non-domain joined Windows 8.1 PC.

Just as with a function in a script, we start by declaring the name, but in this case, we use configuration instead of function. After that we can require or ask for parameters to our DSC and the last part is the actual configuration per node that we encounter. The node part could match on a specific operator like an If-statement does so that we could verify that the group is created only on machines where the name starts with the letters SE for Sweden or US from USA.

A simple DSC configuration script that makes sure that a local group exists.

Our script file then goes ahead and creates the actual configuration file on row 15 by executing the configuration. A configuration file is a MOF file that you can open up in Notepad or actually write from scratch in Notepad. When the creation is completed, the file will be stored in a subfolder called the same as the configuration, in this case ViaMonstraLocalGroups.

To start and apply the configuration, you run the command Start-DscConfiguration and enter the path to the folder containing the MOF files.

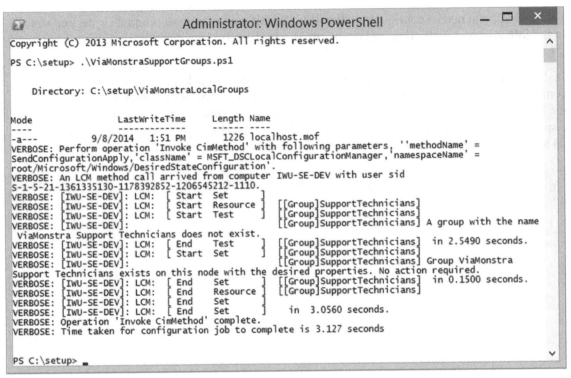

Execution of a DSC configuration script.

When you have executed the script, you can see in the Computer Manager that a new local group now exists on your PC.

Get-FileHash

Now and then there is a need to verify the integrity of a file. One example can be when you have copied a file from a network share or over the Internet, and you need to verify that it is the same file you expected. With a file hash validation, you can be fairly certain that the file hasn't been altered and that it isn't corrupt.

Before PowerShell 4.0, you had to invoke features in the .NET Framework to calculate a file hash value, but now there is a cmdlet to do this for you, so all you need to do is to tell the cmdlet which file you want to calculate for a file hash and optionally what hash mechanism you want to use.

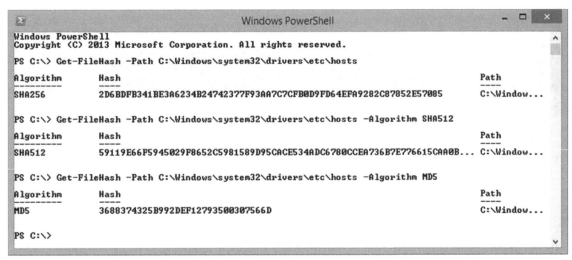

The Hash value for the hosts file using different algorithms.

When validating file hashes, it is important to use the same hash algorithm both times or you won't get a match.

Save-Help

Most, if not all, people who have been using PowerShell over the years have been acquainted with the cmdlet Update-Help in order to get the latest bits and bytes on how to use a cmdlet. Update-Help was introduced in PowerShell 3.0, and what it does is download and install the latest information for the different modules installed on your PC from the Internet. This could be somewhat troublesome on servers that lack Internet connection.

With Save-Help, it is now possible to use one machine to download all the new information to a local store, such as a network path where the other machines can access it in order to update their own local store. Save-Help can be executed as follows to store the information to a local path on the system drive based on the DestinationPath parameter:

```
Save-Help –DestinationPath C:\Setup\PowerShell-Helpfiles
```

Note: The C:\Setup\PowerShell-Helpfiles folder must exist.

It is important to know that Save-Help will only download help files for modules installed on the local machine. When looking at it, it is rather obvious why. PowerShell can by no means know where to download the help files for all the different PowerShell modules in the world. Therefore, if you want to update the help files for Active Directory Domain Services from a Windows 8.1 PC, you must first install that module on the PC, for example by installing the RSAT tools.

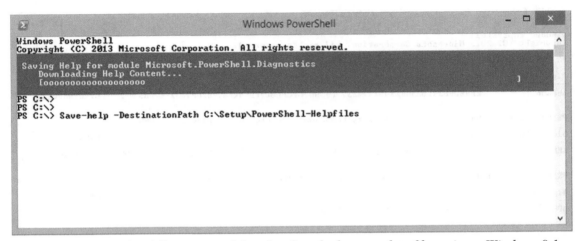

Save-Help command in full progress of downloading the latest update files using a Windows 8.1 PC.

Run the preceding command on a machine on which you have all modules installed, and then move or copy the folder to a host without Internet access and run the following command. The two paths don't have to be the same on the two machines.

```
Update-Help –SourcePath C:\Setup\PowerShell-Helpfiles
```

Test-NetConnection

With the latest versions of Windows, a dear program for many IT professionals has been removed. Telnet has been used for ages to verify network connectivity between two systems. The benefit with the telnet client is that you can select any TCP port that you want to test. New in PowerShell 4.0 is a cmdlet that does just that. This allows you to omit the extra installation of the telnet feature on servers and clients. And, as we all know, fewer installed features equals fewer potential patches and attack vectors for malicious code.

To use the new cmdlet, there isn't really anything that you need to do except start PowerShell on a system with the new version of PowerShell. The cmdlet can be used against IP addresses as well as hostnames and FQDN, if working name resolution exists on the machine, of course.

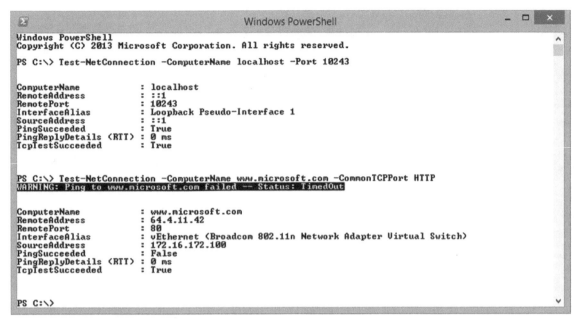

Using Test-NetConnection to verify connectivity in the absence of telnet.

In order to use a specific port, the –Port parameter can be used as well as the –CommonTCPPort parameter for services such as HTTP. Using the –InformationLevel parameter with the value Detailed gives a lot of information and can be quite useful when troubleshooting systems network connectivity. For instance, the command **Test-NetConnection –InformationLevel Detailed** could be part of a remote troubleshooting kit that service desk uses on PCs when troubleshooting and collecting log files.

Appendix A

Build the POC Environment

Here are the detailed steps for installing and configuring the hydration kit provided in the book sample files. This hydration kit allows you to build the same environment that is used for this book in a virtual environment. We recommend using Hyper-V in Windows Server 2012 R2 as your virtual platform, but in addition to Windows Server 2012 R2, we have tested the hydration kit on Hyper-V in Windows 8.1 and in VMware.

> **Note:** The password for the accounts created by the hydration kit is P@ssw0rd (including the Administrator account).

To follow the guides in this appendix, you need to download the book sample files that are available on http://deploymentfundamentals.com.

> **Real World Note:** As you learned in the book's "Introduction," you use virtual machines for the proof-of-concept environment, and if you have a powerful host, you can run them all on the same machine (for lab and test purposes). If you assign the minimum amount of memory, you can complete all steps on a host with 16 GB of RAM, even though 32 GB of RAM is preferred. If you are doing this on your own laptop or desktop, make sure to run the virtual machines on an SSD disk.

The Base Servers

Using the hydration kit, you build the following servers.

New York Site Servers (192.168.1.0/24)

- DC01, Domain Controller, DNS, and DHCP
- CM01, Member Server, System Center 2012 R2 Configuration Manager
- FS01, Member Server, File Services
- DPM01, Member Server, System Center 2012 R2 Data Protection Manager
- SM01, Member Server, System Center 2012 R2 Service Manager

The Base Clients

In addition to the servers, you also use a few clients throughout the book guides. Using this appendix, you build the following list of clients. PC0001 is deployed using either the hydration kit or the manual steps, and PC0002 is deployed as a part of Chapter 3 where you deploy Windows 8.1 using Configuration Manager 2012 R2.

New York Site Clients (192.168.1.0/24)

- PC0001, Windows 7 Enterprise SP1 x64

- PC0002, Windows 8.1 Enterprise x64 (again, deployed in Chapter 3)

Setting Up the Hydration Environment

To enable you to quickly set up the servers and clients used for the step-by-step guides in this book, we provide you with a hydration kit (part of the book sample files) that builds all the servers and clients.

How Does the Hydration Kit Work?

The hydration kit that you download is just a folder structure and some scripts. The scripts help you create the MDT 2013 Lite Touch offline media, and the folder structure is there for you to add your own software. The overview steps are the following:

1. Download the needed software

2. Install MDT 2013 and Windows ADK 8.1

3. Create an MDT 2013 deployment share using a PowerShell script

4. Populate the folder structure with the downloaded software

5. Generate the MDT 2013 media item (big ISO)

6. Create a few virtual machines, boot them on the media item, select which servers they should become, and about an hour later you have the environment ready to go.

Prepare the Downloads Folder

These steps should be performed on the machine (Windows 8, Windows 8.1, Windows Server 2012, or Windows Server 2012 R2) that you use to manage Hyper-V or VMware. If you have enabled the Hyper-V role locally, this machine also can be the host machine.

Download the Software

1.   On the Windows machine that you use to manage Hyper-V or VMware, create the **C:\Downloads** folder.

2.   Download the following mandatory software to the **C:\Downloads** folder:

   o   The book sample files (http://deploymentfundamentals.com)

   o   BGInfo

   o   MDT 2013

   o   Windows ADK 8.1

   o   Windows Server 2012 R2

   o   Windows 7 Enterprise SP1 x64

   o   .NET Framework 4.0.

   o   Windows Management Framework 3.0 (KB 2506146)

Prepare the Hydration Environment

On the Windows machine you use to manage Hyper-V or VMware, make sure you have administrator rights because MDT 2013 requires local administrator rights/permissions.

Note: You need to have at least 45 GB of free disk space on C:\ for the hydration kit and at least 300 GB of free space for the volume hosting your virtual machines. Also make sure to run all commands from an elevated PowerShell prompt.

Create the Hydration Deployment Share

1.   On the Windows machine that you use to manage Hyper-V or VMware, install **Windows ADK 8.1 (adksetup.exe)** selecting only the following components:

   o   **Deployment Tools**

   o   **Windows Preinstallation Environment (Windows PE)**

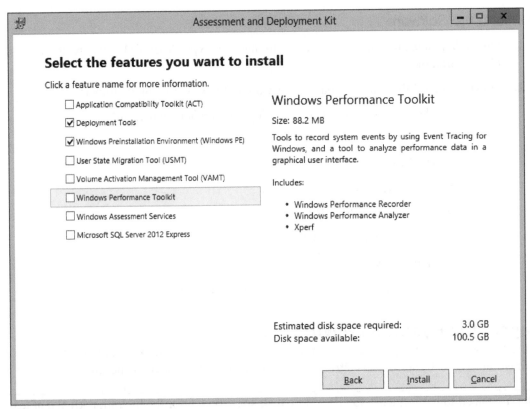

The ADK setup.

2. Install **MDT 2013 (MicrosoftDeploymentToolkit2013_x64.msi)** with the default settings.

3. Extract the book sample files and copy the **HydrationECM** folder to **C:\.**

4. You should now have the following folder containing a few subfolders and PowerShell scripts:

   C:\HydrationECM\Source

5. In an elevated (run as Administrator) **PowerShell** command prompt, configure **Execution Policy** in PowerShell by running the following command:

   ```
   Set-ExecutionPolicy Unrestricted -Force
   ```

6. In the **PowerShell** command prompt, navigate to the hydration folder by running the following command:

   ```
   Set-Location C:\HydrationECM\Source
   ```

7. Still at the **PowerShell** command prompt, with location (working directory) set to **C:\HydrationECM\Source**, create the hydration deployment share by running the following command:

   ```
   .\CreateHydrationDeploymentShare.ps1
   ```

Populate the Hydration Deployment Share with the Setup Files

1. Copy the **BGInfo** file (**bginfo.exe**) to the following folder:

    C:\HydrationECM\DS\Applications\Install - BGInfo\Source

2. Copy the **Windows Server 2012 R2** installation files (the content of the ISO, not the actual ISO) to the following folder:

    C:\HydrationECM\DS\Operating Systems\WS2012R2

3. Copy the **Windows 7 Enterprise SP1 x64** installation files (again, the content of the ISO, not the actual ISO) to the following folder:

    C:\HydrationECM\DS\Operating Systems\W7SP1X64

4. Copy the **.NET Framework 4.0** installation file (dotNetFx40_Full_x86_x64.exe) to the following folder:

    C:\HydrationECM\DS\Applications\Install - NET FrameWork 4.0\Source

5. Copy the **Windows Management Framework 3.0** installation file (Windows6.1-KB2506143-x64.msu) to the following folder:

    C:\HydrationECM\DS\Applications
    Install - Windows Management Framework 3.0\Source

Create the Hydration ISO (MDT 2013 Offline Media Item)

1. Using **Deployment Workbench** (available on the **Start screen**), expand **Deployment Shares**, and expand **Hydration Enterprise Client Management**.

2. Review the various nodes. The **Applications**, **Operating Systems**, and **Task Sequences** nodes should all have some content in them.

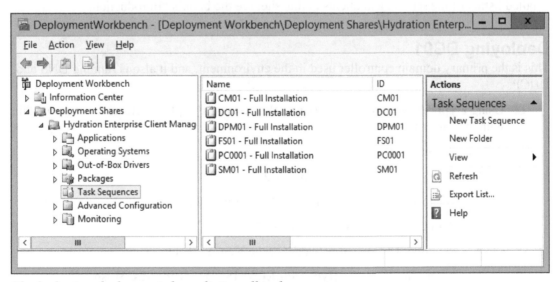

The hydration deployment share, listing all task sequences.

3. Expand the **Advanced Configuration** node, and then select the **Media** node.

4. In the right pane, right-click the **MEDIA001** item and select **Update Media Content**.

Note: The media update will take a while to run, a perfect time for a coffee break. ☺

After the media update, you will have a big ISO (**HydrationECM.iso**) in the **C:\HydrationECM\ISO** folder. Depending on media used (Microsoft now provides ISO files that also include updates), the HydrationECM.iso will be at least 7.3 GB in size.

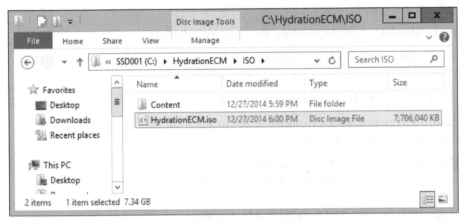

The HydrationECM.iso media item.

Deploying the Virtual Machines

In these steps, you deploy and configure the virtual machines for the New York Site. For a detailed listing of the servers and clients in this site, see the book's "Introduction."

Deploying DC01

This is the primary domain controller used in the environment, and it also is running DNS and DHCP.

1. Using **Hyper-V Manager** or **VMware Workstation/vSphere**, create a virtual machine with the following settings:

   a. Name: **DC01**

   b. VM Generation (Hyper-V only): **2**

   c. Memory: **1 GB** (minimum, 2 GB recommended)

   d. Hard drive: **127 GB** (dynamic disk)

   e. Network: The virtual network for the New York site

   f. Image file (ISO): **C:\HydrationECM\ISO\HydrationECM.iso**

2. Start the **DC01** virtual machine. After booting from **HydrationECM.iso**, and after
    WinPE has loaded, select the **DC01** task sequence.

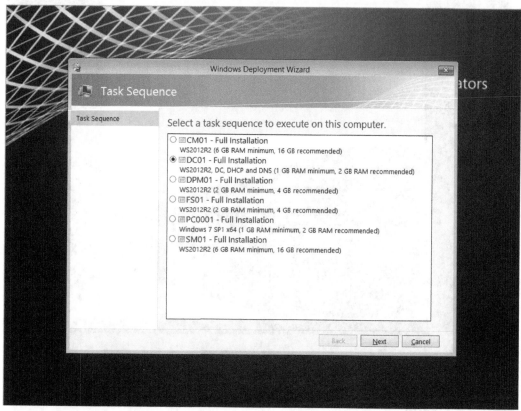

The Task Sequence list showing the hydration task sequences.

3. Wait until the setup is complete and you see the **Hydration completed** message in the
    final summary.

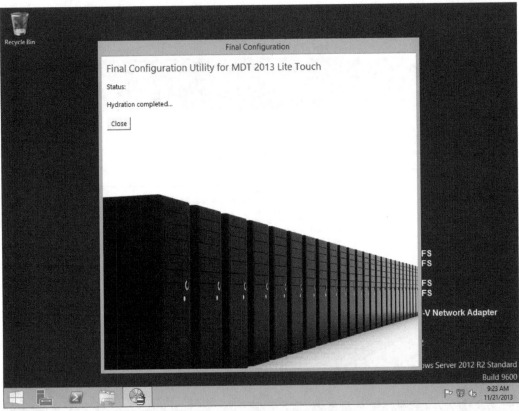

The deployment of DC01 completed, showing the custom final summary screen.

Deploying CM01

CM01 is the server used for Configuration Manager 2012 R2.

1. Using **Hyper-V Manager** or **VMware Workstation/vSphere**, create a virtual machine with the following settings:

   a. Name: **CM01**

   b. VM Generation (Hyper-V only): **2**

   c. Memory: **6 GB** (minimum, recommended 16 GB)

   d. Hard drive: **300 GB** (dynamic disk)

   e. Network: The virtual network for the New York site

   f. Image file (ISO): **C:\HydrationECM\ISO\HydrationECM.iso**

2. Start the **CM01** virtual machine. After booting from **HydrationECM.iso**, and after WinPE has loaded, select the **CM01** task sequence. Wait until the setup is complete and you see the **Hydration completed** message in the final summary.

> **Real World Note:** Microsoft does not support running Configuration Manager 2012 R2 on less than 16 GB of RAM (when running SQL locally), but 6 GB works in a small lab and test environment.

Deploying FS01

FS01 is the file server used in this book.

1. Using **Hyper-V Manager** or **VMware Workstation/vSphere**, create a virtual machine with the following settings:

   a. Name: **FS01**

   b. VM Generation (Hyper-V only): **2**

   c. Memory: **2 GB** (minimum, recommended 4 GB)

   d. Hard drive: **300 GB** (dynamic disk)

   e. Network: The virtual network for the New York site

   f. Image file (ISO): **C:\HydrationECM\ISO\HydrationECM.iso**

2. Start the **FS01** virtual machine. After booting from **HydrationECM.iso**, and after WinPE has loaded, select the **FS01** task sequence. Wait until the setup is complete and you see the **Hydration completed** message in the final summary.

Deploying DPM01

DPM01 is the server for Data Protection Manager 2012 R2 used in this book.

1. Using **Hyper-V Manager** or **VMware Workstation/vSphere**, create a virtual machine with the following settings:

   a. Name: **DPM01**

   b. VM Generation (Hyper-V only): **2**

   c. Memory: **4 GB** (minimum, recommended 8 GB)

   d. Hard drive: **300 GB** (dynamic disk)

   e. Network: The virtual network for the New York site

   f. Image file (ISO): **C:\HydrationECM\ISO\HydrationECM.iso**

2. Start the **DPM01** virtual machine. After booting from **HydrationECM.iso**, and after WinPE has loaded, select the **DPM01** task sequence. Wait until the setup is complete and you see the **Hydration completed** message in the final summary.

Deploying SM01

SM01 is the server for Service Manager 2012 R2 used in this book.

1. Using **Hyper-V Manager** or **VMware Workstation/vSphere**, create a virtual machine with the following settings:

   a. Name: **SM01**

   b. VM Generation (Hyper-V only): **2**

   c. Memory: **6 GB** (minimum, recommended 16 GB)

   d. Hard drive: **300 GB** (dynamic disk)

   e. Network: The virtual network for the New York site

   f. Image file (ISO): **C:\HydrationECM\ISO\HydrationECM.iso**

2. Start the **SM01** virtual machine. After booting from **HydrationECM.iso**, and after WinPE has loaded, select the **SM01** task sequence. Wait until the setup is complete and you see the **Hydration completed** message in the final summary.

Deploying PC0001

This is a client running Windows 7 Enterprise SP1 x64 in the VIAMONSTRA domain.

1. Using **Hyper-V Manager** or **VMware Workstation/vSphere**, create a virtual machine with the following settings:

   a. Name: **PC0001**

   b. VM Generation (Hyper-V only): **1** (Windows 7 does not support generation 2)

   c. Memory: **1 GB** (minimum, recommended 2 GB)

   d. Hard drive: **127 GB** (dynamic disk)

   e. Network: The virtual network for the New York site

   f. Image file (ISO): **C:\HydrationECM\ISO\HydrationECM.iso**

2. Start the **PC0001** virtual machine. After booting from **HydrationECM.iso**, and after WinPE has loaded, select the **PC0001** task sequence. Wait until the setup is complete and you see the **Hydration completed** message in the final summary.

Deploying PC0002

This is an empty client that you deploy in Chapter 3.

1. Using **Hyper-V Manager** or **VMware Workstation/vSphere**, create a virtual machine with the following settings:

   a. Name: **PC0002**

   b. VM Generation (Hyper-V only): **2**

   c. Memory: **1 GB** (minimum, recommended 2 GB)

   d. Hard drive: **127 GB** (dynamic disk)

   e. Network: The virtual network for the New York site

2. Review the **PC0002** virtual machine UEFI boot order, noting the Network Adapter listed first.

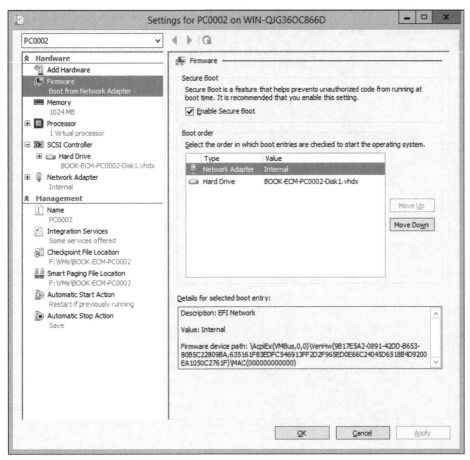

PC0002 Firmware settings.

Appendix B

Remote Server Administration Tools

Regardless of whether you are managing Windows clients or Windows servers, there are many tools you just cannot miss out on. They are a part of Remote Server Administration Tools (RSAT) and include management consoles for all server features. The consoles include, for instance, the Group Policy Management console, Active Directory Users and Computers snap-in, DNS Management console, and many more.

The trick is that you install RSAT on your Windows clients and use the tools from there to manage group policies, users, security groups, DNS, DHCP, and so forth. This is much more efficient than logging into each server through Remote Desktop and then managing whatever you are trying to manage from that particular server.

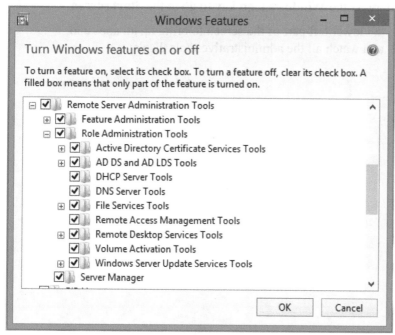

Included with RSAT are a great number of tools that allow you to manage all server features.

All Management Consoles Are Installed with RSAT

When you installed RSAT for Windows Vista or Windows 7, the tools were not actually installed during that installation. You had to enable them manually before you could use any of the management consoles. In RSAT for Windows 8 and 8.1, it is the complete opposite—all management consoles are enabled by default.

Install Remote Server Administration Tools

This guide assumes that you have downloaded the Remote Server Administration Tools from https://www.microsoft.com/en-us/download/details.aspx?id=39296 and have them available on PC0002.

1. On **PC0002**, log on as **VIAMONSTRA\Administrator**.

2. Using **File Explorer,** navigate to the where you have downloaded RSAT and start the installation by opening the file **Windows8.1-KB2693643-x64.msu** update. Use the default settings for the installation. The installation takes a couple of minutes to finish.

3. When **RSAT** is installed, press the **Windows logo key** to go to the **Start screen**.

4. Click the down arrow in the lower left part of the screen to bring up all apps and applications on PC0002, and watch all the administrative tools display.

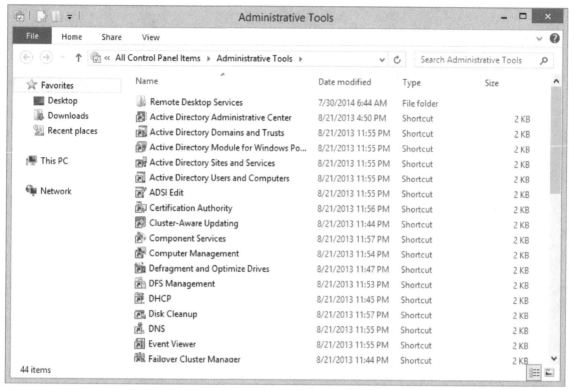

When RSAT has been installed, you will see many additional control panel applets in the Administrative Tools control panel.

Index

Beyond the Book – Meet the Experts

If you liked the book, you will love to hear them in person.

Live Presentations

Andreas frequently speak at Microsoft conferences around the world, such as Microsoft TechEd. You also can find him at local events like Microsoft TechDays or various user group meetings. For current information on Andreas, check out his blog:

> www.theexperienceblog.com

Tim speaks at webinars, user group events, and conferences, both locally in Sweden and abroad. Follow him on his blog for the most up-to-date information on presentations:

> www.infoworks.tv

Live Instructor-led Classes

Andreas conducts scheduled, instructor-led classes in Europe. For current dates and locations, see the following site:

> www.addskills.se

Twitter

Andreas tweets on the following alias:

> @AndreasStenhall

Tim tweets on the following alias:

> @TimNilimaa

CPSIA information can be obtained at www.ICGtesting.com
Printed in the USA
LVOW02s1923190215

427606LV00008B/288/P